The AR-15 Controversy

The AR-15 Controversy:
Semiautomatic Rifles and the Second Amendment

Dennis P. Chapman

THIRD BRIGADE PRESS

Third Brigade Press, Springfield Virginia, USA

First Edition June 2021

(Rev 09/21)

ISBN-13 978-0-578-92803-6

To Charles Minot "Minnie" Dole, and those that volunteered, and those that never came home.

Vires Montesque Vincimus

Table of Contents

Preface

As a retired Army officer and former infantryman, I have observed the debate about firearms, and especially so-called "assault" weapons—AR-15s and similar rifles—with interest. I quickly took note that activists portrayed the utility of these firearms and their more controversial features in a manner inconsistent with my experience using them both recreationally and professionally, as a soldier. This discontinuity troubled me, all the more so as public figures continued to make pronouncements about the AR-15 that seemed incorrect.

Eventually I realized that much of the discourse about firearms in America rests on certain *assumptions* about how controversial guns work, their capabilities, and their legitimate uses that no one had taken the trouble to examine. So I undertook to examine those assumptions myself. I set out on this project intending to publish the results as an article in a law journal or similar publication. When the result proved too large for that format I condensed some of the key points into a much-reduced form, which was duly published in a law review as originally intended.[1] Although pleased, I still wanted to present my findings to the public in full. This book is the result.

---

[1] Dennis P. Chapman, "Firearms Chimera: The Counter Productive Campaign to Ban the AR-15 Rifle." *Belmont Law Review*, Volume 8, No. 1, Fall 2020, 191.

Chapter 1
Firearms Technology in the Courts: The Tragic Case
of Alexander Ripan

On October 25th, 1919, Romanian immigrant Loas (Luca) Tipurla failed to return to his home in Saginaw County, Michigan. He was found shot dead the next day in a railway ditch only fifty yards from his residence.[2] According to Tipurla's wife, he had been in an altercation with his neighbor, Alexander Ripan, a few days earlier; she further alleged that Ripan owned a revolver.[3] Questioned by police, Ripan confirmed he kept a revolver in a trunk at his home; police confiscated the trunk with the pistol inside.[4] To ascertain whether Ripan's gun had fired the fatal round, prosecutor Riley Crane and the local sheriff consulted gunsmith Henry Krogsman, who inserted the spent .32 caliber round that killed Tipurla into the barrel of Ripan's pistol. When Krogsman shook the pistol, the expended round "dropped easily through the barrel"[5] into Krogsman's hand. Krogsman then repeated the procedure with an unfired .32 caliber bullet, but could only force the unfired bullet through the revolver's chamber with difficulty.[6] Krogsman performed this demonstration at trial before Ripan's jury.[7] Ripan was convicted and sentenced to life in prison.[8]

Eventually Crane learned of "advancements in ballistics technology" that raised doubt whether Ripan's pistol was actually the murder weapon.[9] But in 1929, before Crane could act on this new

---

[2] Ann E. Miller, *National Registry of Exonerations*, https://www.law.umich.edu/special/exoneration/Pages/casedetailpre1989.aspx?caseid=272 (retrieved January 27th, 2019).

[3] *Id.*

[4] *Id.*

[5] Judge Jerome Frank and Barbara Frank. *Not Guilt* (Doubleday & Company, Inc, 1957), 186 – 187.

[6] Miller.

[7] *Ripan v. State of Michigan*, 1 Mich. Ct. Cl. 19, 1940 WL 12950 (1940); Miller.

[8] Frank, 187.

information, Ripan escaped, fleeing to Chicago where he established a shoe repair business. A former inmate recognized him in 1935 and Ripan was promptly returned to prison.[10] On December 19th, 1936, State Police ballistics expert LeRoy F. Smith and Saginaw County Police Department firearms expert John D. Leppert wrote to the Commissioner of Pardons and Paroles that "based on certain ballistics tests they had performed, the bullet recovered from the Tipurla's body could not have come from Ripan's gun."[11] Only in 1939 did Ripan regain his freedom, a new trial having been ordered at which the murder charge against him was *nolle prossed*[12] because "a bullet fired from a revolver could not be inserted in the barrel of that same weapon without great difficulty."[13]

Alexander Ripan was the victim of a great tragedy in which "the very evidence that had sent [him] to the penitentiary [later] proved him innocent."[14] How did this happen? Not because of corruption or malfeasance: the very prosecutor that charged Ripan led the effort to free him, with the assistance of the jurisdiction that had originally he charged him.[15] Crane also represented Ripan before the Michigan Court of Claims in an unsuccessful bid for compensation for the hard labor he had performed while in prison.[16]

Clearly the miscarriage of justice for both Ripan, imprisoned for a crime that he did not commit, and Tipurla, for whom justice was never obtained, resulted from error by police and prosecutor. It redounds to their credit that they diligently worked to correct their error once discovered. Nonetheless, the odor of negligence hangs about the case. The State of Michigan attributed the exposure of the error to "recent discoveries in the ballistics field"[17] which led them to

---

[9] Miller.
[10] *Id.*
[11] *Id.*
[12] *Id.*
[13] Frank, 187 – 188.
[14] Frank, 188.
[15] Miller.
[16] *Ripan v. State of Michigan.*
[17] Frank, 188.

realize that the fatal bullet could not have come from Ripan's revolver. That this information was unavailable at the time of Ripan's trial is dubious however, as firearms technology was already in an advanced state by then. Rifled barrels had been used since long before the American Revolution and saw substantial combat for the first time in that struggle;[18] the National armories at Springfield and Harpers Ferry completed the transition to manufacturing firearms with interchangeable parts by the late 1840s;[19] revolvers became commercially viable before the Civil War,[20] which also "saw... the first widespread use of integrated metal cartridges."[21] The "first significant use of breechloaders by a military force" occurred during the American Revolution at the Battle of Kings Mountain, where British troops under the command of Major Patrick Ferguson employed a breech loading flintlock musket of his design;[22] the US Army had adopted the breach loading Hall Rifle in 1819,[23] and breach loaders permanently displaced muzzle loading arms in US service with the adoption of the Model 1873 Trapdoor Springfield.[24]

[18] C.H.B. Pridham, *Superiority of Fire: A Short History of Rifles and Machine-Guns* (Hutchinson's Scientific and Technical Publications, 1945), 8 – 10.

[19] Merritt Roe Smith, *Harpers Ferry Armory and the New Technology: The Challenge of Change* (Cornell University Press, 1977), 280 – 284.

[20] Matthew Moss. "How the Colt Single Action Army Revolver Won the West." *Popular Mechanics*, November 3rd, 2016. https://www.popularmechanics.com/military/weapons/a23685/colt-single-action/. Retrieved July 10th, 2019.

[21] Sam Bacetta. "The Complete History of Small Arms Ammunition and Cartridges." *Small Wars Journal*, nd. https://smallwarsjournal.com/jrnl/art/complete-history-small-arms-ammunition-and-cartridges. Retrieved July 3rd, 2019.

[22] *NRA Firearms Factbook*, Third Edition (National Rifle Association of America, 1989), 36; Newton A. Strait. *Alphabetical List of Battles, 1754 – 1900* (Washington, DC, 1900), 228.

[23] "Day 2: Hall Model 1819 Breechloading Rifle." National Firearms Museum. *NRABlog*, December 2nd, 2016. https://www.nrablog.com/articles/2016/12/day-2-hall-model-1819-breechloading-rifle/. Retrieved July 3rd, 2019.

[24] Nick McGrath. "The Springfield Model 1873 Rifle." Army Historical Foundation, September 9th, 2016. https://armyhistory.org/the-springfield-

Prussia successfully employed its breechloader, the Dreyse needle gun, in combat in 1848, 1866, and 1870.[25] Semiautomatic pistols were introduced as early as 1892,[26] with the US Army adopting its famous semiautomatic pistol in 1911. Semiautomatic rifles were introduced as early as 1894,[27] and the US Army adopted its first selective firearm (that is, a firearm that can fire either semiautomatically or automatically)—the M1918 Browning Automatic Rifle—even before Tipurla's murder.[28]

By the time of Ripan's trial in 1920, certain principles had been firmly established in firearms technology, including the rifled barrel. The internal surface of a rifled firearm's bore comprises two components: raised *lands* and recessed *grooves*.[29] "Bullets fired in rifled arms are usually about a thousandth of an inch larger than the diameter across the grooves of the arm in which they are used. This means that they are larger than the diameter of the bore."[30] This is necessary to force the lands to grip the bullet and the grooves to engrave themselves upon it, imparting the stabilizing spin necessary for improved accuracy.[31] In effect, the bullet is *swaged* through the

---

model-1873-rifle/. Retrieved July 3rd, 2019.

[25] Pridham, 13.

[26] R.K. Wilson. *Textbook of Automatic Pistols* (Small Arms Technical Publishing Company, Plantersville, South Carolina, 1943; reprinted by Palladium Press for the Firearms Classics Library, 1999), 53.

[27] Melvin M. Johnson and Charles T. Haven. *Automatic Arms, Their History and Use* (William and Morrow Company, 1941), 51.

[28] Paul Richard Huard. "Meet the Browning Automatic Rifle: The Best Machine Gun of All Time?" *The National Interest*, February 19, 2019. https://nationalinterest.org/blog/buzz/meet-browning-automatic-rifle-best-machine-gun-all-time-44992. Retrieved July 3rd, 2019.

[29] Michael E. Bousard, Stanton L. Wormley, Jr., (authors), and John Zent (editor), *NRA Firearms Sourcebook*, Third Edition (National Rifle Association of America, 2010),141 – 143.

[30] J.S. Hatcher. *Textbook of Firearms Investigation, Identification, and Evidence, together with the Textbook of Pistols and Revolvers* (Small Arms Technical Publishing Company, 1935), 47.

[31] Bousard and Wormley, 294 – 295.

barrel. "When a lead bullet is fired, the soft metal expands sideways under the impact of the pressure at its base, and fills every available bit of space in the barrel."[32] Jacketed bullets—those with a soft lead core encased in a hard metal jacket — "do not fill up the grooves completely," but still expand enough to engage the lands and grooves, and will still "show the marks left by ... the tops of the lands ... and the center of the groove."[33] For these reasons, a bullet of the proper caliber for a firearm will not pass easily through the barrel even before it has been fired, much less after.

All of this was well known at the time of Ripan's trial. The 1921 Sacco-Vanzetti case included substantial forensic testimony as to the characteristics of the firearms, spent cases, and bullets recovered during the investigation of that crime.[34] Other contemporary cases show that American courts were well aware of the need to take care to avoid admitting unreliable firearms evidence. In the 1923 Illinois case of *People v. Berkman*, Adam Berkman was charged with shooting a railroad security guard, in part on the strength of the testimony of a police officer to the effect that the pistol found at the scene of the crime matched a bullet removed from the victim's body. As reported by the Court:

> The state undertook to prove by the opinion evidence of Officer Dickson that this revolver was the identical revolver from which the bullet introduced in evidence was fired on the night Rahn was shot. The state sought to qualify him for such remarkable evidence by having him testify that he had had charge of the inspection of firearms for the last fivwe years of their department; that he was a small arms inspector in the

---

[32] *Id.*, 75.

[33] *Id.*, 77.

[34] For an extensive analysis of the firearms ballistics aspects of the Sacco-Vanzetti trial, as well as the treatment of such evidence in other trials in the late 19th and early 20th centuries, see Jack Disbrow Gunther and Charles O. Gunther, *The Identification of Firearms* (John Wiley & Sons, 1935).

National Guard for a period of nine years; and that he was a sergeant in the service in the field artillery, where the pistol is the only weapon the men have, outside of the large guns or cannon. He was then asked to examine the Colt automatic 32 aforesaid, and gave it as his opinion that the bullet introduced in evidence was fired from the Colt automatic revolver in evidence. He even stated positively that he knew that that bullet came out of the barrel of that revolver, because the rifling marks on the bullet fitted into the rifling of the revolver in question, and that the markings on that particular bullet were peculiar, because they came clear up on the steel of the bullet.[35]

On appeal the Court rejected this testimony out of hand, holding that

[t]here is no evidence in the case, by which this officer claims to be an expert, that shows that he knew anything about how Colt automatic revolvers are made and how they are rifled. There is no testimony in the record showing that the revolver in question was rifled in a manner different from all others of its model, and we feel very sure that no such evidence could be produced. The evidence of this officer is clearly absurd, besides not being based upon any known rule that would make it admissible.[36]

Berkman is quite similar to *Ripan*: In each case, the trial court accepted unreliable firearms evidence based upon the testimony of a witness with some firearms knowledge, but without sufficient expertise to conduct a proper forensic analysis. Another example is *Jack v. Commonwealth*, 1928, where the Supreme Court of Kentucky "held that a trial court had committed error by admitting as expert testimony the opinions of two witnesses for the Commonwealth that

---

[35] *People v. Berkman*, 307 Ill. 492, 139 N.E. 91 (Ill., 1923).
[36] *Id.*

a fatal bullet had been discharged from the defendant's pistol."[37] Per the Court,

> [t]he Commonwealth introduced two witnesses, one a tax collector, formerly a deputy sheriff and jailer, the other being the present jailer, who testified that they had had some experience in handling firearms and had made a study of catalogs issued by the various firearms companies. They stated that the pistol introduced in evidence was a special make and carried a 32-20 Winchester cartridge, which is a flat nosed bullet. They had made a test of the barrel with an ordinary magnifying glass and had also examined the bullet which killed Douglas, and from the rifles in the pistol and the marks on the ball they could identify that particular ball as having been fired from that pistol. They had also procured cartridges for the pistol and fired one into a sack of bran, and made a magnifying glass test with both bullets and found that the two corresponded. They were not, however, prepared to measure the width nor depth of the rifles nor the distance between them, nor to make such measurements upon the bullets, nor to make any scientific test nor comparison between them.[38]

The Court then noted the advanced state of ballistic forensic science at that time, listing and describing certain scientific instruments employed and the procedures for their use.[39] Concluding that "[i]t thus appears that this is a technical subject, and in order to give an expert opinion thereon a witness should have made a special study of the subject and have suitable instruments and equipment to make proper tests," the Court reversed the conviction.[40]

---

[37] Gunther and Gunther, 265.
[38] *Jack v. Commonwealth*, 222 Ky. 546, 1 S.W.2d 961 (Ky., 1928).
[39] *Id.*, citing Major Calvin H. Goddard, *Popular Science Monthly*, November, 1927.

By 1920 firearms technology, expertise, and forensic techniques were clearly both sufficiently advanced and available to have enabled the authorities in Ripan's case to determine that the round that killed Tipurla could not have been fired from Ripan's gun. Why then did neither prosecutor Crane nor Ripan's defense counsel discover these facts? The reason is as simple as it is tragic: *they simply didn't know what they didn't know.* Crane and Krogsman *assumed* that they knew more about firearms than they actually did, resting their judgment on untested assumptions about how firearms work, it never occurring to them that what seemed intuitively obvious might actually be wrong.

---

[40] *Id.*

Chapter 2
The Emergence of Semiautomatic Firearms Technology

Alexander Ripan suffered much because of the trial court's reliance upon a flawed, incorrect assumption about how firearms work. Unfortunately, courts and litigants today continue to make the same mistake, basing both arguments and rulings on unsubstantiated assumptions and beliefs about certain types of firearms that, while they may seem intuitive to some, are actually false. This is particularly true regarding certain civilian semiautomatic rifles that share features with military arms, stigmatized by some with the pejorative label "assault weapons." These civilian rifles are subject to particularly fervent attack by activists and judges based on unfounded claims about their relative dangerousness in the hands of criminals as compared to other civilian firearms—a set of flawed assumptions that I have termed "The Weapons of War Myth."[41]

One challenge in discussing firearms is that some words are used both as terms of art in legal practice and as esoteric jargon in the shooting sports community differently than the way the word is used in the wider culture. One such is the word "machinegun." In the law "[t]he term 'machinegun' means any weapon which shoots, is designed to shoot, or can be readily restored to shoot, automatically more than one shot, without manual reloading, by a single function of the trigger."[42] This definition includes crew-served machineguns such as the venerable Browning M2 .50 caliber machinegun, the Vietnam era M60 machinegun, and the current US Army standard M240 machinegun; military rifles such as the German STG-44 *Sturmgewehr*, the Soviet Kalashnikov family of rifles, the US military M14 Rifle, and the M16 of family rifles; smaller shoulder fired weapons firing pistol caliber ammunition traditionally thought of as

---

[41] Dennis P. Chapman, "The Weapons of War Myth." www.linkedin.com/pulse/weapons-war-myth-dennis-chapman/, December 2015.
[42] 26 US Code § 5845(a).

submachine guns, such as the M1928A1 Thompson Submachine Gun and the M3 Submachine Gun, commonly called the "grease gun"[43]; all the way down to tiny machine pistols such as the Beretta 93R *Raffica*, a selective fire version of Beretta's famous 92-series pistol capable of firing either semiautomatically (one shot per pull of the trigger) or burst (three shots per trigger pull).[44] For purposes of this book, however, I shall use the term "machinegun" as I used it in the Army and as it is used in the vernacular, to refer to weapons that produce *automatic fire only* with no semiautomatic setting, are usually belt fed,[45] [46]often "requir[ing] a mount for firing and [often] served by a team rather than a single gunner."[47] A selective fire weapon "is a firearm that fires in semiautomatic or fully automatic (or, perhaps, burst-fire) modes at the option of the firer."[48] All other self-loading firearms—that is, firearms that fire a single shot with each pull of the trigger, and then "reload themselves every time a shot is fired,"[49] with "all other elements of the firing cycle being performed without action by the gunner, are termed *semiautomatic*" (emphasis in original).[50]

---

[43] Bruce N. Canfield. "The M3 and M3A1 'Grease Guns." *American Rifleman*, May 20th, 2016, https://www.americanrifleman.org/articles/2016/5/20/the-m3-and-m3a1-grease-guns/. Retrieved February 23rd, 2019.

[44] J.B. Wood. *Beretta Automatic Pistols: The Collector's and Shooter's Comprehensive Guide* (Stackpole Books, 1985), 174 – 181.

[45] "Machinegun." *Encyclopedia Britannica*. https://www.britannica.com/technology/machine-gun. Retrieved January 27th, 2019.

[46] As an exception, where I quote from an original source using the alternative form "machine gun," I retain that spelling.

[47] Charles E. Balleisen. *Principles of Firearms* (John Wiley and Sons, Inc., 1945), 2.

[48] *NRA Firearms Factbook*, 313. Also, selective fire is "At [sic] term used to describe a firearm that has multiple methods of firing. Typically, this term is applied to firearms that have the option to fire a given number of rounds for each pull of the trigger or to fire continuously until the trigger is released." Bousard and Wormley, 456.

[49] Johnson and Haven, 85.

[50] Balleisen, 2.

Until the late 20th Century, gun control efforts in the United States focused on handguns, as made clear by one commentator in 1930:

> In the United States, for the past two decades, there has been a constantly increasing hue and cry against the 'menace of the pistol!' State after state has enacted legislation restricting the sale, ownership, and use of this weapon, so that, where once it was as common an article of household furniture as the frying pan, it has now fallen to such low estate that the few reputable citizens who still possess them must go through a third degree to secure a purchase license, another to transport them on their persons and a third to engage in the practice necessary to perfect themselves in their use. The net effect is that, as the result of the combined efforts of a group of persons who have fastened upon the pistol as the root of all crime, this erstwhile honorable weapon has become an outcast, hunted to its lair by a pack of ravening uplifters, and, once captured, smashed to bits with sledge on anvil, or consigned to the depths of lake or ocean as an unspeakable instrument which is to be destroyed at all costs, and without benefit of clergy.[51] [52]

By contrast, "[f]rom the beginning of the Republic, rifles and long guns were not subject to public controversy."[53] This lack of controversy extended to semiautomatic long guns. Notwithstanding the relatively recent controversy over certain semiautomatic rifles,

---

[51] Calvin Goddard. "This Pistol Bogey," 1 Am. J. Police Sci., 178 (1930).

[52] This would appear to be the same Calvin Goddard that authored the article on firearms ballistics relied upon by the Court in *Jack v. Commonwealth*.

[53] Stephen P. Halbrook. "Reality Check: The 'Assault Weapon' Fantasy and Second Amendment Jurisprudence." *The Georgetown Journal of Law and Public Policy*, Winter 2016, Volume 14, Number 1.

semiautomatic firearms are old technology. As R.K. Wilson noted, "[i]n 1863 one Orbea of Eiber produced a gas-operated semiautomatic pistol … in the same year (1863), Regulus Pilon, an American, took out a patent for a small caliber rifle which was recocked by the recoil of the barrel."[54] One W.T. Curtis "patented a gas-operated weapon which could be used either as a single-shot rifle or as a fully automatic machinegun" in 1866; further attempts at semiautomatic pistols were made in 1870 and 1872. [55]A patent for a gas-operated revolver was filed in 1886, but "the honor of producing the first self-loading pistol to be sold as a practical weapon belongs to Austria" with the introduction of the Schonberger pistol by *Osterreichische Waffenfabrik* in 1892.[56] The next year another semiautomatic pistol was introduced, this time by Andrea Schwarzlose.[57] In 1894 the Mannlicher pistol was introduced, which was the first semiautomatic handgun to use the blow-back system.[58] Weapons designer Theodore Bergman introduced two successful self-loading arms in 1897 and 1903.[59] "The year 1898 is something of a landmark in the history of the self-loading pistol, for it saw the advent of the first really successful self-loading pistol … [t]he famous 7.63mm. Mauser", which had been patented in 1896 but which first gained widespread attention in the 1899—1903 Boer War.[60] John Browning, who "must rank, after Maxim, as the greatest and most successful inventor of automatic arms of all time," produced his Old Model Browning .32 pistol in 1899, and brought out the first .38 Colt in 1900.[61] By 1910,

> there were a score or more of different makes of
> small pocket loading pistols with varying degrees of
> reliability on the market, and the now ubiquitous .25

[54] Wilson, 7.
[55] *Id.*, 7.
[56] *Id.*, 9.
[57] *Id.*, 5, 10.
[58] *Id.*, 5, 11.
[59] *Id.*, 13
[60] *Id.*, 15.
[61] *Id.*, 18 – 19.

(6.35 mm.) had appeared, in Europe as the Baby Browning (1908) and in America as the Vest Pocket Colt ... in 1900 G. Luger ... filed his specification for [the] pistol that became famous ... as the Parabellum, known in America as the Luger ...[62]

The Luger appeared in 1902 in 7.65 mm and in 1908 in 9mm.[63] The US Army adopted the Colt Government Model in 1911 as the "Model of 1911 US Army," and "[i]n 1914 all combatant nations took the field with self-loading pistols, except Great Britain (and Montenegro)", though in Russia and France officers carried self-loading pistols at their own expense in lieu of the officially adopted arms.[64]

Semiautomatic rifles are equally venerable. "Among the earlier [semi]automatic rifles of the beginning of the modern type—although none of them were successful to the point of any general use—was the Griffiths and Woodgate, English, 1894 ... English inventors were also responsible for the Clausin (1895) and the Ross (1896)," neither of which got much beyond the experimental stage. The United States tested several semiautomatic rifles including the Murphy Manning, White Greenman, Farquhar Hill, and designs of the Springfield and Rock Island Armories.[65] The first semiautomatic rifle accepted by a military power for service is widely accepted to have been the *Mondragón* rifle, "a gas-operated 10-shot gun, feeding from a box magazine."[66] The *Mondragón* was designed by Mexican Army General Manuel *Mondragón*; "patented in 1907, [it] was officially adopted by the Mexican Army in 1908 as the '*Fusil Porfirio Diaz Systema Mondragón*'; manufacturing orders were issued to Swiss-based SIG Arms because Mexico had no proper arms making facilities," but because of the political turmoil besetting Mexico at the time, the

---

[62] *Id.*, 22 – 23.

[63] *Id.*

[64] *Id.*, 23.

[65] Johnson and Haven, 51, and plate preceding page 53.

[66] *Id.*, 51 and 52, plate following page 56.

14

Mexican Army took possession of only a few *Mondragón* rifles.[67] The Mexican government cancelled the order after delivery of only 1,000 rifles, "leaving SIG with 3,000 finicky rifles not paid for."[68] SIG found a buyer for some of these rifles upon the outbreak of the First World War, when the German air corps "adopted [the *Mondragón*] as the *Flieger-Selbstlader-Karabiner 15* (Self-Loading Aircraft Carbine, Model 1915) as a stopgap measure to give aerial observers a firearm that could be effectively used in flight. For this use, the guns were equipped with a 30-round snail drum type magazine."[69] Near the end of the war, the United States developed the so-called "Pederson Device" which could convert the bolt action Model 1903 Springfield into a semiautomatic rifle. Approximately 85,000 were manufactured, only to see the war end in November 1918 before they could be deployed.[70] Most were destroyed, and functional Pederson Devices are very rare and valuable collector's items today.

Winchester introduced the first semiautomatic rifle sold commercially in the United States—a blowback-operated .22 rifle with a tubular magazine in the buttstock—in 1903.[71] The company introduced semiautomatic rifles chambered for the .32 and .35 Winchester Auto cartridges in 1905; a similar rifle chambered in .351 was introduced in 1907 and one chambered for the .401 Winchester Auto Cartridge was introduced in 1910. Winchester introduced the "popular-priced .22 auto rifle, listed as Model 74" in the late 1930s, and from 1911 to 1925 Winchester sold a recoil operated shotgun.[72]

---

[67] "Mondragon." https://modernfirearms.net/en/military-rifles/self-loading-rifles/mexico-self-loading-rifles/mondragon-eng/.   Retrieved January 20th, 2021.

[68]   "Mexican   Mondragon."   *Forgotten   Weapons.* https://www.forgottenweapons.com/early-semiauto-rifles/mexican-mondragon/. Retrieved February 3rd, 2019.

[69] *Id.*

[70] Johnson and Haven, 52 – 53.

[71] *Id.,* 53,

[72] *Id.,* 54,

Remington brought out its first semiautomatic rifle, the Model 8 Autoloading Rifle, in 1906, modernizing it as the Model 81 in 1936. Remington issued its first .22 semiautomatic rifle in 1914, the Model 16, reissuing it in improved form as the Model 24 in 1922. In the early 1940s Remington introduced the Series #550 Automatic Sporting Rifle, and the company introduced its first autoloading shotgun in 1910.[73] Other examples of commercially available semiautomatic firearms from the first decades of the 20th Century include the Standard Gas-Operated Automatic Rifle; the Marlin .22 Automatic Rifle; the Stevens No. 57 Automatic Rifle and the Stevens .22 Automatic Rifle Model 76; the Savage .22 Automatic Rifle Models 6, 6-S, 7, 7-S, and the Savage Automatic Shotgun Model 720; and the Mossberg .22 Automatic Rifle Models 50 and 51.[74]

The first semiautomatic rifle adopted as the standard infantry arm by any country was the .30 M1 Garand, officially adopted but the US Army in 1936 after nearly 16 years of experimentation by its inventor, John C. Garand of the US Army's Springfield Armory.[75] The US adopted another standard issue semiautomatic rifle—the M1 Carbine—in 1941, with the rifle first seeing service in 1942.[76]

What all of this means is that semiautomatic firearms technology is old technology, developed by civilian designers and adopted commercially for private use long before being adopted by any military organization. It is only comparatively recently that semiautomatic firearms, and particularly semiautomatic rifles in any form, have been controversial.

---

[73] *Id.*, 55 – 56.

[74] Johnson and Haven, plates between pp 58 and 59.

[75] *Id.*, 65.

[76] Dave Campell. "A Look Back at the M1 Carbine." *American Rifleman*, September 12th, 2017. https://www.americanrifleman.org/articles/2017/9/12/a-look-back-at-the-m1-carbine/. Retrieved February 3rd, 2019.

Chapter 3
The Campaign Against "Assault" Weapons

While "[h]andguns had previously been the primary target of gun prohibitionists,"[77] gun control activists failed to achieve outright bans on handguns save for a few instances such as those in the District of Columbia and Chicago.[78] Given this failure, gun control advocates shifted focus away from handguns in favor of a strategy of pursuing the prohibition of semiautomatic rifles such as the AR-15, expressly relying on their external appearance and the misperceptions about them in the public mind to foment fear and build support for their prohibition. As the Violence Policy Center's Josh Sugarman wrote in 1988,

> [t]he weapons' menacing looks, *coupled with the public's confusion* over fully automatic machineguns versus semiautomatic assault weapons—*anything that looks like a machinegun is assumed to be a machinegun*—can only increase the chance of public support for restrictions on these weapons. In addition, few people can envision a practical use for these weapons (emphasis added).[79]

Sugarman's report careens back and forth between inconsistent objectives. In the main, it cultivates the image of "menacing" semiautomatic weapons by associating them with various frightening bad actors:

---

[77] Stephen P. Halbrook. "Reality Check: The 'Assault Weapon' Fantasy and Second Amendment Jurisprudence." *The Georgetown Journal of Law and Public Policy*, Winter 2016, Volume 14, Number 1, 47.

[78] Josh Sugarman. *Assault Weapons and Accessories in America* (The Violence Policy Center, 1989). http://www.vpc.org/studies/awaconc.htm. Retrieved January 27th, 2019.

[79] *Id.*

Across America, the firepower in the hands of gun owners of varying stripes is increasing dramatically. The reason: assault weapons. Drug traffickers are finding that assault weapons—in addition to "standard issue" handguns—provide the extra firepower necessary to fight police and competing dealers. Right-wing paramilitary extremists, in their ongoing battle against the "Zionist Occupational Government," have made these easily purchased firearms their gun of choice.[80]

Sugarman further asserts that these rifles are favorites of "[d]rug [t]raffickers [and] [p]aramilitary groups"[81] and characterizes them as the "preferred weapons of the Jamaican posses," a Tampa, Florida gang and "the weapon of choice for … America's right-wing paramilitary extremists;" he also alleges that "[a]lthough many drug traffickers and members of paramilitary organizations are convicted felons, they are often able to illegally buy these weapons from retail sales outlets," and complains that "[i]n every state, assault rifles … are sold under the same lax restrictions that apply to hunting rifles and shotguns."[82] Yet the report does not substantiate these claims beyond a few anecdotes. It also makes bald, unsupported assertions about the applications of semiautomatic "assault" weapons, claiming that "[m]ost assault weapons have no legitimate hunting or sporting use," and that they "often have pistol grips and folding stocks and are typically lighter and more concealable than standard long guns."[83] The report shamelessly exploits racial tensions, class divisions, and anxiety about violent crime to incite fear and hostility toward a certain class of firearms, claiming that "[t]he fact that assault weapons

---

[80] *Id.*, http://www.vpc.org/studies/awaintro.htm, retrieved January 27th, 2019.

[81] *Id.*, http://www.vpc.org/studies/awadrug.htm, retrieved January 27th, 2019.

[82] *Id.*, http://www.vpc.org/studies/awadrug.htm, retrieved January 27th, 2019.

[83] *Id.*, http://www.vpc.org/studies/awaintro.htm, retrieved January 27th, 2019.

are increasingly being equated with America's drug trade may play a major role in motivating the public to call for their restriction."[84] It also accuses the National Rifle Association (NRA) of exaggerating the gun control movement's objectives:

> ... the NRA presents the controversy over assault weapons as a broader attack on all semiautomatic firearms, including hunting rifles with semiautomatic mechanisms. By framing the debate as one concerning all semi-autos, as opposed to a specific category of semi-auto, the NRA is able to present efforts to restrict assault weapons as a threat to hunters. The NRA recognizes the fact that it is far easier to mobilize its membership and non-NRA outdoorsmen with images of banning their trusted hunting rifles as opposed to UZIs or TEC-9s ... While the NRA struggles to turn the assault weapons debate into a semi-auto debate for public relations purposes, legislators and members of the press have been making it into one inadvertently. Neither of America's national handgun restriction organizations has come out in favor of restricting or banning all semi-autos, and have only recently begun dealing with long guns (there is no national organization calling for restrictions on all guns). Yet in discussions of assault firearms, those urging restrictions on these weapons have used the terms assault, paramilitary, and semiautomatic weapon interchangeably. This misusage apparently stems from an unfamiliarity with weapons terminology and a lack of understanding of the wide range of weapons covered by the term semiautomatic. As the result of this lack of knowledge, and the difficulties in defining assault weapons in legal terms, laws have been proposed on

---

[84] *Id.,* http://www.vpc.org/studies/awaconc.htm, retrieved January 27th, 2019.

the state level that would place waiting periods on all semi-auto weapons. In August 1988, The New York Times ran two editorials in favor of such a law on the Federal level, as well as urging a ban on the sale of assault weapons.[85]

Sugarman's claims to the contrary notwithstanding, his report makes clear that the Violence Policy Center intended to leverage any success in restricting "assault" weapons to achieve further restrictions, including on handguns:

> Assault weapons are increasingly being perceived by legislators, police organizations, handgun restriction advocates, and the press as a public health threat. As these weapons come to be associated with drug traffickers, paramilitary extremists, and survivalists, their television and movie glamour is losing its luster to a violent reality. Because of this fact, assault weapons are quickly becoming the leading topic of America's gun control debate and will most likely remain the leading gun control issue for the near future. *Such a shift will not only damage America's gun lobby, but strengthen the handgun restriction lobby for the following reasons* ... It will be a new topic in what has become to the press and public an 'old' debate ... [and] Efforts to stop restrictions on assault weapons will only further alienate the police from the gun lobby. ... [86] (emphasis added).

Finally, the report links efforts to ban semiautomatic weapons that share some features with military rifles directly to the corresponding effort to ban or restrict handguns:

---

[85] *Id.*, http://www.vpc.org/studies/awadebat.htm, retrieved January 27th, 2019.
[86] *Id.*, http://www.vpc.org/studies/awaconc.htm, retrieved January 27th, 2019.

Efforts to restrict assault weapons are more likely to succeed than those to restrict handguns. Although the majority of Americans favor stricter handgun controls, and a consistent 40 percent of Americans favor banning the private sale and possession of handguns, many Americans do believe that handguns are effective weapons for home self-defense and the majority of Americans mistakenly believe that the Second Amendment of the Constitution guarantees the individual right to keep and bear arms. Yet, many who support the individual's right to own a handgun have second thoughts when the issue comes down to assault weapons. Assault weapons are often viewed the same way as machine guns and 'plastic' firearms— a weapon that poses such a grave risk that it's worth compromising a perceived Constitutional right.[87]

One commentator has summarized this strategy thus:

> People who know better [than to believe that banning "assault" weapons would lead to a reduction in crime] may nevertheless support "assault weapon" bans as a tactic for achieving more stringent gun restrictions down the road. "No one should have any illusion about what was accomplished," the *Washington Post* editorialized after President Bill Clinton signed the 1994 ban into law. "Assault weapons play a part in only a small percentage of crime. The provision is mainly symbolic; its virtue will be if it turns out to be, as hoped, a stepping stone to broader gun control." *The faulty logic of such legislation actually works to the benefit of those who support "broader gun control." Once people realize that banning these firearms has no measurable effect on*

---

[87] *Id.,* http://www.vpc.org/studies/awaconc.htm, retrieved January 27th, 2019.

violence, they may be primed to accept more ambitious measures[88] (emphasis added).

The gun control movement has labored to promote a series of myths about AR-15 rifles: That they are more deadly than other firearms; that they can produce rates of fire comparable to their selective fire counterparts; that certain features they share with military firearms—most notably pistol grips, "barrel shrouds"[89], and detachable magazines—have no legitimate civilian application; that these weapons are the special favorites of criminals and mass shooters; that they are not commonly used for lawful purposes; and that violent crime is analogous to infantry combat. In short, they have worked tirelessly to create a "weapons of war myth" surrounding AR-15 rifles and similar weapons in pursuit of their campaign to ban them and many other firearms.

In *District of Columbia v. Heller*[90] and *McDonald v. City of Chicago*[91] the US Supreme Court repudiated Sugarman's pinched reading of the Second Amendment, finding that it embodies an individual right to keep and bear arms separate and apart from militia membership, enforceable against both the Federal Government and the states. Nonetheless, court after court has sought to circumscribe the right to keep and bear arms to within as narrow an operative scope as possible, often relying on precisely the sort of unsubstantiated myths, misconceptions, and mistaken beliefs about firearms listed above.

---

[88] Jacob Sullum. "'Assault Weapons' Explained: How a Scary Name for an Arbitrary Group of Firearms Distorts the Gun Control Debate." *Reason*, Volume 50, No. 2, June 2018, 57, citing "Hyping the Crime Bill," *The Washington Post*, September 15th, 1994.

[89] The term "barrel shroud" appears to be a neologism coined by the legislators, regulators, and/or the American gun control movement. The term does not appear in any of the US Military firearms doctrinal manuals that I reviewed in the course of preparing this paper. As we shall see below, the proper term for these components is "handguard."

[90] *District of Columbia v. Heller*, 554 US 570, 128 S.Ct. 2783 (2008).

[91] *McDonald v. City of Chicago*, 561 US 742, 130 S.Ct. 3020 (2010).

Chapter 4
The "Weapons of War" Myth: Combat, Crime, and Legitimate Shooting Applications

The *public* rationale for banning the AR-15 and similar rifles was concisely stated in a 1999 Justice Department study assessing the 1994 Federal Assault Weapons Ban, asserting that the offending features were banned because they "*appeared* useful in military and criminal applications but that were *deemed* unnecessary in shooting sports" (emphasis added).[92] The words chosen are very illuminating: the word "appear" has been defined as "to *seem* or *look* to be" (emphasis added),[93] and "deem" as "to have an opinion; suppose,"[94] or "to have an opinion: believe."[95] These qualifiers show that the authors of the 1994 Assault Weapons Ban rested the enactment upon nothing more than their own guesses about what the capabilities and uses of these firearms might be, and that they made no effort to validate these assumptions.

Crime and Infantry Combat: Fundamentally Different Phenomena

The call to ban the AR-15 rests upon a fatally flawed premise: that crime and combat are equivalent phenomena. They are not. Dismounted infantry combat—the only type of combat relevant to this discussion—is a phenomenon in which a collective entity cooperatively seeks to "close with the enemy by means of fire and maneuver to defeat or capture him, or to repel his assault by fire, close combat, and counterattack."[96] It occurs in a context in which

---

[92] Jeffrey A. Roth and Christopher S. Koper. *Impacts of the 1994 Assault Weapons Ban: 1994–96* (National Institute of Justice Research Brief, March 1999), 2.

[93] *The American Heritage Dictionary*, Second College Edition (Houghton Mifflin Company, 1986).

[94] *Id.*

[95] *Merriam Webster Dictionary.* www.merriam-webster.com/dictionary/deem, Retrieved February 2nd, 2019.

the contending forces are presumed capable of offering meaningful resistance, and operations are planned accordingly, each side mustering any supporting fires and other combat multipliers available to destroy or defeat the opposing force. By contrast, violent crime, whether a street mugging or a mass shooting, is ordinarily a phenomenon wherein one or more assailants attack an unprepared victim or group of victims, whom the assailant presumes to be unarmed and unable to offer meaningful resistance.

Except in the most unusual circumstances, violent crime is an entirely different activity than small unit infantry combat. A key goal in dismounted infantry combat is the achievement of fire superiority: that is, directing such a high volume of fire against the enemy that he is prevented from firing or maneuvering effectively in response. It is for this purpose that soldiers are equipped with machineguns and selective fire weapons. In infantry combat, the enemy is presumed capable of resisting effectively, necessitating concentration of overwhelming combat power to facilitate subduing them without absorbing unacceptably high losses oneself. The attacking commander must carefully plan his attack and coordinate to bring massive combat power to bear on his enemy. Doing anything else invites unnecessary casualties and defeat.

By contrast, a violent offender at large among the populace faces no such daunting considerations in planning his depredations. He faces a different and less intimidating task: to attack and overcome a victim whom he presumes to be unarmed, unsuspecting, and unprepared. The criminal achieves "fire superiority" by the mere brandishing of a weapon of *any* kind—possibly even physical strength alone. *He can do this because he has selected targets he believes to be unarmed.* If a criminal has chosen an unarmed victim, his introducing a weapon into the situation vests him with an overwhelming superiority of force against that person, creating an imbalance of power so greatly

---

[96] *FM 7-8, Infantry Rifle Platoon and Squad* (Department of the Army, 22 April 1992) paragraph 1-1; See also *FM 3-21.20, The Infantry Battalion* (Department of the Army, 13 December 2006), 1-1.

in the criminal's favor that any marginal advantage offered by the features of the criminal's weapons are simply surplus to requirements—he doesn't need them. Virtually any weapon, particularly a firearm (semiautomatic or not) is sufficient to completely overwhelm an unarmed victim, with or without features such as pistol grips, adjustable stocks, and detachable magazines. Any qualitative advantages of one type of firearm over another in this scenario is simply overwhelmed by and subsumed into the huge disparity of power between the armed assailant and the unarmed victim inherent in the presence of a firearm of any kind; a criminal doesn't need a semiautomatic firearm to wreak havoc, much less one with supposedly "military" features.

Conflating Civilian Semiautomatic Firearms with Selective Fire Military Arms

As foreshadowed by Sugarman, the beliefs of many Americans about the AR-15 and similar rifles have indeed been strongly shaped by the mistaken belief that a firearm outwardly resembling an arm used by the military must be a machinegun. But this belief is indeed mistaken, as one earthy, colloquial source explains:

> AR-15s, civilian semi-auto AK-47 clones, etc., ARE NOT MACHINEGUNS. The most common AK-47 variant in the US civilian market is the Romanian-built WASR-10, imported by Century Arms, because it is the least expensive AK. Although similar in appearance, they DO NOT fit the definition of MACHINEGUN because they fire one and only one round with a single pull of the trigger, which means they are semiautomatic. An AR-15, despite its similarity to an M-16, is not the same thing. Vietnam era M-16s were true MACHINEGUNS also, capable of fully automatic fire. The Pentagon brass found this to be a waste of ammo and restricted later models to three round burst mode as the only option for

selective fire. Machineguns are mainly carried by the military and only rarely found in civilian hands … Most ordinary Americans can't tell the f*cking difference between a real machinegun and a semiautomatic like the WASR-10 or AR-15. Unfortunately the News media and politicians are similarly misinformed, to the detriment of all (emphasis in original).[97]

Exaggerating Semiautomatic Rifle Rates of Fire

The perception that the AR-15 is equivalent to a machinegun has been "industriously circulated … [and] spread abroad"[98] by firearms prohibitionists in their zeal to narrow the scope of the Second Amendment as much as possible. One way that they have done this is to attribute fantastical rates of fire to the AR-15. Shortly after the 2016 Orlando Nightclub Massacre, Congressman Alan Grayson had this to say to about the AR-15:

If [Mr. Mateen] was not able to buy a weapon that shoots off 700 rounds in a minute, a lot of those people would still be alive … If somebody like him had nothing worse to deal with than a Glock pistol … he might have killed three or four people and not 50. It's way too easy to kill people in America today, and we have to think long and hard about what to do about that.[99]

[97] "Machine gun." *The Urban Dictionary*, March 20, 2008, https://www.urbandictionary.com/define.php?term=Machine%20gun. Retrieved February 10th, 2019.
[98] Jane Austen. *Pride and Prejudice*, in *Jane Austen, the Complete Novels* (Gramercy Books, 1981), 343.
[99] Douglass Ernst. "Alan Grayson claims AR-15s can fire '700 rounds in a minute' after Orlando attack." *The Washington Times*, June 13th, 2016, https://www.washingtontimes.com/news/2016/jun/13/alan-grayson-

The gross inaccuracy of this claim was shown, perhaps ironically, in a piece found in the left-leaning *Vice News* entitled "Glock pistols are the overlooked weapon in American mass shooting:"

> A list of mass shootings between April 1999 and January 2013 prepared for lawmakers in Connecticut showed that rifles were used in ten incidents and shotguns in ten others, while handguns were used in 42. Glock brand pistols turned up in nine of those cases. Another compendium of mass shootings since 2009 by the *New York Times* showed that handguns were used in thirteen incidents, compared to five in which a rifle was the primary weapon. Glocks were recovered from six of the perpetrators.[100]

The piece further describes mass shootings carried out with Glock pistols at Killeen, Texas; Virginia Tech University; Jared Lee Loughner's attack on Representative Gabby Gifford; a "rampage" at an apartment complex in Hialeah, Florida; Dylann Roof's attack on an African-American church in Charleston, South Carolina; and Vester Lee Flanagan II's shooting of a reporter and cameraman during a live broadcast in Roanoke, Virginia.[101]

Representative Grayson is not the only public figure retailing inaccurate claims about AR-15 rifles. Jonathan Lowy of the Brady Center did as well in 2013, derisively declaring that they "would shred your venison before you could eat it, or put a trophy up on the wall" if you use one for hunting;[102] he later doubled down, declaring that

---

claims-ar-15-rifles-can-fire-700-roun/. Retrieved February 10th, 2019.
[100] Francisco Alvarado. "Glock pistols are the overlooked weapon in American mass shootings," *Vice News*, June 21st, 2016, https://news.vice.com/en_us/article/gy9nj4/glock-pistol-omar-mateen-orlando-mass-shooting. Retrieved May 31st, 2019.
[101] *Id.*
[102] Jonathan Lowy: Lowy, Jonathan and Malcolm, John G. "Gun Control: Assessing Constitutionality and Effectiveness." Federalist Society Podcast,

"the pistol grips enable a mass killer to spray fire, it was the old military usage of spray and pray."[103] Lowy's comments plainly distort reality: a hunter cannot "shred" his prey with a single round or even a series of individually fired rounds, and a soldier cannot "spray" fire one shot at a time as a semiautomatic rifle is constrained to. These assertions seek to create the false impression that a semiautomatic AR-15 has a rate of fire equivalent to that of a selective fire M16 rifle.

These claims cannot not withstand scrutiny, as the *Washington Examiner* reports:

> Conrad Close, the conservative editor-in-chief of *American Crossroads* ... offered $50,000 to the charity of Mr. Grayson's choice if he accomplish[ed] the feat ... "Let's do some math here," replied one reader. "700 rounds / 30 rounds per mag = 23.333 magazines. For round numbers, 23 mags. 60 seconds per minute / 23 magazines = 2.6 seconds *per magazine*. 30 rounds per mag / 2.6 seconds per magazine = 11.53 rounds per second. Not to mention, you'd have to sustain this for a full 60 seconds, no time factored for changing magazines ..."[104] (emphasis added).

According to self-defense expert Massad Ayoob, "the average person [can] fire a gun with a long trigger pull and reset, such as a double action revolver, at a rate of four shots per second measuring from first shot to last, and a semiautomatic pistol with short trigger pull and reset at five rounds per second (*world champions* can shoot at roughly twice that speed)"[105] (emphasis added). While Ayoob refers

April   3rd,   2013,   50:21   –   50:28.
https://fedsoc.org/commentary/podcasts/gun-control-assessing-constitutionality-and-effectiveness-podcast. Retrieved February 10th, 2019.
[103] *Id.*, 48:51 - 51:53, retrieved July 8th, 2019.
[104] Ernst, 96.
[105] Massad Ayoob. *Straight Talk on Armed Defense* (Gun Digest Books, 2017), 119 (citing "[n]oted gun expert John Farnam").

to handguns in this quote, there is absolutely no difference between pulling the trigger on a semiautomatic rifle and a semiautomatic pistol. As to rates of fire for such arms, while "world champions" may achieve rates of fire at something like ten rounds per second, this is simply beyond the typical shooter: In their work *Automatic Arms*, Melvin M. Johnson, Jr. and Charles T. Haven observed that "[i]t is customary to consider rapid fire in terms of how many shots are fired in one minute. *This is unreal and very misleading*. The true criterion and measure of efficiency are expressed in terms of how many shots are necessary to fire the necessary number of effective shots"[106] (emphasis added). Their work shows conclusively the meaninglessness of many claims about semiautomatic rifles. It included the results of various shooting tests comparing the bolt action M1903 Springfield Rifle and a semiautomatic rifle (most likely the M1 Garand). Based upon their tests,

> [c]omparisons [of the M1903 bolt-action rifle could] now be submitted with the semiautomatic rifle, caliber .30. The actual ratio of firing speed of both types of rifles *in expert hands* proves the following: 1.5 shots in 3 seconds, M1903, *unaimed* [and] 10 shots in 1.5 seconds, semiautomatic, *unaimed*[107] (emphasis added).

Thus, attempting to replicate automatic fire with a semiautomatic weapon would produce only wild, inaccurate, and comparatively ineffective fire. Haven and Johnson provide data from shooting tests conducted at various ranges by expert marksmen. Their data shows that semiautomatic rifles can clearly produce fire much faster than bolt action rifles, and in the hands of experts can produce impressive feats of rapid and accurate fire. Nevertheless, their findings also show that the *practical* rates of fire for semiautomatics are measured in *seconds per shot*, not the scores of shots per second often claimed.

---

[106] Johnson and Haven, 189.
[107] *Id.*, 190.

Rates of Fire as Set Forth in
Military Doctrine

Calls to ban the AR-15 rely on the implicit claim that such rifles are, as Virginia Lieutenant Governor Justin Fairfax described them, "essentially automatic."[108] Because this claim is made to conflate semiautomatic rifles with selective fire M16 rifles in the public's mind, an examination of the military doctrine on semiautomatic weapons is in order.

Of the many US military doctrinal publications I examined preparing this book, only one—published in 1923—made any claim as to the ability of a marksman to replicate automatic fire with a semiautomatic weapon, and that publication was skeptical. Addressing the then relatively new selective fire M1918 Browning Automatic Rifle (the famous BAR), *Training Regulation 150-30, Marksmanship: The Automatic Rifle*, stated that "[a] well trained automatic rifleman can, if necessary, deliver practically the same volume of fire with semiautomatic fire as with automatic fire … "[109] but it denigrated the attempt, stating that "[u]se of automatic fire is exceptional, since it is inaccurate even at close ranges, hard on the rifle due to excessive heat and vibration, and a waste of ammunition. Its only advantage is the effect on morale of friendly troops and that of the enemy."[110] The claim that semiautomatic fire could replicate automatic fire does not hold up to scrutiny, and the Army had dropped it from the doctrinal manual by 1940, instead stating only that "an excessive rate [of fire] wastes ammunition without corresponding effect."[111] This change is just as well, as the findings of

---

[108] Jim Geraghty. "What the Heck Is an 'Essentially Automatic Weapon'?" *National Review Online*, October 5th, 2017. https://www.nationalreview.com/corner/what-heck-essentially-automatic-weapon/. Retrieved February 10th, 2019.

[109] *TR 150-30, Marksmanship, the Automatic Rifle*, (War Department, November 21, 1923), 37.

[110] *Id.*

Johnson and Haven conclusively show that semiautomatic rifles cannot effectively replicate automatic fire.[112]

More enlightening is US military doctrine relating to the M16 family of rifles, the selective fire rifle with which gun control activists seek to confuse the AR-15. The M16 was first introduced in large numbers in the US Army as the XM16E1, when the Department of Defense placed an order with Colt for a "one time buy" of 85,000 rifles in November 1963,[113] with the first examples arriving in 1964.[114] "In February 1967 ... the XM16E1 rifle was accepted as a standard service weapon and re-designated the M16A1."[115] The M16 series has remained in service as the US military's primary individual arm ever since.

The US Army measures a firearm's rate of fire in three ways: cyclic, maximum effective, and sustained. All selective fire weapons have a maximum—cyclic—"rate of fire that is expressed as rounds per minute (r.p.m.)."[116] This is the *theoretical* number of cartridges which could be fired automatically in one minute"[117] (emphasis

---

[111] *FM 23-20, Basic Field Manual, Browning Automatic Rifle, Caliber.30, M1918, Without Bipod* (War Department, 1940), 178.

[112] Johnson and Haven, 190.

[113] R. Blake Stevens and Edward C. Ezell. *The Black Rifle – M16 Retrospective* (Collector Grade Publications, 2004), 118; *FM 23-9, M16A1 Rifle and Rifle Marksmanship* (Department of the Army, June 1974), Appendix F, "M16A1 Rifle History," 175; *American Rifleman*, December 1963, 32.

[114] Stevens and Ezell, 149.

[115] *FM 23-9*, June 1974, 175.

[116] *Assault Rifle Fact Sheet #1*. The Institute for Research on Small Arms in International Security, https://guncite.com/assausup.txt, retrieved February 10th, 2019.

[117] *Operator's Manual for: Colt Carbine* (Colt's Manufacturing IP Holding Company, LLC. November 2015), 10. See also, *FM 23-8, US Rifle 7.62MM, M14 and M14E2* (Headquarters, Department of the Army, May 1965), 5; *FM 23-8, M14 and M14A1 Rifles and Rifle Marksmanship* (Headquarters, Department of the Army, April 1974), 7; and *FM 23-9, M16A1 and M16A2 Rifle Marksmanship* (Headquarters, Department of the Army, July 1989),

added). The *effective*, as opposed to the theoretical, rate of fire is limited by the rate of fire at which a shooter can fire and *still achieve hits*,[118] and the physical limitations of the firearm itself—notably, its propensity to overheat and therefore to malfunction under hard use.[119] The US Army has defined the *maximum effective* rate of fire as "[t]he highest rate of fire that can be maintained and still achieve target hits."[120] Finally, the US Army has further defined the *sustained* rate of fire as the "[r]ate of fire that a weapon can deliver for an indefinite period without overheating."[121]

Because semiautomatic rifles such as the AR-15 fire only one round for each pull of the trigger, they do not have a cyclic rate of fire, properly understood, and can only be intelligently said to have maximum effective and sustained rates of fire. Because the operating cycle of an AR-15 is identical to that of an M16 operating in semiautomatic mode, the rates of fire for AR-15 rifles can be illuminated by reference to the semiautomatic operating characteristics of the M16 family of rifles as set forth in US Army doctrine.

According to the US Army, the *cyclical* rate of fire for the M16 family of rifles—that is, the rate at which they will theoretically fire in automatic mode given a constant supply of ammunition and no mechanical malfunctions (a highly dubious assumption), is between 700 and 800 rounds per minute for the M16A1[122] and 700—900

Glossary, 5.

[118] *FM 23-9*, July 1989, Glossary, 7.

[119] *Id.*, Glossary, 11; *FM 23-8*, May 1965, 5; *FM 23-8*, April 1974, 7.

[120] *FM 23-9, July 1989*, Glossary, 7.

[121] *Id.*, Glossary, 11; see also *FM 23-8*, May 1965, 5; *FM 23-9, Rifle, 5.56-MM, XM16E1*, 1966, 5; and *FM 23-8*, April 1974, 7.

[122] *FM 23-9, Rifle, 5.56-MM, XM16E1* (Headquarters, Department of the Army, January 1965, reprinted by Cornell Publications, 2019), 4. *FM 23-9, Rifle, 5.56-MM, XM16E1*,1966, 5; *FM 23-9, Rifle, 5.56-MM, M16A1* (Headquarters, Department of the Army, March 1970), 4; *FM 23-9, M16A1 Rifle and Rifle Marksmanship*, June 1974, 6; *FM 23-9*, July 1989, 2-3; and *SH 21-25, The Infantryman's Handbook* (United States Army Infantry School,

rounds per minute for the M16A2/A3 and M4 Carbine,[123] although the manufacturer has claimed cyclical rates of fire of 700—950 rounds per minute for the M16A1[124] and 700—970 rounds per minute for the M4 Carbine.[125] As noted above, however, these stated cyclical rates of fire are "unreal and very misleading"[126] given the practical constraints at play in the operation of a firearm.

More important are a rifle's *maximum effective* and *sustained* rates of fire. For the M16 series, the maximum effective rate of fire in automatic mode is 150—200 rounds per minute depending upon the model, whereas the maximum effective rate of fire in semiautomatic mode is 45 to 65 rounds per minute (depending upon the version of the rifle), with 45 rounds per minute being the current rating for the M4 Carbine. [127]Thus, contrary to the inferences that firearms prohibitionists would have us draw, a selective fire M16 rifle employed in automatic mode produces effective fire, on average, over three times faster than can a semiautomatic AR-15. To put yet a finer point on the comparison, the 700-round per minute rate of fire attributed to AR-15 rifles by Representative Grayson is almost 13 times faster than an AR-15 can *effectively* fire. Some versions of the M16, such as the M16A2, are configured to fire three-round bursts.

March 1985), 39.

[123] *FM 3-22.9 (FM 23-9), Rifle Marksmanship M16A1, M16A2/3, M16A4, AND M4 Carbine* (Headquarters, Department of the Army, April 2003, with changes 1-4), Table 2-1.

[124] *M16A1 Operator's Manual* (Colt Industries Firearms Division, 1975), 1.

[125] *Operator's Manual for Colt Carbine* (Colt's Manufacturing IP Holding Company LLC, November 2015), 10.

[126] Johnson and Haven, 189.

[127] *FM 3-22.9(FM 23-9),* April 2003, with changes 1 – 4, 2-1; *FM 23-9, Rifle, 5.56-MM, XM16E1,* 1965, 4. *FM 23-9, Rifle, 5.56-MM, XM16E1,* 1966, 5; *FM 23-9,* 1970, 4; *FM 23-9,* June 1974, 6; *FM 23-9,* July 1989, 2-3; *SH 21-25,* 39; *M16A1 Operator's Manual,* 1975, 1; *Professional Facts for Infantry Combat Platoon Leaders* (United States Army Infantry School, Fort Benning GA, September 1974), 30; *TM 9-1005-249-10, Operator's Manual for Rifle, 5.56-MM, M16 (1005-00-856-6885), Rifle, 5.56-MM, M16A1 (1005-00-073-9421)* (Headquarters, Department of the Army, February 1985), 1-4.

Even for these rifles, the maximum effective rate of fire in burst mode is 90 rounds per minute—twice the maximum effective rate of fire of the semiautomatic AR-15.[128]

Even this does not tell the full story of the extent to which gun control advocates like Representative Grayson—whether willfully or out of ignorance—have exaggerated the capabilities of the AR-15. The rates of fire set forth above are *maximum* rates, to be employed for short durations only. The sustained rate of fire for the both the M16 and the AR-15—the rate at which they can fire for an indefinite period without overheating—is 12 to 15 rounds per minute,[129] for an average of 13.5 rounds per minute—*almost 52 times slower* than the 700 rounds per minute claimed for the AR-15 by Representative Grayson.

Semiautomatic rifles such as the AR-15 cannot even approximate—much less replicate—the effective rates of fire of machineguns or selective fire weapons, and they cannot even remotely approach the extreme capabilities that some poorly informed commentators attribute to them. This observation is not limited to the AR-15. The "rate of effective sustained fire [was] about 40 rounds per minute" in semiautomatic mode for the selective fire M1918 BAR[130]—less than one seventeenth of Representative Grayson's alleged 700 rounds per minute; the selective fire M14 Rifle in semiautomatic mode had a maximum effective rate of fire of approximately 40 rounds per minute, with a sustained rate of fire of fifteen rounds per minute—17.5 and 46.7 times slower than the Representative Grayson's 700 rounds per minute, respectively.[131, 132]

---

[128] *FM 3-22.9(FM 23-9),* April 2003, with changes 1 – 4, 2-1.

[129] *Id.; FM 23-9,* January 1965, 4; *FM 23-9,* July 1966, 5; *FM 23-9,* March 1970, 4; *FM 23-9,* June 1974, 6; *FM 23-9,* July 1989, 2-3; *SH 21-25,* March 1985, 39; *M16A1 Operator's Manual,* 1975, 1; *Professional Facts for Infantry Combat Platoon Leaders,* 30.

[130] *FM 23-20,* 1940, 1.

[131] *FM 23-8,* May 1965, 5; *FM 23-8,* April 1974, 7.

[132] In fact, one early reference on the M14 Rifle rated its capabilities somewhat lower, listing its maximum effective rate of fire in semiautomatic

For the venerable M1 Garand, the semiautomatic mainstay of US forces during the Second World War and after, estimated rates of fire range from about twelve rounds per minute in 1958[133], to 16—24 round per minute (for an average of 20) in 1965—35 times slower than Representative Grayson's 700 rounds per minute.[134]

Mischaracterizing the Purpose of Pistol Grips and Handguards

Gun control activists have compounded their exaggerations about AR-15 rates of fire by falsely characterizing the purpose of certain features to make them seem more dangerous than they actually are. The archetypal example of this is their obsession with pistol grips. It will come as a surprise to many that the term "pistol grip" is actually more ambiguous than gun control proponents know. As traditionally understood before the AR-15 and other semiautomatic rifles became controversial, a pistol grip was *"the curved part of the stock behind & below the action on the rifle or shotgun"* (emphasis added)[135]—in other words, a "pistol grip" as traditionally understood was simply the breach-end grip on what gun control advocates would view as a traditionally configured rifle, as opposed to the handguard or forearm where the shooter grips the firearm forward of the trigger. In the 1994 Assault Weapons Ban, gun prohibitionists appropriated this term and recast it as something sinister and dangerous, including "a pistol grip that protrudes conspicuously beneath the action of the

---

mode as 20 – 30 rounds per minute and its sustained rate as 8 – 10 rounds per minute, "[b]ased on limited tests." *FM 23-8, US Rifle 7.62-MM M14* (Department of the Army, December 1959, reprinted by Normount Armament Company), 5.

[133] Extrapolated from a rapid fire drill in which nine rounds are fired in 50 seconds. *FM 23-5, US Rifle Caliber 30, M1* (Department of the Army, September 1958), 124.

[134] *FM 23-5, US Rifle Caliber.30, M1* (Department of the Army, May 1965), 3.

[135] R. A. Steindler. *The Firearms Dictionary* (Stackpole Books, 1970), 114 – 115.

weapon" as one of the features that counted as indicative of a so-called "assault weapon." [136]

As with other enacted or proposed semiautomatic rifle regulations, this focus on pistol grips is entirely misplaced. The purpose of the pistol grip is the same, whether in its earlier form of "the curved part of the stock behind & below the action,"[137] or of the contemporary type "protrud[ing] conspicuously beneath the action of the weapon."[138] In either configuration,

> [t]he pistol grip gives the trigger hand a grasping surface & enables the shooter to pull the gun tighter into his shoulder, thus not only adding support to the gun, but also lessening the effect of the recoil.[139]

Thus, the pistol grip in either form is an essential component for accurate shooting—essential, in fact, to operating the rifle at all. The contemporary pistol grip of the type that gun control advocates seek to ban is an improvement over the earlier form to be sure, providing a more comfortable, surer grip. In the words of one commentator, "what the pistol grip does is allow you to stabilize the gun so that your second shot is not going to be indiscriminate but is going to be focused on your target."[140] The modern pistol grip, so loathed by gun control advocates, arguably performs its function better than the pistol grip in its earlier form; yet it is still performing the same function: enabling the shooter to securely grasp and

---

[136] Public Law 103-322, September 13th, 1994, previously codified at 18 US Code §921(a)(30)(B)(ii), part of the so-called "Assault Weapons Ban" of 1994, which expired in 2004.

[137] Steindler, 114.

[138] 1994 Assault Weapons Ban.

[139] Steindler, 115.

[140] John G. Malcolm. Malcolm, John G. and Jonathan Lowy. *Gun Control: Assessing Constitutionality and Effectiveness – Podcast* (The Federalist Society, April 3rd, 2013). https://fedsoc.org/commentary/podcasts/gun-control-assessing-constitutionality-and-effectiveness-podcast, 52:40 – 53:11. Retrieved November 28th, 2020.

stabilize the rifle to be able to hit what he is aiming at. While the modern pistol grip is an ergonomic improvement over earlier designs, it is not the great leap forward in lethality that gun control advocates claim. As convenient as it is, the modern pistol grip is merely an incremental improvement on an earlier advancement in firearms technology, the *receiver*, which is

> [t]he basic unit of a firearm that houses the firing and breach mechanism and to which the barrel and stock are assembled. In revolvers, pistols and break-open guns, it is called the "frame."[141] [142]

In early firearms, the wooden stock functioned both as stock and receiver: The barrel was bedded in a channel carved for that purpose and fixed in place by steel barrel bands, while the firing action, or lock, was assembled on a steel lockplate secured to the stock via screws. The firing components attached to the lockplate—the mainspring, tumbler, bridle, sear, sear spring, and associated screws—were housed inside a cavity in the stock. The early form of pistol grip to which gun control advocates seek to bind shooters in perpetuity was a necessary compromise in a weapon where the stock did double duty both as the contact point between the firearm and the shoulder and as the platform upon which the firing components are assembled.

The installation of the firing action of the gun into a metal receiver was introduced in the nineteenth century. Early examples were the Hunt Volitional Rifle (with the receiver styled as the "lock-case")[143] and the Lewis Jennings Breach Loading Firearm, both

---

[141] Bousard and Wormley, 450.

[142] See also Steindler, 189: The receiver is "that part of the firearm (excepting hinged frame guns) that houses the bolt, firing pin, mainspring, the trigger group, & the magazine or ammunition feed system."

[143] Walter Hunt. US Patent No. 6,663, *Combined Piston-Breach and Firing-Cock Repeating-Gun*, August 21st, 1849. http://pdfpiw.uspto.gov/.piw?PageNum=0&docid=00006663&IDKey=D 3ED9E34B725&HomeUrl=http%3A%2F%2Fpatft.uspto.gov%2Fnetahtm

patented in 1849.[144][145] Evolution was slow thereafter, with decades passing before repeating arms of any type superseded breach loaders in American service. But eventually the metal receiver, freeing the stock from double duty and leaving it to its sole duty of serving as a brace against the shoulder, opened the way for new design innovations including the modern pistol grip as we know it, positioned below the firing action in such a manner as to provide a more natural, comfortable, and effective grasp of the rifle. It is this purpose, and no other, for which the modern pistol grip is intended.

Given the innocuous purpose of the modern pistol grip, gun control advocates have resorted to attributing functions to it far beyond its actual use. Whether this has been an intentional propaganda effort or an honest mistake is unknown. What is clear is that gun control advocates have aggressively seized upon the modern pistol grip as the emblem and evidence of the iniquity they attribute to the AR-15 and similar rifles. The principal charge against modern pistol grips was succinctly stated by the District of Columbia Council's Committee on Public Safety and the Judiciary in their 2008 *Report on Bill 17-843, Firearms Registration Amendment Act of 2008*, asserting that so-called "[a]ssault weapons also have features such as pistol grips ... Pistol grips help stabilize the weapon during rapid fire *and allow the shooter to spray fire from the hip position*" (emphasis added).[146]

---

l%2FPTO%2Fpatimg.htm. Retrieved February 16th, 2019.

[144] Lewis Jennings. US Patent No. 6,973, *Improvement in Breach Loading Firearms*, December 25th, 1849. http://pdfpiw.uspto.gov/.piw?docid=00006973&SectionNum=4&IDKey =06FFA4B55622&HomeUrl=http://patft.uspto.gov/netahtml/PTO/pati mg.htm. Retrieved February 16th, 2019.

[145] For a brief overview of the development of lever action firearms, including the evolution of the corporate entities that produced them, see Dr. James R. Lucie, *Volcanic and Henry Firearms*, (The American Society of Arms Collector, nd), http://americansocietyofarmscollectors.org/wp-content/uploads/2013/03/B010_Lucie.pdf, retrieved February 16th, 2019.

[146] *Report on Bill 17-843, "Firearms Registration Amendment Act of 2008"* (District of Columbia Council Committee on Public Safety and the Judiciary, November 25th, 2008), 7.

Lowy restated this position at a Federalist Society conference at the National Press Club in 2019, claiming that "things like barrel shrouds [handguards] they enable [sic] you to hold the gun, *particularly in conjunction with the rear pistol grip* where you can spray an area and kill large amounts of people …"[147]

Gun control advocates allege that pistol grips and handguards as they appear on AR-15 exist to enable the shooter to *spray fire from the hip*. Does this claim hold up?

US Military Doctrine Does Not Support the Claim that Pistol Grips and Handguards are Intended to Facilitate Spray Firing from the Hip

AR-15 rifles are not military arms, irrespective of what features they share with military selective fire weapons. Nonetheless, because firearms prohibitionists insist upon conflating them with their selective fire look-alikes, US Army marksmanship doctrine provides a very useful benchmark against which to compare the prohibitionists' claim that pistol grips and handguards facilitate rapid firing "from the hip." But first, it will be helpful to clarify certain terms of reference. Those who advocate banning AR-15s use the term "barrel shroud" to describe "a shroud that is attached to, or partially or completely encircles, the barrel of a firearm so that the shroud protects the user of the firearm from heat generated by the barrel", while expressly excluding "a slide that partially or completely encloses the barrel; or an extension of the stock along the bottom of

---

[147] Jonathan Lowy, *et al.*, *The Second Amendment in The New Supreme Court*, Panel 2: "Are Semiautomatic Rifles, aka 'Assault Weapons,' Protected by the Second Amendment?" (The Federalist Society, Civil Rights Practice Group, at the National Press Club, Washington, D.C., January 25th, 2019, 59:21 – 1:00:52). https://fedsoc.org/conferences/the-2nd-amendment-in-the-new-supreme-court?#agenda-item-panel-2-are-semiautomatic-rifles-aka-assault-weapons-protected-by-the-second-amendment. Retrieved February 16th, 2019.

the barrel which does not encircle or substantially encircle the barrel." [148]

But the term "barrel shroud" is not a term of art in use in the firearms community or in military doctrine; even at least one Department of Justice internal reference implicitly rejects the term, stating that "the [M16's] barrel is surrounded by two aluminum-lined fiberglass handguards which are notched to permit air to circulate around the barrel, and further serve to protect the gas tube."[149] The term appears to be nothing more than a legal or regulatory neologism. Whatever the source of the term "barrel shroud," I prefer the term "handguard"—which appears frequently in the military and sporting literature on semiautomatic rifles—to describe firearms components or groups of components that fairly meet the definition of "barrel shroud," Though I use both terms interchangeably here. Where the firer's hand is protected only by an extension of the stock forward of the trigger or a grip forward of the trigger, we shall use the term "forearm."[150]

What Military Doctrine Says About Firing from the Hip

---

[148] S. 150, 113th Congress, 1st Session, January 24th, 2013, "Assault Weapons Ban of 2013," Section 2, Definitions, (a)(38)(A) and (B).

[149] *Colt M16 Rifle Operation and Field Maintenance Handbook* (US Department of Justice Drug Enforcement Administration, nd), 2-1. This publication is undated, but given that the rifles illustrated are depicted with early style collapsible buttstocks and some with Colt 4x20 scopes no longer manufactured, it is likely that this publication appeared not later than the 1980s or 1990s.

[150] Note that I deviate somewhat in my use of terminology from the usage of some others. Some refer a "forearm" as the forward part of a one-piece stock forward of the trigger (see Steindler, 106; and Bousard and Wormley, 426). However, not everyone follows that convention. For example, an early reference on the Browning Automatic Rifle described the separate wood grip forward of the receiver, which was not part of the stock, as a "forearm" (*TR 150-3,* November 21st, 1923, 5).

In assessing the claims about pistol grips and handguards, I reviewed US Military references covering many firearms from 1923 to 2012, as well as commercial publications. Based upon this review, it is clear that there is not the slightest evidence that either pistol grips or handguards were developed or deployed intending to facilitate the spraying of fire from the hip.

Firing "from the hip" is a species of "quick fire" or "quick kill" firing techniques long present in US Army marksmanship doctrine. However, such techniques have never occupied more than an extremely minor place in that doctrine; they have been disfavored techniques to the extent that they were accepted at all; they have received very little attention in marksmanship training programs; and, even to the limited extent that they existed in the doctrine, they are implicitly obsolete. Importantly, these techniques have been present in doctrine irrespective of whether the firearm in question had either a pistol grip, "barrel shroud" handguards, both, or neither.

One of the earliest selective fire individual weapons adopted by the US Army was the M1918 Browning Automatic Rifle (BAR). The BAR was configured in what was then the traditional firearms layout: a buttstock with the then traditional curved "pistol grip" behind and below the trigger like that of all other long guns adopted by the US Army prior to that time, and a forearm grip forward of the trigger that left the upper portion of the barrel exposed—in sum, the BAR had neither a modern pistol grip nor a handguard ("barrel shroud").[151] An early publication setting forth the characteristics of the training program and techniques for employment of the BAR, mentioned previously, was *Training Regulation (TR) 150-3, Marksmanship, Automatic Rifle*, published in 1923. Despite the absence of either the pistol grip or "barrel shroud" allegedly deployed to facilitate "hip" firing, *TR 150-3* provided a quick fire technique for the BAR called "assault fire," in which the operator would hold "the butt [of the rifle] under the armpit, clasped firmly between the body and the upper portion of the arm, sling over the left shoulder."[152]

---

[151] *FM 23-20*, 1940, 2 – 3.

41

Training on this technique comprised firing at three prone silhouette targets.[153] That so-called "assault fire" constituted little more than a niche technique is shown by the amount of real estate the regulation devoted to it—nine lines and one illustration out of a 42 page document[154]—as well as the dim view taken toward automatic fire, dismissed as "a waste of ammunition."[155]

The next selective fire weapon adopted by the US Army was the M1928A1 Thompson submachine gun. The Thompson had previously been used by the Marine Corps providing security on postal trains to quell a series of armed train robberies; the Marines later "took their Thompsons along to various hotspots around the globe in the late 1920s and 1930s, including Nicaragua and China, where they proved very effective."[156][157] Simplified versions were adopted during World War II as the Thompson M1 and M1A1 submachine guns.[158] While the Thompson was the first individual weapon adopted by the US Army with a modern pistol grip, it did not have a handguard or "barrel shroud," being equipped instead only with a wooden forearm (styled a "fore grip").[159] Despite having

---

[152] *Training Regulation (TR) 150-3, Marksmanship, Automatic Rifle* (War Department, November 21, 1923), 23.

[153] *Id.*

[154] *Id.*

[155] *Id.*, 37.

[156] Bruce N. Canfield. "'Almost Perfect'? The G.I. Thompson in World War II." *American Rifleman*, March 2019, 51.

[157] For a less glowing assessment of the Marine Corps' experience with the Thompson during operations prior to World War II, see *Small Wars Manual* (United States Marine Corps, 1940, paragraph 2-40, 47 (reprinted as *Small Wars Manual*, Sunflower University Press, Manhattan, KS., nd; and *Fleet Marine Force Reference Publication (FMFRP) 12-15, Small Wars Manual*, US Marine Corps, 1990).

[158] Canfield, "Almost Perfect," 53 – 54; "Object Record: US Thompson M1 Submachine Gun." *The Price of Freedom: Americans at War*, Smithsonian National Museum of American History. Retrieved March 3rd, 2019, https://amhistory.si.edu/militaryhistory/collection/object.asp?ID=714.

[159] *FM 23-40, Thompson Submachine Gun, Caliber.45, M19281A1*, with changes

only one of the features gun prohibitionists associate with firing from "the hip," Army doctrine did acknowledge firing "from the hip while marching" as a permissible firing technique for the Thompson.[160] As with the BAR, however, this technique was at best a niche method, openly denigrated as a "relatively ineffective" technique that "should rarely be used."[161]

The US Army adopted the venerable M1 Garand, dubbed by General George S. Patton as "the greatest battle implement ever devised,"[162] in 1936,[163] making it the "first semiautomatic rifle to be adopted as standard by any nation"[164] (the *Mondragón*, adopted earlier, was never the standard arm of any country). The M1 has a three-piece handguard ("barrel shroud") system consisting of a long "stock group" with an integral forearm extending well forward of the trigger,[165] a rear handguard that covers the upper portion of the barrel not covered by the stock group forearm, and a front handguard that encircles the barrel forward of the stock group.[166] It does not have a modern pistol grip, and it is capable of semiautomatic fire only.[167] Like all rifles, the M1 Garand is designed to be fired from shoulder, even in a close quarters assault: "Assault fire is fire delivered by the unit while advancing at a walk. Riflemen halt individually and *aim and fire* standing"[168] (emphasis added). "When the attacking troops reach the assault phase, they are normally deployed as skirmishers and

---

1, 2, 3, & 4, 31 (War Department, December 1941), 2.
[160] *Id.*, 34.
[161] *Id.*, 35.
[162] "Springfield Armory: The Best Battle Implement Ever Devised." National Park Service, August 4th, 2017. https://www.nps.gov/articles/springfieldarmoryww2.htm. Retrieved February 20th, 2019.
[163] W.G.B. Allen. *Pistols, Rifles, and Machine Guns* (The English Universities Press, Ltd., 1964), 145.
[164] Johnson and Haven, 65.
[165] *FM 23-5,* May 1965, 2.
[166] *FM 23-5, US Rifle, Caliber.30, M1* (War Department, 1940), 2.
[167] *FM 23-5,* 1965, 3.
[168] *FM 23-5,* 1940, 191.

advance at a rapid walk toward the objective. The riflemen … deliver a heavy volume of fire by *firing well-aimed shots from the shoulder* every two or three steps until they are within 30 or 35 yards of the objective" (emphasis added).[169] The M1 has no modern pistol grip, and having no full automatic setting it is not capable of "spraying" anything. Yet, despite the fact that the Garand lacks a pistol grip—the quintessential "assault weapon" feature adopted, in the view of firearms prohibitionists, to "allow the shooter to spray fire from the hip position"[170]—US military doctrine did provide a quick-firing technique for the Garand—specifically, the underarm position also provided for the BAR, discussed above.[171] The M1 Garand could be "fired in the prone, sitting, squatting, kneeling and *underarm* positions"[172] (emphasis added), as well as a "crouch position" which a soldier could employ in "a sudden engagement with the enemy at extremely short ranges…"[173] When coming within 30—35 yards of the enemy, soldiers armed with Garands were to "shift [from firing from the shoulder] to the underarm position and fire *well-directed* shots at suspected enemy locations as well as observed enemy soldiers" (emphasis added).[174] Note that US Army doctrine did *not* call for "indiscriminate" or "spray" fire as claimed by gun control advocates—*it provided for well-aimed fire, even when firing from under the arm.*

The US Army adopted the M1 Carbine design in late October 1941. The carbine first saw service in 1942 in the European theater. More than six million M1 Carbines were made during World War II, compared to 1.3 million Thompson submachine guns made and even surpassing the 5.4 million M1 Garands, "making it the most popularly produced long gun of that era."[175] It was ultimately

---

[169] *FM 23-5,* September 1958, 265.

[170] *Report on Bill 17-843,* 144.

[171] *TR 150-30,* 1923.

[172] *FM 23-5,* September 1958, 84; the underarm fire technique is described in detail at 106 – 110.

[173] *Department of the Army Field Manual FM 23-1 / Department of the Air Force Technical Order TO 39A-5AC-11, US Rifle Caliber.30, M1,* (Departments of the Army and the Air Force, October 1951), 189 – 192.

[174] *FM 23-5,* September 1958, 265.

produced in four versions: the basic model semiautomatic M1 Carbine;[176] the M1A1, "identical with the Carbine M1 with the exception of the stock. A separate grip is attached to the stock of the M1A1 and a metal skeleton folding stock extension is hinged to the grip and to the rear end of the stock;"[177] the M2, outwardly identical, but with the crucial difference of being selective fire;[178] and the M3, which "is identical with the ... M2, except that the top of the receiver is designed to accommodate special sighting equipment (sniper scope)."[179] All four versions have a two-part handguard arrangement ("barrel shroud") consisting of a forearm stock extension beneath the barrel and a detachable handguard on top; two of the four versions are selective fire, and two are semiautomatic only; and only one has a perpendicular pistol grip.[180] Only one of the four (the M1A1) possesses both of the features purported by gun prohibitionists as specially adapted to firing from the hip—a handguard and a perpendicular pistol grip; and only two have the selective fire capability necessary to "spray" fire (the M2 and the M3). Notably, the one version with the pistol grip—the M1A1—is not among the selective fire versions. US military doctrine for employment of the M1 Carbine and its variants provided for several firing positions, including the prone, sitting, kneeling, squatting, standing, and crouch positions.[181] Doctrine made no distinction in the employment of these firing positions between the selective fire and semiautomatic variants of the weapon, nor, significantly, between the M1A1 variant equipped with a pistol grip and the others not so equipped. In fact, in the illustrations depicting the crouch firing position, the soldier

---

[175] Campbell. "A Look Back at the M1 Carbine."

[176] *FM 23-7, US Carbine, Caliber.30 M1* (War Department, May 20, 1942); *Department of the Army Field Manual FM 23-7 / Department of the Air Force Manual AFM 50-4, Carbine Caliber.30 M1, M1A1, M2, and M3* (Departments of the Army and the Air Force, January 1952), 2 – 3.

[177] *Id.*, 2 – 4.

[178] *Id.*, 2 – 5.

[179] *Id.*, 5 – 6.

[180] *FM 23-7*, May 20, 1942, 2; and *FM 23-7 / AFM 50-4*, January 1952, 1 – 6.

[181] *FM 23-7 / AFM 50-4*, 130 – 156.

modeling the position is equipped with the M1 or M2 version—
without a pistol grip—*not* with the M1A1 version with one.[182]

The "US Submachine Gun, Caliber.45, M3"—known
colloquially as the Grease Gun—was recommended for adoption by
the US Army in December 1942 and was officially approved on
January 11, 1943. The slightly modified M3A1 was standardized in
December 1944, with 606,694 M3 and 15,469 M3A1 submachine
guns being made during the Second World War.[183] It fired the .45
ACP cartridge used by the M1911 pistol and the Thompson
submachine gun.[184] Unlike every other individual firearm discussed
here, the M3 could operate only in one mode: full automatic.
However, "because of the very low cyclic rate, a little practice [would]
enable a gunner to fire single rounds whenever he desire[d]."[185] Like
the Thompson, the Grease Gun is equipped with a pistol grip.
However, it does not have a handguard, its diminutive 8" barrel being
completely exposed along nearly its entire length; when firing, the
shooter grips the magazine and magazine well.[186] US Army doctrine
for M3 and M3A1 submachine guns provided for several firing
positions: Standing, sitting, kneeling, prone, and assault. One of these
firing positions—the assault position—is fired from the hip.[187]
However, as with the Thompson submachine gun, the same doctrinal
manual that describes this position also denigrates it, cautioning that
"the soldier must have a great deal of practice before he can do
accurate shooting" in this position.[188]

The "Rifle, 7.62mm, M14" was adopted in 1957.[189] Although
more than 1.5 million M14s were made, the M14 had one of the

---

[182] *FM 23-7 / AFM 50-4*, 154 – 156.

[183] Bruce N. Canfield. "The M3 and M3A1 'Grease Guns.'"

[184] *FM 23-41, Submachine Gun, Caliber.45, M3* (War Department, 30 October
1943), 1 – 3.

[185] *Id.*, 1. See also *FM 23-41, Submachine Guns Caliber.45 M3 and M3A1*
(Department of the Army, July 1957), 2.

[186] *FM 23-41*, July 1957, 5, 55.

[187] *Id.*, 55.

[188] *Id.*, 54.

[189] Patrick Feng, "M14 Rifle." Army Historical Foundation, June 22nd, 2017.

shortest runs of any standard issue firearm in US history. The last M14 contract was let in 1964, with the M16 being named its replacement that year, and though some would remain in reserve component service for a bit longer, the M14 was largely phased out by 1968—only eleven years after its adoption.[190]

The M14 is a selective fire battle rifle equipped with a two-part handguard assembly ("barrel shroud") consisting of a forearm forward of the trigger integral to the stock which covers the bottom portion of the barrel, and a separate handguard attached to the barrel receiver group.[191] The M14 was produced in two configurations: the basic configuration (the M14), with the same basic stock as the M1 Garand Rifle with its traditional-style curved pistol grip and integral forearm ahead of the trigger; and the less familiar M14A1 (previously known as the M14E2), which was equipped with a modern, perpendicular pistol grip, a foregrip, and a bipod,[192] so that one version (the less common one) had both of the features that gun control proponents claim exist to facilitate rapid fire from the hip, while the more common version was missing the pistol grip most loathed by gun control activists. M14 doctrine provided six standard firing positions: prone, prone supported, kneeling, kneeling supported, standing, and foxhole.[193] It also provided for a hip firing technique, the familiar underarm position employed with both the M1918 BAR and the M1 Garand, as discussed above. Importantly, however, M14 doctrine provided for the use of this underarm firing position with both the pistol grip equipped M14A1,[194] and with the

---

https://armyhistory.org/m14-rifle/. Retrieved February 23rd, 2019.

[190] Metesh T. Logan. "A Brief History of the M14 Rifle: A Time of Transition." *NRA Blog*, January 4th, 2017. https://www.nrablog.com/articles/2017/1/a-brief-history-of-the-m14-rifle-a-time-of-transition/. Retrieved February 23rd, 2019.

[191] *FM 23-8, US Rifle 7.62-MM M14*, Headquarters, Department of the Army, December 1959, 11 and 25.

[192] *FM 23-8, US Rifle 7.62MM, M14 and M14E2*, 1965, 4; *FM 23-8, M14 and M14A1 Rifles and Rifle Marksmanship*, April 1974, 6.

[193] *FM 23-8*, April 1974, 71.

[194] *Id.*, 129.

standard, *no pistol grip* M14 configuration,[195] showing that the perpendicular pistol grip of the M14A1 was **NOT** provided to facilitate firing from the hip.

This recapitulation of the relevant US Army marksmanship doctrine shows that the chimera of the alleged spray and hip fire enabling pistol grip and "barrel shroud" handguards—the principle demons of the gun control movement—have feet of clay, as the pertinent marksmanship references indubitably show that *there is no correlation between the presence or absence of either a perpendicular pistol grip or a handguard encircling the barrel for a particular weapon and the provision of a hip firing or quick fire technique in the marksmanship doctrine for that weapon.* Such provisions existed in the manuals for selective fire and semiautomatic rifles; for rifles with neither a pistol grip nor a "barrel shroud" handguard; for rifles equipped with one but not the other; and for arms equipped with both. But even where doctrine did provide for such techniques, it accorded them little more than cursory attention, and sometimes *actually denigrated* them.

But what of the firearm most loathed and feared by firearms prohibitionists, the great "bogey" with which they have toiled tirelessly to smear the AR-15 by association—the M16 rifle? Contrary to the position of the gun control movement, marksmanship doctrine for the M16 follows the same pattern set forth above: while hip firing or quick fire techniques exist in the doctrine they are decidedly secondary, receiving scant emphasis to the point almost of being an afterthought. Furthermore, doctrine and practice began to move away from such techniques soon after the M16's adoption—a transition that by now is all but complete.

The first Field Manual for the M16 series of rifles was *FM 23-9, Rifle, 5.56-MM, XM16E1,* January 1965. All M16-series rifles have a two-piece assembly that completely surrounds the barrel (which the manual calls "handguards," not a "barrel shroud)."[196] At Chapter 3,

---

[195] *Id.*, 133.
[196] *FM 23-9, Rifle, 5.56-MM, XM16E1*, 1965, 4 and 12.

"Marksmanship Training," the manual provides that "[t]he rifle can be fired ... from any of the eight positions outlined in *FM 23-71*."[197] In an odd case of discontinuity, the version of *FM 23-71, Rifle Marksmanship* in effect at the time (the July 1964 edition) actually identified six basic firing positions, together with a host of variations upon them. The basic positions included the prone (supported and unsupported), sitting (open-legged, cross-ankle, cross-legged), squatting, kneeling (supported and unsupported), standing, and foxhole;[198] and situational variations, including the rubble pile, log, bunker, barricade, and rooftop positions.[199] The next version of *FM 23-71*, dated December 1966, contained a substantially similar list of approved firing positions.[200] This first version of *FM 23-9*, the doctrine devoted to the M16 in particular, contained the old "underarm position" previously described for the M1918 BAR, the M1 Garand, and the M14 Rifle—none of which have pistol grips and one of which does not have a handguard ("barrel shroud")—describing this position as "[t]he most effective position for delivering assault fire."[201] However, this early version of *FM 23-9* further specified that "[c]ourses of fire with the XM15E1 [sic] are those prescribed in *FM 23-71*,"[202] and neither the July 1964 nor the December 1966 version of *FM 23-71* makes mention the underarm or any hip firing technique, nor make any provision for training or qualifying in such techniques.[203] Had the Army viewed the M16, with its distinctive pistol grip and handguards, as specially designed,

---

[197] *Id.*, 32.

[198] *FM 23-71, Rifle Marksmanship* (Department of the Army, July 1964), 16 – 26.

[199] *Id.*, 101 – 108.

[200] *FM 23-71, Rifle Marksmanship* (Department of the Army, December 1966), 14 – 23 and 179 – 184.

[201] *FM 23-9*, 1965, 32 and 34.

[202] *Id.*, 34.

[203] *FM 23-71*, July 1964, Appendix III, Rifle Marksmanship Courses, 129 – 168, and Appendix IV, Premobilization Readiness Proficiency "C" Courses, 169 – 188; *FM 23-71*, December 1966, Appendix C, Rifle Marksmanship Courses, 136 – 170 and Appendix D, Premobilization Proficiency "C" Courses, 171 – 187.

intended, or particularly suited to spraying fire from the hip, then it would have done more than make cursory reference to a more than 50-year-old firing technique previously associated with other weapons lacking those features, and it would have made more provision for training soldiers on "firing from the hip." That the Army made no such effort further establishes that facilitating "spray fire" from the hip had nothing to do with the adoption of pistol grips and handguards that encircle the barrel of a rifle.[204]

Abandonment of "Hip Firing" Techniques

Were the signature features of the AR-15 and similar firearms really designed with "spraying" fire "from the hip" in mind as gun control activists claim, such techniques should have gained greater prominence in military marksmanship doctrine with the adoption of

---

[204] The 1964 and 1966 versions of *FM 23-71* point to the irrelevance of so-called "firing from the hip" with respect to adoption of pistol grips and handguards in another interesting way. Each of these references contain an unusual appendix setting forth, in thumbnail fashion, some of the important milestones in the development individual or military weapons (*FM 23-71*, July 1964, Appendix VIII, "Evolution of Military Weapons," 223 – 226; *FM 23-71*, December 1966, Appendix H, "Evolution of Military Rifles," 222 – 225). Both focus on the M1 and M14 rifles. Neither makes any reference to the unique design of the M16 rifle or any other rifle like it. Granted, the first version of *FM 23-71* was published in 1964, after the Army's first bulk order of M16 rifles but before formal adoption of the rifle. But the 1966 version was published after the Department of Defense had not only purchased large numbers of M16 rifles, but had actually published the first two versions of the *FM 23-9*, the doctrinal manual for the M16 (January 1965, and July 1966); furthermore, the 1966 version actually made note of some of the unique attributes of the M16, stating that "the much-argued-for superiority of lightweight alloys, plastics, and glass compounds must be balanced against the yet-to-be-confirmed field observations of their wearing qualities and stress resistances" (*FM 23-71*, December 1966, 225).

the M16. In fact, the opposite happened: already largely ignored, quick fire techniques from the hip became even further marginalized.

The discrediting of hip and underarm firing techniques manifested itself in combat employment of the M16 rifle early on, as described by US Army Major (Ret) John L. Plaster. Major (Ret) Plaster served with the Military Assistance Command—Vietnam (MACV) Studies and Observations Group (SOG), fighting "a secret war behind enemy lines."[205] Major(Ret) Plaster's principal weapon was the CAR-15, a compact carbine version of the M16, which he characterized as a superior weapon, claiming that "not once did [my CAR-15] fail me during a cross-border mission; [and] I don't know of a single instance of another SOG man's CAR-15 malfunctioning either."[206][207] According to Plaster, "[t]he great benefit of the CAR-15 was its dexterity ... *Though you used the sights*, you hit targets not by aiming, but by thinking about aiming" (emphasis added).[208] As this comment shows, even in the cramped and constrained environment of the Southeast Asian jungle, *Plaster and his compatriots fired from the shoulder, not from the hip*, even when employing instinctive quick fire techniques.

The significance of the already unimportant underarm or hip firing technique shrank further with the publication of *FM 23-9, Rifle, 5.56-MM, XM16E1*, July 1966. Unlike the 1965 edition, the 1966 version contained a substantial amount of material on marksmanship training and employment of the M16; largely a recapitulation of material developed for the M14 rifle, it explicitly stated that "[w]ith very few exceptions, the preparatory marksmanship training for the XM16E1 is identical to that for the M14 (*FM 23-71*) and the M14A2," and that "the techniques of aiming the XM16E1 rifle are

---

[205] John L. Plaster. "Behind Enemy Lines with the CAR-15." *American Rifleman*, February 2019, 44.
[206] *Id.*, 50.
[207] For a less sanguine assessment of the CAR-15 in Vietnam, see Tom Carhart, *The Offering* (William Morrow and Company, 1987), 24 - 25.
[208] Plaster, 48.

the same as for the M14 Rifle (*FM 23-71*)."[209] It specified substantially the same group of firing positions previously presented for the M14 Rifle: prone, sitting (open-legged, cross-ankle, cross-legged), squatting, kneeling (unsupported and supported), standing, and foxhole.[210] *FM 23-9* (1966) also provided for the "underarm position," the same position described for more than 55 years going back to the M1918 Browning. *Were the pistol grip and handguards intended to enable hip firing, the references would not have specified that the firing techniques for the M16 were substantially the same as for the M14.*

However, this version made a subtle but significant change, one very relevant to the debate over the AR-15 rifle: *FM 23-9* (1966) identified three firing positions for use with automatic fire: modified versions of the prone and foxhole positions also used with semiautomatic fire, and the underarm position. Unlike previous doctrine, the 1966 version of *FM 23-39* identified the underarm firing position as an automatic firing position only, making no reference to it in the section devoted to semiautomatic firing,[211] the only mode in which the AR-15 rifle can fire at all. *FM 23-39* (1966) contains about two dozen photographs of soldiers holding the M16 at the shoulder in various firing positions, while presenting only one image of a soldier holding the M16 in the underarm position; out of approximately 31 pages of marksmanship instructional materials, it devotes only the equivalent of about a half a page of text and a single photograph to the underarm technique; and finally, it makes repeated reference to *FM 23-71* which, as we have seen, makes no reference to underarm or any similar hip firing position.[212] The next version of *FM 23-9* (March 1970) omitted all marksmanship training material altogether, limiting itself instead to covering the battlesight zero and citing *FM 23-71, Rifle Marksmanship* (which contains no reference to any hip firing techniques) in the references section.[213] This

---

[209] *FM 23-9,* July 1966, 32.

[210] *Id.,* 35 – 42.

[211] *Id.,* 42 – 43.

[212] *Id.,* 32 – 63.

[213] *FM 23-9, Rifle, 5.56-MM, M16A1.* (Department of the Army, March

banishment of the underarm firing technique continued in the next version of *FM 23-8*, June 1974, which stated that "the six standard semiautomatic firing positions … are the prone, prone supported, kneeling, kneeling supported, standing, and the foxhole,"[214] while continuing to limit the underarm technique to automatic fire only[215] which, again, the semiautomatic AR-15 cannot produce. The manual contains more than two dozen images of soldiers operating the M16A1 rifle from a shoulder-firing position as opposed to one depicting the underarm position,[216] and none of the firing tables or courses of fire illustrated in it make any provision for qualification fire with the underarm or other hip fire position.

Even as the Army was fielding the M16 and developing marksmanship doctrine for it, elements within the Army were looking for alternatives to the so-called hip firing position gun control advocates view as the *raison d'être* of the AR-15. An early attempt at such emerged in 1967, when the US Army Infantry School produced *Training Text 23-71-1, Principles of Quick Kill*. This publication set forth techniques for marksmen to rapidly acquire and engage targets both on the ground and in the air, and for practicing those techniques. For training purposes, *Principles of Quick Kill* prescribed the use of a Daisy lever action air rifle, which notably lacked a pistol grip.[217] The technique described required the shooter to lock the weapon into the pocket of the shoulder with the weapon "stockwelded to the jaw."[218] *Principles of Quick Kill* contains eleven images of soldiers in shooting position, all depicting soldiers firing from the shoulder.[219]

In 1971, a detailed study of Army marksmanship training was conducted for the Department of the Army Office of the Chief of

---

1970), Chapter 3, 48 – 51; Appendix A, "References," 52.

[214] *FM 23-9, M16A1 Rifle and Rifle Marksmanship*, June 1974), 64.

[215] *Id.*, 110.

[216] *Id.*, 57 – 113.

[217] *Training Text 23-71-1, Principles of Quick Kill* (US Army Infantry School, May 12th, 1967), 2 - 3, 10 – 23, 38 – 39, and 67.

[218] *Id.*, 10 and 21.

[219] *Id.*, 13 – 19, 22 – 23, and 28.

Research and Development (the HumRRO study).[220] It reviewed various aspects of marksmanship technique and training, including aimed fire, "the Quick Fire technique [which was] included as a method of pointing fire,"[221] and the underarm (hip firing) technique discussed so much above. Significantly for this discussion, the study evaluated hip / underarm firing specifically. The results do not appear to support the theory that handguards and a pistol grip facilitate deadly spraying of fire. Per the authors,

> to check the possibility that the underarm position might be superior to shifting to the shoulder position for firing the weapon, this comparison was also made ... *Firing from the underarm position was grossly inferior to firing from the shoulder position in both speed and accuracy*, even though the individual firing from the shoulder position had to raise the rifle from the underarm carry before he could fire[222] (emphasis added).

The HumRRO study represents an early appearance of what would eventually become, in effect, the standard combat carry position: carrying the rifle oriented with the buttstock held high at or near the soldier's shoulder—what the study authors termed the "British ready position." According to the HumRRO report,

> a modification of the British ready position was compared with an underarm carry position. In the modified British ready position the butt of the weapon is placed high in the shoulder pocket so that when the weapon is raised, a minimum head movement is required of the shooter. For a right-handed individual, the right hand is on the pistol grip,

---

[220] James W. Dees; Magner, George J.; and McCluskey, Michael R. *Technical Report 71-4, An Experimental Review of Basic Combat Rifle Marksmanship: Phase I* (Human Resources Research Organization, March 1971).
[221] Dees, *et. al.*, v.
[222] *Id.*, 15.

the left hand is on the stock beyond the carrying handle, and weapon is slanted downward to the left across the body. The British ready position was superior to the underarm carry in time to first hit, but the two positions were equal in the number of trigger pulls required to hit the target. Thus, there was no accuracy difference, *but the modified British ready position was faster. In this study, the gun was always fired from the shoulder* (emphasis added).[223]

Thus, by 1971 it was clear that hip or underarm firing was inferior to any firing technique from the shoulder. This finding was acknowledged in Army doctrine in 1974. Although the hip / underarm position was not eliminated, its importance was diluted by the incorporation of the Quick Fire technique into the doctrine alongside it. Both *FM 23-8, M14 and M14A1 Rifles and Rifle Marksmanship (April 1974)*, and *FM 23-9, M16A1 Rifle and Rifle Marksmanship* (June 1974), incorporate Quick Fire techniques. *FM 23-8* (April 1974—M14 Rifle) states that the "[f]irer … make[s] a slight jabbing motion at his target *as he brings the weapon to his shoulder and stock welds the weapon to his jaw*"[224] (emphasis added). He then looks over the rifle, not using the sights, aligning the muzzle with the target not by "consciously align[ing] [sic] his barrel when picking his target," but rather by "relat[ing] himself to it" the way a driver aligns his vehicle on the road while keeping his focus on the horizon."[225] *FM 23-9* (June 1974, M16A1) describes the technique in nearly identical terms.[226] Each manual's inclusion of this Quick Fire technique demonstrates further the irrelevance of the old hip fire underarm technique since the adoption of the M16 rifle, rather than the greater emphasis upon it that should have occurred if spraying fire from the hip really was the purpose of the pistol grip and handguards.

---

[223] *Id.*, 15.
[224] *FM 23-8*, April 1974, 152.
[225] *Id.*, 151.
[226] *Id.*, 123.

The Army persisted in diluting of the hip firing technique in the next version of its marksmanship doctrine, *FM 23-9, M16A1 and M16A2 Rifle Marksmanship*, July 1989. This version describes two Quick Fire techniques: Aimed (fired from the shoulder), and Pointed, in which the soldier fires his weapon from the side. As found by the 1971 HumRRO study, *FM 23-9* (July 1989) states what, while Pointed Fire is a fraction of a second faster, Aimed Quick Fire is much more accurate: "A soldier well trained in pointed quick fire can hit an E-type silhouette target at 15 meters, although the shot may strike anywhere on the target, [while] a soldier well trained in aimed quick fire can hit an E-type silhouette target at 25 meters, with the shot or burst striking 5 inches from the center of mass."[227] The relative *unimportance* of hip firing techniques in the employment of AR-15 style rifles is further shown by the techniques employed elsewhere. In an early handbook on the employment of the M16, the Drug Enforcement Administration (DEA) described the proper techniques for employment of the rifle. These included "carefully plac[ing] the rifle buttstock firmly into the pocket formed by the right shoulder," with the "cheek … firmly placed on the rifle buttstock."[228] The same reference includes prone, sitting, kneeling, and standing firing positions for semiautomatic fire, and one full automatic firing position, in all of which the weapon is fired from the shoulder.[229] In his 1999 book *The Tactical Rifle*, Gabriel Suarez delves deep into the training for and employment of tactical carbines like the AR-15 and M16 in the law enforcement context. Over the course of 247 pages and dozens of photographs, Suarez's focus is clearly on firing rifles from the shoulder; he devotes only one page to a hip firing technique—the underarm technique described above (here, called the "close combat position"), with the technique relegated to "[w]eapon retention situations, or when contact is likely at extreme [close] contact situations."[230] And while Suarez asserts that "CQB [close

---

[227] *FM 23-9, M16A1 and M16A2 Rifle Marksmanship*, (Department of the Army, July 1989), 4-12.
[228] *Colt M16 Rifle Operation and Field Maintenance Handbook*, Drug Enforcement Administration, 9-4 to 9-5.
[229] *Id.*, 9-1 – 9-15.

quarters battle] is the natural home of full auto," he makes no inference that firing from the hip is the natural position of "full auto." In fact, he does quite the opposite, depicting the proper full auto position as fired from the shoulder with the shooter's "weight slightly forward in an aggressive stance"—nothing like the underarm technique provided in military doctrine or the "spraying fire" from the hip envisioned by gun control activists.[231]

Doctrine for the employment of the M16 continued on the same tack with the publication of *FM 3-22.9(FM 23-9), Rifle Marksmanship, M16A1, M16A2/3, M16A4, and M4 Carbine* in April 2003. This reference contains more than two score depictions of soldiers with the M16 rifles in firing or ready position at the shoulder, compared to only two of a soldier firing underarm—in one of which the soldier is expected to bring is rifle to the shoulder when firing.[232] It keeps the Quick Fire doctrine adopted in 1974 (evening using the same illustrations used in the 1989 version of *FM 23-9*), and continues to diminish the importance of underarm (hip) firing by including the shoulder fired Aimed Quick Fire technique along with the underarm Pointed Quick Fire technique; and while it liberalizes both techniques slightly by allowing for their use in either semiautomatic or full automatic / burst modes,[233] it eclipses them to the point of irrelevance by including an entirely new section on "Short Range Marksmanship Training."[234] This short range marksmanship program provides for two ready carrying positions— the "High Ready Position [in which] [t]he butt of the weapon is held under the armpit," and the "Low Ready Position … [in which] [t]he butt of the weapon is placed firmly in the pocket of the shoulder with the barrel pointed down at a 45-degree angle;"[235] whichever ready position is used, the manual explains that "when engaging targets the

---

[230] Gabriel Suarez. *The Tactical Rifle* (Paladin Press, 1999), 226.
[231] *Id.*, 225.
[232] *FM 3-22.9(FM 23-9)*, April 2003, with changes 1 – 4, 1 – 4, 7-16 – 7-17.
[233] *Id.*, 7-15 – 7-18.
[234] *Id.*, 7-37.
[235] *Id.*, 7-39.

gunner holds the weapon with the butt of the weapon *firmly against his shoulder* and the firing side elbow close against the body" (emphasis added).[236] The August 2008 version of *FM 3-22.9* continues this trend.[237] Although both versions of *FM 3-22.9* retain the underarm quick fire technique that has long been a part of US Army marksmanship doctrine, they also explicitly recognize its obsolescence, admitting that

> *[m]odern short range combat (SRC) techniques emphasize carrying the rifle with the butt high, so the rifle sights can be brought into display as quickly as firing a hasty unaimed shot.* In extremely dangerous moments, special reaction teams (SRTs) commonly advance with *weapons shouldered,* aiming as they advance (emphasis added).[238]

The M16 is also the standard arm of the US Marine Corps, and Marine Corps doctrine shows even more clearly that pistol grips and handguards like those used on the M16 and AR-15 were *not* designed with "spraying fire from the hip" in mind. Of over 100 images of Marines bearing rifles in ready or firing positions depicted in *MCRP 3-01A, Rifle Marksmanship,*[239] all are depicted with the rifle at the shoulder. The one exception is "Tactical Carry with the Web Sling," in which the Marine carries the rifle in something like a forward-pointed port arms; however, as the *MRCRP 3-01A* states, "[t]he Marine carries the Service rifle at the tactical carry [only] if *no immediate danger is present*" (emphasis added).[240]

---

[236] *FM 3-22.9(FM 23-9),* April 2003, with changes 1 – 4, 7-38 – 7-39.

[237] *FM 3-22.9(FM 23-9), Rifle Marksmanship, M16A1, M16A2/3, M16A4, and M4 Carbine, August 2008,* with change 1 (Department of the Army, February 10th, 2011), 7-18 – 7-21.

[238] *FM 3-22.9(FM 23-9),* April 2003, with changes 1 – 4, 7-17; *FM 3-22.9(FM 23-9), August 2008,* 7-20.

[239] *MCRP 3-01A, Rifle Marksmanship* (US Marine Corps, October 11th, 2012).

[240] *Id.,* 4-18 – 4-19.

MRCRP 3-01A also highlights an interesting development further undermining the claim that the existence of a pistol grip and handguard encircling the barrel renders a rifle particularly amendable to "spraying" fire from the hip: *The use of one-point and three-point slings.* As shown in *MRCRP 3-01A*, page 4-17, one-, two- or three-point tactical slings are used to keep the buttstock of the rifle high, near the firing shoulder, to facilitate rapidly brining the firearm to bear at the shoulder for firing and to facilitate transitioning to a backup weapon while retaining control of the rifle.[241] Tactical slings have come into near universal use in law enforcement and military applications, at the expense of any practical ability to fire the weapon from the hip, further discrediting the claim by gun control advocates that pistol grips and handguards exist to facilitate spraying fire from the hip.

---

[241] For a brief overview of these types of slings, see "Two-Point, Three-Point or Single-Point Tactical Slings?" *Guns.com*. https://www.guns.com/news/2015/03/12/opinion-two-point-three-point-or-single-point-tactical-slings-video. Retrieved February 3rd, 2019.

Chapter 5
Gun Control Advocates Are "Shooting from the Hip" About the AR-15 Rifle

According to *The Free Dictionary*, to "shoot from the hip" means, *inter alia*, "[t]o act or speak on a matter without forethought"[242]— a particularly apt definition in the context of the debate over the AR-15, given the persistent efforts to convince the public that it is equipped with vertical pistol grips and handguards ("barrel shrouds") to facilitate indiscriminate "spraying of fire" from the hip.

As shown above, there is no foundation for this claim. US Army marksmanship doctrine has incorporated hip firing in the form of the underarm technique for at least a century, dating back to the adoption of the M1918 BAR. Contrary to gun control advocates' claims, there is no correlation whatsoever between the presence of either a pistol grip or a "barrel shroud" type handguard and the provision of a hip or underarm firing in the doctrine for that firearm. Such a technique has been present in the doctrine for every individual long-arm adopted by the US Army from the M1918 BAR onward, including firearms equipped with neither a pistol grip nor a "barrel shroud" handguard; firearms equipped with a pistol grip but no such handguard; firearms equipped with a "barrel shroud" handguard but no pistol grip; semiautomatic firearms; selective fire firearms; and in the case of the M3 Grease Gun, automatic firearms with no semiautomatic setting.

Even to the extent that the hip or underarm firing position has been present in US marksmanship doctrine, it has never been more than a niche technique; has never received much emphasis in training; and has been denigrated to varying degrees in the same doctrinal manuals that presented it.

---

[242] "Shoot from the Hip." *The Free Dictionary*. https://idioms.thefreedictionary.com/shoot+from+the+hip. Retrieved February 16th, 2019.

Finally, there is the evolution of marksmanship doctrine since the United States adopted the M16. If the AR-15 and M16 rifles really were designed to facilitate indiscriminate spraying of fire from the hip, then one would expect the underarm firing position or a technique like it to have become more prominent in US military doctrine since the Army adopted the M16. In fact, the opposite has occurred. The underarm firing position has not merely continued to occupy the same insignificant place in US marksmanship doctrine since the adoption of the M16 that it occupied for fifty years before that: it has actually *become less important*, having been eclipsed both in theory and practice by other tactics, techniques, and procedures, all of which emphasize firing *from the shoulder*.

As large as the pistol grips loom the minds and claims of gun control advocates, it is noteworthy that they are rarely mentioned in firearms technical literature. They are depicted and appear on parts lists and in assembly instructions for the firearms that bear them[243] but there is little or no discussion about the special utility of modern pistol grips compared to the earlier form of pistol grip, nor about special techniques for their employment. From the perspective of the technical literature, pistol grips are largely invisible, taken for granted, with no discussion of their historical development, evolution, or employment. Like animal phyla leaping into existence seemingly from nowhere during the Cambrian explosion,[244] the perpendicular pistol grip appeared in the taxonomy of modern long guns without comment. Circumstantial evidence suggests that, in addition to the

---

[243] One exception to this seems to be in on-line discussion about the utility of pistol grip-only shotguns (niche-weapons themselves, to be sure) versus those equipped with buttstocks. Examples of the discussion of such shotguns include MDPrepper, "Pistol Grip Only Shotguns: A Bad Idea," April 12th, 2015, https://www.youtube.com/watch?v=EkMc2AHgz-k, retrieved March 9th, 2019; and Jeff Johnson, "Pistol Grip Shotguns: Great or Gimmick?" https://www.nrafamily.org/articles/2017/4/18/pistol-grip-shotguns-great-or-gimmick/, April 18th, 2017, retrieved March 9th, 2019.

[244] "Cambrian Period." *National Geographic Science and Innovation*, nd. Reference. https://www.nationalgeographic.com/science/prehistoric-world/cambrian/, Retrieved March 9th, 2019.

evolution of the metal box receiver noted above, the origin of the pistol grip as a feature of individual long guns is attributable simply to the realization that it provides a handy way to give "the trigger hand a grasping surface [and to] enable[] the shooter to pull the gun tighter into his shoulder."[245] That it this mundane purpose and not some spectacular ability to spray fire from the hip for which the modern pistol grip was adopted is, perhaps ironically, illustrated by the evolution of certain truly military firearms: machineguns and submachine guns. Early infantry machineguns were not particularly mobile.[246] Generally intended to be fired from "fixed platforms,"[247] wheeled carriages, or tripods,[248] some early machine guns had no provision for the gunner to handle and fire the weapon without the mount, often even omitting a buttstock. Examples of such include the early Maxim machineguns,[249] the Hotchkiss M1914,[250] and the Browning Machine Gun, Model of 1917.[251] While these machineguns were not intended to be handled during firing in the manner of traditional shoulder arms, the gunner nonetheless needed a place to grab on to the weapon while pulling the trigger. One solution was a pair of spade grips at the breach, as used on the Maxims and on the venerable Browning M2 machinegun,[252] adopted in 1921 and still in service today.[253] The other solution—employed on the M1917 Browning[254] and the Hotchkiss M1914,[255] was the perpendicular

---

[245] Steindler, 115.

[246] Marvin M. Johnson. *Rifles and Machine Guns* (William Morrow & Co., 1944), 12.

[247] Pridham, 75.

[248] Johnson, 12–13; Pridham, 35 (illustration), 32, 40 – 41, 45, 51, 75, 117.

[249] Pridham, 35, 75 (illustrations).

[250] Johnson, back of page 207 (illustration).

[251] *Id.*, plate following page 207 (illustration).

[252] *Id.*, 287 (illustration).

[253] Barrett Tillman. "The .50-cal. Browning Machine Gun – The Gun That Won The War." *American Rifleman*, February 23rd, 2017. https://www.americanrifleman.org/articles/2017/2/23/the-50-cal-browning-machine-gun-the-gun-that-won-the-war/. Retrieved March 9th, 2019.

[254] Chris Eger. "The Browning M1917 Machine Gun: Browning's Water-

pistol grip. That the pistol grip was used on these machine guns simply as a handy way to grab onto the weapon when firing, and not because of some innate ability to enhance automatic firing, is demonstrated by the development of numerous automatic and selective fire shoulder weapons introduced with or after them, many of which did not have pistol grips, such as the German Bergmann,[256] the Beretta Submachine Gun,[257] the Finnish Suomi,[258] and the Russian PPSh-41.[259] Further support comes from a rather unexpected quarter: the battleship USS *Iowa*, BB 61. Photographs of the forward plot rooms for both the 16-inch guns of the ship's primary armament and the 5-inch secondary guns reveal three brass pistol grips protruding from the Mk 41 Stable Vertical and the Mk 6 Stable Element—devices that measured the pitch and roll of a ship and provided this data to the ship's fire control computer.[260] These brass pistol grips housed the triggers by which the ship's gunners would fire the guns remotely, at a position separate from the guns themselves. They can have served only one purpose—to give the sailor a grasping surface when actuating the trigger. I also observed these pistol grips at first hand during a visit to another museum ship, USS North Carolina, BB 55, at Wilmington, North Carolina.

Cooled Heavy." *Guns.com*, March 28th, 2013. https://www.guns.com/news/2013/03/28/the-browning-m1917-machine-gun-brownings-water-cooled-heavy. Retrieved January 21st, 2021.

[255] Ian McCollum. "Hotchkiss 1914: A French and American WWI Heavy MG." *ForgottenWeapons.com*. https://www.forgottenweapons.com/hotchkiss-1914-a-french-and-american-wwi-heavy-mg/. Retrieved January 21st, 2021.

[256] Johnson, 249.

[257] *Id.*, 250.

[258] *Id.*, 251, plate following page 256.

[259] *Id.*, 226, 250 – 251; Ruslan Budnik. "PPSh-41 – The Most Mass-Produced Submachine Gun of WWII." *War History Online*. https://www.warhistoryonline.com/instant-articles/ppsh-41-submachine-gun.html, retrieved March 9th, 2019.

[260] *Official Battleship IOWA Crew Handbook*, Second Edition (Pacific Battleship Center, April 28th, 2017), 43 and 49.

The chimera of handguards and modern pistol grips facilitating the spray of bullets indiscriminately from the hip has absolutely no basis in fact, either in the historical development of automatic, selective fire, and semiautomatic firearms technology, nor in the tactics, techniques and procedures for their employment.

"Barrel Shroud" Handguards

Gun control advocates "no longer think[] we need to worry about bayonet mounts,"[261] which were dropped from the list of assault weapons features as set forth in the "Assault Weapons Ban of 2013;"[262] but the rebooted 2013 ban added the "barrel shroud"—the handguard encircling the barrel—as a proscribed feature.[263] The purpose of these handguards is straightforward: it is "a covering that protects the shooter's hand from the heat generated by firing a rifle."[264] Gun control advocates of are at pains to associate this feature with mass shootings, as did Lowy when he said that that they are "useful because with the barrel shroud … the guns heating up with this tremendous amount of fire … your hand is protected and it is … shielded from the heat," that "they are put in for military purposes … to spray an area fire," and that they "have no legitimate self-defense purpose."[265]

---

[261] Sullum, 56 – 57.

[262] As well they might be: even the United States Army dropped bayonet training from the program of instruction for basic training in 2010; see "One less skill for soldiers to master at boot camp: bayonet training," *Christian Science Monitor* online, 10 September 2010. http://www.csmonitor.com/USA/Military/2010/0928/One-less-skill-for-soldiers-to-master-at-boot-camp-bayonet-training. Retrieved March 17th, 2019.

[263] S.150 — 113th Congress (2013-2014), Assault Weapons Ban of 2013, Sec. 2(a)(36)(A)(v), https://www.congress.gov/bill/113th-congress/senate-bill/150/text, retrieved March 17th, 2019.

[264] Sullum, 57.

[265] Lowy, *Jonathan Lowy, et al., The Second Amendment in The New Supreme Court, Panel 2: "Are Semiautomatic Rifles, aka 'Assault Weapons,' Protected by the Second Amendment?"* 59:21 – 1:00:52.

This contention does not bear scrutiny. Like the semiautomatic firing mechanism itself, "barrel shroud" handguards are old technology. An early rifle so equipped was the Short Magazine Lee-Enfield (S.M.L.E.), "which first came into use around 1904," and was equipped with "[a] new feature [which] was the complete covering of the barrel by the wooden stock, thus protecting the hands from the overheating barrel during rapid firing."[266, 267] This "rapid firing" is not the sprayed fire envisioned by Mr. Lowy; British doctrine called for their soldiers to be able to fire fifteen rounds per minute[268]—much less than the maximum effective rate of fire for the AR-15 and comparable to its sustained rate of fire. It would appear that rates of fire less than fifteen rounds per minute also required this protective feature. The German Gewehr 1898, used by that power throughout World War I, had a "bolt action very awkward for rapid loading and firing, especially as compared to the S.M.L.E."[269] Yet the Gewehr 98 was equipped, along with the forearm covering most of the underside of the barrel, and a handguard covering part of the upper side;[270] a subsequent iteration of this remarkable weapon—the Mauser 98K[271]—had a handguard and forearm encircling most of the barrel, as with the S.M.L.E.. Given that rifles have been equipped with "barrel shroud" handguards for more than 100 years and that the first rifles so equipped were bolt action, it is self-evident that like pistol grips, the employment of handguards that encircle the barrel has nothing to do with spraying fire from the hip, for while the six-armed *Gegenees* might have been able to fire bolt action rifles from the hip at Jason and the Argonauts, [272] no mere two armed mortal could hope to carry out such a feat of arms.

---

[266] Pridham, 16 – 17.

[267] For an illustration of an S.M.L.E, see Johnson, 96.

[268] Pridham, 67.

[269] *Id*, 20.

[270] Christopher Mace. "Gewehr 98 Mauser – The Cutting Edge Bolt Action." *GunsAmerica Digest*, August 17th, 2018, https://www.gunsamerica.com/digest/gewehr-98-mauser-the-cutting-edge-bolt-action/. Retrieved March 17th, 2019.

[271] Johnson, 84.

It takes a rate of fire much lower than the extravagant rates that gun control advocates ascribe to the AR-15 to heat a rifle barrel sufficiently to cause injury. Just how much less was shown in a 1975 Rock Island Arsenal study of external barrel temperatures at various points along the barrel's length for various rates and modes of fire.[273] While the study was conducted under "a product improvement program to improve the accuracy of the M16A1 Rifle's barrel,"[274] its findings are of interest for our purposes as well, as they show that rifle barrels can reach dangerous temperatures at low rates fire. For example, the study found that after firing 140 rounds at the rate of one round every 6 seconds (10 rounds per minute), external temperatures ranged from 265 to 585 degrees Fahrenheit at various points along the barrel.[275] Further, the study results show that external barrel temperatures at some points along the barrel reached temperatures of 200 degrees Fahrenheit (93.33 degrees Celsius) and higher *after the first shot fired*.[276] This is a critically important safety concern, as one study has shown that partial skin thickness burns occur after one second of contact at less than 70 degrees Celsius, and full skin thickness burns occur after one second of contact at around 95 degrees Celsius.[277] Another study found that damage to porcine skin in contact with a surface heated to just over 61 degrees Celsius (143.6 degrees Fahrenheit) occurred at only one second of contact.[278]

---

[272] David Kravitz. *Who's Who in Greek and Roman Mythology* (Clarkson N. Potter, Inc., 1976), 105.

[273] Ronald E. Elbe. *External Barrel Temperature of the M16A1 Rifle* (GEN Thomas J. Rodman Laboratory, Rock Island Arsenal, distributed by the National Technical Information Service, US Department of Commerce) July 1975. https://apps.dtic.mil/dtic/tr/fulltext/u2/a019649.pdf. Retrieved March 17th, 2019.

[274] *Id.*, 1.

[275] *Id.*, Table II, page 10.

[276] *Id.*, Figures 4 – 10, pages 13 – 21.

[277] J.C. Lawrence, and Bull, J.P., "Thermal conditions which cause skin burns," Institution of Mechanical Engineers, *Engineering in Medicine*, Volume 5 Issue 3, July 1976, 61.

[278] A.R. Moritz and Henriquez, F.C., "Studies of thermal injury," *American*

In sum, "barrel shroud" type handguards exist to protect shooters from injury by contact with hot rifle barrels during ordinary, routine shooting activities, not just during extreme circumstances like combat.

Relating an experience from his military service, a childhood friend of mine once showed me the importance of the wrap-around handguard or "barrel shroud" to operating a firearm safely. He served in the infantry with the 82nd Airborne Division. He related to me his unit's experience with the M249 Squad Automatic Weapon (SAW), a light machine gun employed by the US Armed Forces. When first fielded, this weapon was equipped, not with a handguard, but with only a polymer forearm similar to the wooden one found on the BAR.[279] The top of the barrel was left exposed to the air for its entire length, in the manner that would, in effect, be required by law under Senator Feinstein's proposed Assault Weapons Ban of 2013 (this defect was later corrected). The result was soldiers burning themselves on the barrel. These burns would not have been incurred while firing from the hip in the manner imagined by gun control advocates. While the weapon can be fired that way, that is not its primary mode of employment. These injuries would have been sustained while operating the weapon in its usual manner—firing, reloading, repositioning the gun while shooting in the prone position, and moving from one firing location to another.[280] More such injuries would occur but for the "barrel shroud" handguards loathed by firearms prohibitionists.

Nor are handguards just for the safety of the shooter. As one researcher observed in another context,

---

Journal of Pathology, 23(5), September 1947, 711.

[279] For an image of what the M249 SAW looked like in its original configuration, see *SH 21-25, The Infantryman's Handbook* (United States Army Infantry School, March 1985), 44.

[280] The Army ultimately corrected this, adding a handguard on top of the barrel and forearm, thus completely encircling the barrel. See *FM 23-14, M249 Light Machine Gun in the Automatic Rifle Role* (Headquarters, Department of the Army, 26 January 1994), 1-1.

[i]t is not unusual for a driver of an automobile to listen to the radio, drink a cup of coffee, and drive at the same time—multitasking. We should note, though, that if the driver were to spill the hot coffee on their lap, for some brief period of time the driver's attention to the management of the vehicle and to the songs being played on the radio might be very limited and perhaps these would not be attended to at all.[281]

What might happen in such a scenario? I can attest from experience one possible outcome. Many years ago I dropped a fountain soda on the floor of my Geo Storm while moving in traffic; in scrambling to recover it, I struck the rear of a tractor trailer. The tractor trailer proceeded on, oblivious, while I limped back to work in my damaged vehicle. Now, imagine a similar scenario in which the piece of machinery involved isn't a motor vehicle but a firearm, and the surprise event isn't contact with hot coffee or a dropped soda, but unexpected contact with the hot barrel of a rifle. What might happen? We can get some idea from a real-life tragedy. In 2016, 14-year-old Stephen Brumby was accidentally shot by his father, Clayton Brumby, at a Sarasota, Florida shooting range. The cause:

[w]hen Clayton Brumby fired his last shot, he said a smoking hot casing flew out of the pistol and went down the back of his shirt. Both arms flailed up in the air, he said, his finger still on the trigger. The gun fired … The father said the bullet he fired ricocheted off the ceiling and struck the 14-year-old's jugular vein. The teen was rushed to Sarasota Memorial

---

[281] William Lewinski, "The Attention Study: A Study on the Presence of Selective Attention in Firearms Officers," *Law Enforcement Executive Forum,* November 2008, 109 – 110. https://www.iletsbeiforumjournal.com/images/Issues/FreeIssues/ILEEF%202008-8.6.pdf. Retrieved March 17th, 2019.

Hospital, where deputies said he was later pronounced dead.[282]

While this awful scenario involved a hot shell casing under a shirt, such an outcome would also be plausible where someone accidentally touches the unshielded portion of a hot rifle barrel while or immediately after firing, causing the shooter to temporarily lose muzzle awareness and accidentally squeeze off a round in the wrong direction.

Handguards—"barrel shrouds" if one prefers—reduce the chance of accidental contact between the shooter or others with the hot barrel of the firearm, and correspondingly reduce the risk of accidents and injury. Attempting to curb gun violence by proscribing or restricting the use of such handguards would be akin to fighting drunk driving by banning cup holders in cars: it would prevent no one from violating the open container laws, but it would cause more distracted-driver traffic accidents involving innocent people spilling soda and coffee. Likewise, restricting the use of "barrel shroud" style handguards will not prevent any gun crimes, but may well cause injuries stemming from firearms-related accidents.

Detachable Magazines

Even more divisive than the perpendicular pistol grip is the detachable box magazine. But like the semiautomatic firing mechanism, the detachable box magazine is old technology. "The first handgun to use a detachable box magazine was the ten round Jarre harmonica pistol, patented in 1862."[283] One of the earliest

---

[282] "Sarasota father who accidentally shot his son: 'The gun didn't kill my boy. I did.'" *Tampa Bay Times*, July 6th, 2016. https://www.tampabay.com/news/publicsafety/accidents/father-accidentally-kills-son-at-sarasota-gun-range/2284099. Retrieved March 17th, 2019.

successful rifles to employ it—the Lee-Metford Magazine Rifle—appeared in 1888.[284] Multi-shot arms and magazines existed earlier than that, of course. As noted Second Amendment scholar David B. Kopel has written,

> [w]hen a defender is reloading, the defender is especially vulnerable to attack ... *[w]hen guns are fired defensively*, it is unusual for a single hit to immediately disable an attacker. Accordingly, from the outset of firearms manufacturing, one constant goal has been to design firearms able to fire more rounds without reloading. To this end, manufacturers have experimented with various designs of firearms and magazines for centuries. While not all of these experiments were successful in terms of mass sales, they indicated the directions where firearms development was proceeding (emphasis added).[285]

One of the earliest technically, if not commercially, successful repeating rifles was the .46 Girondoni repeating air rifle, which "could fire up to 40 times before it began losing muzzle velocity," and was equipped with a twenty-two round tubular magazine. It is likely that Lewis and Clark carried one on their transcontinental expedition.[286]

Calls to ban so-called "high capacity" magazines have become a staple of the firearms debate, though what constitutes "high capacity" has not been conclusively decided, and different proposals for an upper limit have been floated over the years. Michigan once limited magazine capacity to sixteen rounds, while Rhode Island once

---

[283] David B. Kopel. "The History of Firearms Magazines and Magazine Prohibitions," *Albany Law Review*, Vol. 78.2, 2014/2015, 856.
[284] Pridham, 15.
[285] Kopel, 852.
[286] David Harsanyi. *First Freedom: A Ride Through America's Enduring History with the Gun* (Threshold Editions, 2018), 90 – 91.

limited capacity to twelve rounds and Ohio to eighteen rounds. All three limits have since been repealed.[287] The 1994 Federal Assault Weapons Ban limited magazine capacity to ten rounds. Maryland, Connecticut, the District of Columbia, California, and Hawaii (for handguns only) all limit magazine capacity to ten rounds, while New Jersey and Colorado limit them to no more than fifteen rounds; New York's "so-called SAFE Act[] ban[s] ... possession of magazines of more than ten rounds and loading more than seven rounds in a magazine;" and New York City bans "long gun magazines of more than five rounds."[288]

While there is little consensus on what constitutes a "high capacity" magazine, there is no doubt what animates those who seek their proscription: the belief that such magazines are particularly suitable for mass murder and useful for nothing else. As one commenter argued,

> [h]igh capacity magazines ... having a hundred round drum that the aurora shooter had, or the 30-round magazine that [Jared Lee Loughner] had in Tucson, these are useful if you are trying to gun down a lot of people without reloading. They have obvious usefulness in military contexts. Not so for facing an intruder in the home.[289]

Or, stated less hyperbolically,

> [a]n important rationale for the [assault weapons (AW)—large capacity magazine (LCM) ban is that AWs and other guns equipped with LCMs are particularly dangerous weapons because they facilitate the rapid firing of high numbers of shots, thereby

---

[287] Kopel, 865 – 865.

[288] *Id.*, 868.

[289] Lowy, *Jonathan Lowy: Lowy, Jonathan and Malcolm, John G. "Gun Control: Assessing Constitutionality and Effectiveness,"* 48:51 – 51:52.

potentially increasing injuries and deaths from gun violence. Although AWs and LCMs were used in only a modest share of gun crimes before the ban, it is conceivable that a decrease in their use might reduce fatal and nonfatal gunshot victimizations, even if it does not reduce the overall rate of gun crime.[290]

The assumption that a magazine having a capacity over ten rounds makes it *ipso facto* a tool of mass murder and of nothing else is false. The "high capacity" magazines of 15, 20 or 30 rounds capacity that gun control advocates denounce are actually very useful in many legitimate shooting applications—including self-defense—but are unnecessary to carry out the mass shootings driving calls to ban them.

Christopher Koper's 2004 report (quoted above) defined a large capacity magazine as one capable of holding more than ten rounds, the limit imposed in the 1994 Assault Weapons Ban. In that same study, he asserted that "[assault weapons—(AWs)] or other semiautomatics with LCMs were involved in 6, or 40%, of fifteen mass shooting incidents occurring between 1984 and 1993 in which six or more persons were killed or a total of twelve or more were wounded."[291] Put another way, 60% of those shootings *did not* involve such weapons. He goes on to state that

> guns equipped with LCMs—of which AWs are a subset—are used in roughly 14% to 26% of gun crimes. Accordingly, the LCM ban has greater potential for affecting gun crime. However, it is not clear how often the ability to fire more than ten shots without reloading ... affects the outcomes of gun

---

[290] Christopher S. Koper. *Updated Assessment of the Federal Assault Weapons Ban: Impacts on Gun Markets and Gun Violence, 1994-2003* (Report to the National Institute of Justice, United States Department of Justice, June 2004), 20.
[291] *Id.*, 14.

attacks... *All of this suggests that the ban's impact on gun violence is likely to be small* (emphasis added).[292]

Conversely, Koper's figure shows that 74% to 86% of gun crimes did not involve such magazines. Later in his report, Koper informs us that

> [t]he few available studies on shots fired show that assailants fire less than four shots on average... a number well within the 10-round magazine limit imposed by the AW-LCM ban, but these studies have not usually presented the full distribution of shots fired for all cases, so it is usually unclear how many cases, if any, involved more than ten shots.[293]

Koper gives us some indication of what the upper limit on firearms victimization might be in the absence of magazines capable of holding more than ten rounds, referring to a study of gun crime in Jersey City:

> Focusing on cases for which at least the type of handgun (semiautomatic, revolver, derringer) could be determined, 2.5% of the gunfire cases involved more than ten shots ... On the other hand, the Jersey City study also implies that eliminating AWs and LCMs might only reduce gunshot victimizations by up to 5%. *And even this estimate is probably overly optimistic because the LCM ban cannot be expected to prevent all incidents with more than ten shots.* Consequently, any effects from the ban ... are likely to be smaller and perhaps quite difficult to detect with standard statistical methods[294] (emphasis added).

---

[292] *Id.*, 19.
[293] *Id.*, 90.
[294] *Id.*, 90 – 91

Koper later reports that "[g]uns with LCMs are used in up to a quarter of gun crimes, but it is not clear how often the outcomes of gun attacks depend on the ability to fire more than ten shots … without reloading."[295] Koper's finding makes it clear that the vast majority of gun crimes at the time of his study did not involve "high capacity" magazines, or if they did, they did not affect the outcome.

Koper's 2004 conclusions indicate that banning magazines capable of holding more than ten rounds would have little impact on gun victimization. But calls to ban so-called "assault weapons" and "high capacity" magazines are not driven by concerns about ordinary crime, but by concern over sensational mass killings such as the Orlando Night Club Shooting in which Omar Mateen "pledge[d] allegiance to ISIS [Islamic State of Iraq and Syria]" and killed 49 people, wounding 53 others;[296] the Norway Shooting in which right-wing extremist Anders Behring Breivik killed 69 and wounded scores of others on Norway's Utoya island in 2011;[297] or the New Zealand Mosque Shootings, in which Australian Brenton Tarrant killed at least 50 people and wounded at least 50 more at two mosques in Christchurch, New Zealand on March 16th, 2019.[298] Gun control advocates claim that "mass killers use [weapons with "high capacity" magazines] [] often."[299] Indeed, Koper asserted that "[a]ssault

---

295 *Id.*, 97.
296 Ralph Ellis, Ashley Fantz, Faith Karimi and Eliott C. McLaughlin. "Orlando shooting: 49 killed, shooter pledged ISIS allegiance." https://www.cnn.com/2016/06/12/us/orlando-nightclub-shooting/index.html. Retrieved March 23rd, 2019.
297 "Norway Terror Attacks Fast Facts." *CNN.com*, https://www.cnn.com/2013/09/26/world/europe/norway-terror-attacks/index.html. Retrieved March 23rd, 2019.
298 Jennifer Williams, Alex Ward, Jen Kirby, and Amanda Sakuma. "Christchurch mosque shooting: what we know so far," *Vox*, March 18th, 2019. https://www.vox.com/world/2019/3/14/18266624/christchurch-mosque-shooting-new-zealand-gunman-what-we-know. Retrieved March 23rd, 2019.
299 Jonathan Lowy: Lowy, Jonathan and Malcolm, John G. "Gun Control: Assessing Constitutionality and Effectiveness," 21:30

weapons and other high capacity semiautomatics appear to be used in a higher share of firearm mass murders (*up to* 57% *in total*), *though data on this issue are very limited*"[300] (emphasis added). But even this figure—which Koper himself concedes may not be reliable— demonstrates that 43% or more of firearm mass murders did not involve "[a]ssault weapons and other high capacity semiautomatics." Clearly, neither an "assault" weapon nor a "high capacity" magazine is necessary for the execution of a mass killing, and there is no reason to believe that most, or even any, of the mass killings in which such magazines or weapons were used would not have occurred absent of such weapons. The implication is clear: some, most, or even all of these shooters would simply have substituted another type of firearm, had an "assault" weapon and /or "high capacity" magazines not been available.

The August 2007 report *Mass Shootings at Virginia Tech, April 16, 2007: Report of the Review Panel* hinted at this conclusion. It reviewed the events of April 16th, 2007, when "Seung Hui Cho, an angry and disturbed student, shot to death 32 students and faculty of Virginia Tech, wounded seventeen more, and then killed himself"[301] using a 9mm Glock 19 semiautomatic pistol and a Walther P22 .22 caliber pistol.[302] During his spree, Cho emptied seventeen magazines, each capable of holding between 10 to 15 rounds[303]—a capacity of one-third to half the capacity of the 30-round magazines standard for AR-15 and Kalashnikov-style rifles. According to the report, "Cho was able to kill 31 people including himself … in about 10 minutes with the semiautomatic handguns at his disposal. Having the

---

[300] Christopher S. Koper; William D. Johnson; Jordan L. Nichols; Ambrozine Ayers; and Natalie Mullins. "Criminal Use of Assault Weapons and High-Capacity Semiautomatic Firearms: an Updated Examination of Local and National Sources." *Journal of Urban Health* 95, 2018, abstract. https://link.springer.com/article/10.1007/s11524-017-0205-7. Retrieved July 8th, 2019.
[301] *Mass Shootings at Virginia Tech, April 16, 2007: Report of the Review Panel* (Virginia Tech Review Panel, August 2007), 1.
[302] *Id.*, 71.
[303] *Id.*, 91.

ammunition in large capacity magazines facilitated his killing spree."[304] Nonetheless, the Review Panel also

> considered whether the previous Federal Assault Weapons Act of 1994 that banned 15-round magazines would have made a difference in the April 16 incidents [and] *concluded that 10-round magazines that were legal would have not made much difference in the incident.* Even pistols with rapid loaders could have been about as deadly in this situation[305] (emphasis added).

So-called "high capacity" magazines are unnecessary for the execution of a mass shooting. In September 2013 Aaron Alexis used a Remington 870 12-gauge shotgun to kill 12 people at the Washington Navy Yard. [306]The Remington 870, introduced in 1950,[307] comes standard with a magazine capacity of 4—6 rounds, individually loaded into a tubular magazine beneath the barrel—hardly suitable for "spraying" fire.[308] In a similar attack, Jarrod Ramos sought revenge on the Annapolis *Capital Gazette* in June 2018 with a shotgun, killing several.[309] In yet another shotgun spree killing, prison parolee

---

[304] *Id.*, 75.

[305] *Id.*

[306] *Report of the Investigation into the Fatal Shooting Incident at the Washington Navy Yard on September 16, 2013 and Associated Security, Personnel and Contracting Policies and Practices* (Department of the Navy, November 8th, 2013), 2 and 40.

[307] Robert Farago. "Remington Model 870 Shotgun, Past and Present." *The Truth About Guns*, https://www.thetruthaboutguns.com/2015/09/robert-farago/remington-model-870-shotgun-past-and-present/. Retrieved March 23rd, 2019.

[308] Dave Campbell. "A Look Back at the Remington 870 Shotgun." *American Rifleman*, February 8, 2016. https://www.americanrifleman.org/articles/2016/2/8/a-look-back-at-the-remington-870-shotgun/. Retrieved January 1st, 2021.

[309] Chase Cook. "Man charged in Capital Gazette shooting asks for time to consider insanity plea," *Capital Gazette*, August 15th, 2018. https://www.capitalgazette.com/news/for_the_record/ac-cn-ramos-plea-

Ben Hoffmann killed four men and injured one woman with a pump action shotgun in the Australian city of Darwin.[310] Although the number of Hoffman's victims was relatively low, magazine capacity had nothing to do with that; taking place at four different locations over the course of an hour,[311] Hoffman had ample time to reload his weapon between attacks and to make provision to continue to kill more people. Even a source as anti-gun as *Mother Jones* established (unintentionally) that "high capacity" magazines are not an essential element of a mass shooting. In a piece analyzing 62 mass shooting incidents from 1982 to 2012—with a "mass shooting" defined as an assailant shooting four or more persons, excluding himself, in a single incident—*Mother Jones* asserted that "more than half of all mass shooters possessed high capacity magazines, assault weapons, or both" (note—*possessed*, not *used*), which admits its converse, that a large share of them possessed neither. The graphic accompanying the article paints a more ambiguous picture, stating that of the 142 weapons possessed by the assailants in these 62 events, "48 would be outlawed by the Assault Weapons Ban of 2013." Of these, 42 would have been banned for being equipped with "high capacity" magazines.[312] Fully 94 of their weapons—more than 66%—would not have been banned under the 2013 proposal.[313]

The underlying logic of those seeking to ban so-called "high capacity" magazines is that with smaller magazines, a killer can shoot fewer people before having to reload, thereby reducing the casualty

---

0816-story.html. Retrieved March 23rd, 2019.

[310] "Four people dead in Darwin city shooting, gunman arrested by NT Police." *The New Daily*, June 4, 2019 (updated June 5th, 2019). https://thenewdaily.com.au/news/state/nt/2019/06/04/darwin-mass-shooting/. Retrieved June 22nd, 2019.

[311] Id.

[312] Mark Follman, Gavin Aronsen and Deanna Pan. "A Guide to Mass Shootings in America." *Mother Jones*, updated February 15th, 2019. https://www.motherjones.com/politics/2012/07/mass-shootings-map/. Retrieved March 23rd, 2019.

[313] For purposes of *Mother Jones'* analysis, a "high capacity magazine is any magazine exceeding 10 rounds capacity.

count of the attack. But this reasoning is insufficient, as the mass killer need only eject the empty magazine and insert a full one to resume his killing spree after the first magazine runs dry.

Limiting magazine capacity, by itself, can have no impact on the lethality of a shooting event: though rarely explicitly stated, the drive to limit magazine capacity assumes that the interval between a shooter's first magazine running empty and his inserting a new magazine and chambering a round provides a window of opportunity in which unarmed victims can either escape or counterattack with improvised weapons. Regrettably, such hope is misplaced. While some victims may seize on such an interregnum to escape or fight, in reality firearms can be reloaded so rapidly that this interregnum provides no reasonable opportunity for them to do so. And this may not be limited to semiautomatic weapons with detachable magazines. Some bolt action rifles not accepting detachable magazines are loaded by inserting an *en bloc* clip containing several rounds directly into the rifle's internal magazine. Examples of this type of loading include Italy's Model of 1891 Mannlicher-Carcano;[314] the Mannlicher Model of 1895;[315] and the French Lebel M1916 and M1934.[316] The semiautomatic M1 Garand is also loaded from an *en bloc* clip.[317] Other firearms are rapidly loaded by chargers and stripper clips in which a feeding device is inserted into an aperture provided for that purpose on the firearm and the rounds are rapidly pushed into the weapon's integral magazine in a single movement. Examples of this type include the Model 1903 Springfield;[318] the Mauser 1898;[319] the Japanese Arisaka;[320] and the Russian semiautomatic Samozaryadny Karabin Sistemy Simonova, (English, Self-loading Carbine of the Simonov system) (SKS) carbine.[321]

---

[314] Johnson, 64.
[315] *Id.*, 66.
[316] *Id.*, 68 – 70.
[317] *FM 23-5, US Rifle, Caliber.30, M1* (Headquarters, Department of the Army, May 1965), 14 – 15.
[318] Johnson, 79.
[319] *Id.*, 84.
[320] *Id.*, 90.

That limiting magazine capacity does not materially limit the rate at which an armed attacker can discharge rounds was clearly shown by Boone County, Indiana Sheriff Ken Campbell in 2013,[322] where Sheriff Campbell narrates several demonstrations timing magazine changes and victim reaction times in a simulated shooting event. One demonstration compares the rate at which a shooter fires 30 rounds from a semiautomatic pistol at three targets in three configurations: two fifteen round magazines; three ten-round magazines; and five 6 round magazines. When executed by an experienced shooter, the shooter expended thirty rounds from two 15 round magazines in 20.64 seconds; from three 10 round magazines in 18.05 seconds; and from five 6 round magazines in 21.45 seconds. An inexperienced shooter performed the same demonstration firing thirty rounds from two 15 round magazines in 22.9 seconds; from three 10 round magazines in 25 seconds; and from six 5 rounds magazines in 26.93 seconds. A similar demonstration was conducted using an AR-15 rifle. In this demonstration the experienced shooter expended the entire twenty rounds from a single magazine in 12.16 seconds and expended 20 rounds from two 10 round magazines in less than 11 seconds. The inexperienced shooter expended 20 rounds from a single magazine in 12.26 seconds and from two 10 round magazines in 14.63 seconds. In another demonstration, an experienced shooter fired 21 rounds from three 7 round magazines from a 1911 pistol in 9.78 seconds.[323]

---

[321]   "SKS Stripper Clip Combat Loading." https://www.youtube.com/watch?v=o9V8qhMzwr4. Retrieved March 24th, 2019.

[322] Rod Rose. "Sheriff narrates video disputing 'high capacity' magazine claims." *Zionsville Times Sentinel,* March 6th, 2013. https://www.timessentinel.com/news/local_news/sheriff-narrates-video-disputing-high-capacity-magazine-claims/article_2c94a1eb-f026-533f-8db3-a976a5697f39.html. Retrieved March 23rd, 2019.

[323] Ken Campbell. "Boone Co. Sheriff Ken Campbell - Proposed Magazine Bans Are Absurd." *Minuteman1969,* March 6th, 2013. https://www.youtube.com/watch?v=8YmF2ULnlhA. Retrieved March 24th, 2019.

The foregoing shows that magazine changes do not materially slow a shooter's rate of fire. But the question remains whether the short interval in which the shooter is changing magazines creates an opportunity in which unarmed victims can act. Sheriff Campbell evaluated this question by running a scenario in which a role playing unarmed "victim" crouched about 25 feet away from the shooter; upon perceiving the shooter's magazine running empty, the "victim" charged the shooter. When this scenario was run with an experienced shooter, the "victim" made it to within about 9 feet of the shooter before the shooter resumed shooting; with the inexperienced shooter, the "victim" got very close to the shooter before the shooter resumed shooting, but still did not move fast enough to have disarmed the shooter.[324] In this test, the role playing "victim" faced no stress or danger. In a real mass shooting scenario, the victims would be delayed in their actions by fear, stress, and uncertainty, slowing their reactions and degrading their ability to seize the interval of reloading effectively.[325]

Sheriff Campbell's demonstration also illustrates the implausibility of the exaggerated the rates of fire attributed to semiautomatic firearms. In Campbell's demonstration, the shooters were expending rounds as fast as possible, with the only aim to ascertain the impact of magazine changes on rates of fire. Target acquisition and accuracy were presumably not considerations. Yet, even under these circumstances, Campbell's shooters could not come close to producing the huge rates of fire attributed by some to semiautomatic weapons.

---

[324] *Id.*

[325] Regrettably, Sheriff Campbell resigned his post in 2014 after it was revealed that he had been involved in an affair with a known prostitute. While this regrettable lapse certainly reflects upon Sheriff Campbell's personal and professional values and judgment, it says nothing about the efficacy of the demonstrations described here. See Vic Ryckaert, "Boone County sheriff resigns amid prostitution investigation," *IndyStar*, June 20, 2014, https://www.indystar.com/story/news/crime/2014/06/19/boone-county-sheriff-resigns-amid-prostitution-probe/11015867/, retrieved March 24th, 2019.

Gun control advocates are most outspoken about "high capacity" magazines when combined with so-called "assault" weapons. However, handguns are smaller, more conveniently transported, more easily concealed, and more readily brought to bear from a concealed or stowed position than are long guns of any type. While handguns do have the drawback of smaller magazine capacity than AR-15s and similar firearms, this is compensated for because an active shooter can potentially carry more rounds of ammunition for a pistol than for a long gun. For example, the standard capacity magazine for a Colt 1911 pistol is seven rounds. Four 1911 magazines containing a total of 28 rounds are roughly equivalent in volume to a single 20-round AR-15 magazine—a 40% increase in potential shots in a comparable space. Eight 7-round 1911 magazines—56 rounds of ammunition—will fit in a space comparable to that occupied by a single standard capacity 30-round AK-47 magazine—an 86% increase in the potential number of shots in a similar amount of space. That same 30-round AK magazine occupies roughly the same space as four Beretta 92-series pistol magazines or four Sig Sauer P320 magazines in 9mm Parabellum, each with a standard capacity of 15 and 17 rounds, respectively. Thus, a shooter can carry roughly twice as many rounds for a typical full sized 9mm semiautomatic pistol as for an AK-series rifle in a similar amount of space. Even considering the ten round magazines required in some jurisdictions, the potential number of shots would be forty rounds for the pistols compared to 30 rounds for the AK—a premium of one-third. Furthermore, in addition to the benefit of being able to carry more rounds of ammunition, a mass shooter equipped with a semiautomatic pistol rather than a long gun will also find his ammunition, being housed in smaller feeding devices, easier to carry, stow, and hide than the "high capacity" semiautomatic rifle magazines so decried by firearms prohibitionists.

Those most adversely affected by magazine capacity restrictions are law abiding citizens wishing to use their firearms for lawful purposes, especially those forced to rely upon their firearms for self-defense. Such restrictions will pose little if any effective constraint upon those who are intent upon misusing firearms.

Collapsible and Folding Stocks

Gun control advocates also worry about adjustable and folding buttstocks that they fear make so-called "assault" weapons "lighter and more concealable than standard long guns,"[326] which in their view can only serve nefarious purposes in the hands of civilians. In fact, they serve legitimate, non-military purposes: to adjust the length of pull of the rifle to the size, stature, clothing and equipment of the shooter; to facilitate easier transportation and stowage of the firearm; or both.

"Length of Pull is the distance from the center of the trigger to the center of the buttplate,"[327] and is

> one of the most important aspects of a gun's dimensions and determines whether the gun will fit you, meaning how comfortable the gun feels to you and how accurate you can shoot it. With the correct length of pull, you will have quick sight acquisition, better control, better accuracy, and feel more comfortable.[328]

And further,

> [m]ost rifles are designed for the average adult male, but many people, especially women, are not built like your average adult male. You will find that many rifles

---

[326] Sugarman. http://www.vpc.org/studies/awaintro.htm. Retrieved July 8th, 2019.

[327] Steindler, 244.

[328] Suzanne Wiley. "What is Length of Pull and why does it Matter?" *The Shooter's Log,* July 10th, 2013. https://blog.cheaperthandirt.com/length-pull-matter/. Retrieved March 24th, 2019.

will not feel comfortable when you shoulder them.
This is because the length of pull … is either too long
or too short for you.[329]

Most people cannot afford to have a rifle custom-stocked to
fit their precise size and shape and certainly cannot afford to have
custom stocks made for each member of their family. Collapsible or
adjustable stocks provide a standard, off-the-shelf solution that
allows each shooter to adjust the rifle to their own body and thus
optimize their shooting experience; adjustable buttstocks enable
multiple members of a family to practice shooting with the same rifle,
optimizing the shooting experience for each. In this respect,
adjustable buttstocks reflect the American shooting tradition, wherein
hunting, target shooting, and arms for self-defense have always been
the province of ordinary working people of modest means, as
opposed to the European tradition wherein the shooting sports were
the domain of the wealthy and privileged classes who could afford to
indulge in fine, handcrafted, and extremely expensive custom
sporting arms. Adjustable buttstocks are more functional than even
this, however:

> The requirements for perfection of length of pull will
> change if the rifle is to be used in more than one
> position. Perhaps this is what confounds the rifle
> shooter who is able to use different positions. Unlike
> a trap or skeet shooter, or maybe someone on Safari,
> the one 'perfect' fit may not exist.[330]

Folding buttstocks serve one principal function: to make the
rifle easier to transport or stow, and there are perfectly

---

[329] "Purchasing a Women's Rifle and What to Consider." *Legacy Sports International*, May 10th, 2017. https://www.legacysports.com/purchasing-a-womens-rifle-and-what-to-consider/. Retrieved March 24th, 2019.
[330] "Rifle Fit: Length of Pull." *Art of the Rifle*, February 27th, 2012. https://artoftherifle.com/rifle-fit-length-of-pull/2012/02/rifle-fit-length-of-pull.html. Retrieved March 24th, 2019.

straightforward, non-criminal reasons as to why a folding stock is useful and appropriate on a civilian firearm. Some people occupy small living quarters, where storage is at a premium. Some drive smaller vehicles with less cargo capacity. Some may wish to carry their rifle to the range in a smaller, possibly less expensive, rifle case. In fact, the military application of folding stocks shows that they do not exist for the nefarious purpose of secreting rifles into vulnerable places in which to unleash mass violence. The default firing position in military doctrine is from the shoulder. Well-trained soldiers do not run around the battlefield employing their rifles in some *faux* gangland style, firing them from the hip with the stocks collapsed. Folding stocks exist in military service to facilitate handling the rifle in cumbersome and awkward situations such as parachuting and boarding or disembarking vehicles. The ability to reduce the size of the rifle by folding or otherwise collapsing the stock is a simple matter of convenience, not of lethality or tactical surprise, and this convenience is of equal utility in civil as well as military life. Consider the ArmaLite AR-7 Explorer survival rifle: introduced in 1959, the AR-7 is a semiautomatic .22 caliber rifle with what might be the ultimate collapsible stock: the entire rifle disassembles and can be stowed inside the buttstock itself, which floats.[331] The purpose of this arrangement is straightforward: to allow the rifle to be stowed in as small a space as possible. This is better illustrated by the version formerly employed by the Israeli Armed Forces. Instead of a floating buttstock that served as a storage case for the rest of the rifle, this version came equipped with a collapsible wire buttstock. Although adopted by a military force, this rifle was not a combat weapon—it was a survival rifle issued to Israeli pilots. The function of the collapsible wire stock was not so much to facilitate the downed pilot's secreting the rifle in his clothing or baggage as he escaped and evaded as it was to make it easier to stow in his aircraft. "[T]he rifles were intended as a survival weapon, to forage for food in the event

---

[331] Jeremiah Knupp. "The Unlikely Resilience of the AR-7 Survival Rifle." *American Rifleman*, December 27th, 2016. https://www.americanrifleman.org/articles/2016/12/27/the-unlikely-resilience-of-the-ar-7-survival-rifle/. Retrieved January 1st, 2021.

of a crash in a remote area, the task for which the AR-7 was originally designed;" the collapsible stock was added to best use "little spare room in the cockpit of a modern fighter jet."[332]

Adjustable and folding buttstocks exist, not for criminal purposes, but for legitimate civilian and military shooting applications. But is there any merit to the contention that these features render the rifles more easily concealed and therefore more deadly in the hands of killers? *In a word, no.* To start with, a rifle with a collapsible or folding stock might or might not be materially lighter than its fixed stock counterpart. The fixed stock M16A2 rifle weighs 7.78 pounds without sling or magazine.[333] At 6.49 pounds, the M4 Carbine weighs just 1.29 pounds less, but is actually slightly heavier than the fixed stock M16A1.[334] The fixed stock Soviet Kalashnikov AKM (*Avtomát Kalášnikova modernizírovannyj*, or Automatic Kalashnikov Rifle, Modernized in English) with an empty Bakelite magazine, weighs 7.3 pounds, whereas the folding stock version of the rifle—the AKMS—also with one empty Bakelite magazine, weighs only a half-pound less at 6.8 pounds.[335] While these weight reductions are helpful to a soldier who must carry is rifle, along with ammunition, helmet, armor, rations and his other equipment for extended periods of time, such modest weight savings cannot be expected to be of much importance in the context of a criminal attack.

Folding and adjustable stocks do not necessarily reduce the weight of a rifle to a material degree, but they do reduce its minimum length. Again comparing M16-series rifles, the fixed stock M16A1 measures 39 inches,[336] and the fixed stock M16A2 measures about 39

---

[332] *Id.*

[333] *FM 23-9,* July 1989, 2-2.

[334] *TM 9-1005-249-10, Operator's Manual for Rifle, 5.56-MM, M16 (1005-00-856-6885); Rifle, 5.56-MM, M16A1 (1005-00-073-9421)* (Headquarters, Department of the Army, February 1985), 1-4.

[335] James F. Gebhardt, Maj. (trans). *The Official Soviet AKM Manual* (Paladin Press, 1989), 94.

[336] *TM 9-1005-249-10, Operator's Manual for Rifle, 5.56-MM, M16 (1005-00-*

and 5/8 inches.[337] The M4 Carbine, by contrast, measures 33 inches with the buttstock fully extended, and 29.75" long with the buttstock fully closed.[338] So, while the difference in length of the M4 Carbine with the buttstock extended versus collapsed is a modest 3.25", the M4 is shorter than the other two M16 versions whether the stock is collapsed or extended. Similarly, the AKM rifle with fixed stock is 34.6 inches, while the AKMS with folded stock is 25.2 inches.[339]

Does this modest reduction in overall length make these collapsible or folding stock rifles "concealable" in any meaningful sense? Again, no. "The AR-15 is an extremely well-designed rifle from a shooting perspective, but it's a bumpy rifle with numerous snags and protuberances that can make deploying it from behind a truck seat or other hiding place a frustrating effort."[340] Features such as the vertical front sight post and the magazine and pistol grip projecting at nearly right angles from the rifle's receiver conspire to make the AR-15 a poor choice if deploying the firearm from concealment is the intention. It is worth noting that it is possible to construct an AR-15 with few or none of the features that gun control advocates seek to ban but, ironically, *such a rifle would actually be easier to conceal for evil purposes than an ordinarily configured AR-15.*[341]

Even setting aside the issue of the odd projections poking out from the receiver and barrel of AR-15 or a Kalashnikov-style rifle,

---

856-6885); *Rifle, 5.56-MM, M16A1 (1005-00-073-9421)* (Headquarters, Department of the Army, February 1985), 1-4.

[337] *TM9-1005-319-10, W/Changes 1-4, Rifle, 5.56-MM, M16A2 W/E (1005-01-128-9936)* (US Marine Corps / US Army, August 1986), 3.

[338] *FM 3-22.9, Rifle MarksmanshipM16-/M4-Series Weapons* (Headquarters Department of the Army, August 2008), 2-1.

[339] Gebhardt, 94.

[340] "Is There Room for a Traditional Civilian Semiauto Rifle?" *The Firearms Blog,* June 11th, 2016. https://www.thefirearmblog.com/blog/2016/06/11/room-traditional-civilian-semiauto-rifle/. Retrieved March 24th, 2019.

[341] An example of such a "featureless" AR-15 can be seen at "Is There Room for a Traditional Civilian Semiauto Rifle?" *The Firearms Blog, id.*

such rifles are simply not readily concealable, even with a folding or collapsible stock—especially by comparison to the epitome of the concealable firearm, the handgun. A few examples will confirm this. An M4 Carbine with an adjustable buttstock fully retracted is 29.75" long, and AKMS rifle with the stock folded in is 25.2" long. By comparison, the venerable Beretta M1951 semiautomatic pistol and its Egyptian clone the Helwan is only 8 inches long—less than a third the length of either rifle—and weighs only 29.8 ounces without the magazine or 31.4 ounces with it (*sans* ammunition)[342]—a fraction of the of the size and weight of either the M4 Carbine or the AKMS. The Beretta 92FS—the commercial version of the US Army's famous M9 pistol—is 8.5" long and weighs 34.4 ounces;[343] the Sig Sauer P320, recently adopted as the M17 pistol by the US Army,[344] is slightly over 8" long and weighs 27.6 ounces with an empty magazine;[345] the full sized, .22 Sig Sauer Mosquito pistol is 7.2" long overall and weighs 22.9 ounces;[346] and finally, the famous Colt Model 1911 Government model in .45 ACP is 8.5 inches long overall and weighs 39 ounces.[347] All of these are much smaller, lighter, and more concealable than the AR-15, whatever stock it has.

The relative concealability of AR-15 and similar rifles equipped with folding or adjustable stocks—as compared to fixed stock versions of the same firearms—simply does not materially increase the lethality or dangerousness of such weapons as instruments of crime, mass shootings or otherwise. A handgun is

---

[342] *Instruction and Safety Manual, Helwan* (Interarms Corporation, 1987), 2; Wood, 121.

[343] *Beretta Series 92 Instruction Manual* (Beretta Pubblicita, June 2012), 47.

[344] Todd C. Lopez. "Modular handgun to begin fielding before Christmas," October 3rd, 2017. https://www.army.mil/article/194787/modular_handgun_to_begin_fieldin g_before_christmas. Retrieved March 24th, 2019.

[345] *P320, P320 X-Series, Operators Manual: Handling and Safety Instructions* (Sig Sauer, nd), 74.

[346] *Mosquito Handling and Safety Instructions* (Sig Sauer, nd), 6.

[347] *Colt Revolvers and Automatic Pistols* (Colt's Patent Firearms Manufacturing Co., Fire Arms Division, October 1933), 36.

vastly easier to conceal and transport undetected to the criminal's target area than any long gun; and while AR-15s and similar rifles equipped with adjustable or folding stocks may be marginally easier to conceal than their fixed stock equivalents, such increased concealability is not such as to make them substantially more dangerous as instruments of crime than their fixed stock analogs. Furthermore, the characteristics AR-15s and similar firearms render them relatively less amendable to being concealed, whether equipped with a folding or adjustable stock or not, than handguns. All things considered, any criminal's "best" choice of firearm—for lack of a better term—is a handgun.

Chapter 6
Military vs. Civilian Firearms

The rationales offered by gun control advocates for banning semiautomatic rifles are as fluid as the shifting sands of the Arabian Desert. One rationale *de jour* is that AR-15 rifles are "weapons of war." The obvious question is, then, just what exactly constitutes a "weapon of war"? But the better question is whether there is any important difference between civilian and military arms *at all*. The answer to this question, *with one important caveat that will be discussed below*, is no: there is no fundamental difference between military and civilian firearms. As the great maneuver warfare theorist B.H. Liddell Hart wrote, "[t]here is no adequate reason why a military rifle should not be treated with the same care as a sporting rifle."[348] The evolution of civilian and military firearms have been inextricably linked and intertwined throughout the history of guns. Many indispensable features of military firearms today were developed by private parties for the commercial market and only accepted for military service after first being introduced commercially—sometimes *long* after. In fact, civilian firearms development has often led the development of military weapons, rather than the reverse.

The most striking example of this is the rifled barrel. Rifling—the spiral grooves cut into the interior of a firearm's barrel—impart the spin to the bullet that vastly enhances accuracy. A military firearm without a rifled barrel would be unthinkable today. Yet the rifled barrel was in civilian use centuries before being adopted as a standard feature of infantry arms. According to David Harsanyi, gun makers in Nuremburg, Germany were proficient in this technology by 1520.[349] The first patent for rifling in a gun barrel was registered by Arnold Rostipen in 1635.[350]

---

[348] John A English. *On Infantry* (Praeger Publishers, 1984), 38, quoting B.H. Liddell Hart, *The Future of Infantry,* and *Thoughts on War.*
[349] Harsanyi, 29.
[350] Pridham, 8.

The Pennsylvania or Kentucky Long Rifle came into existence in the early 18th century, having been developed by German gunsmiths in Pennsylvania who originally made "traditional Jäger rifles" for hunting.[351] For rifling to be effective the bullet must fit tightly in the bore; for muzzle loaders, this required "some force" and a rifle could take "a long time" to load;[352] per Pridham,

> [f]or military purposes, therefore, rifles were rejected, and rifling was confined to sporting weapons where accuracy and range were of greater importance than speed of loading. For this reason we find that rifle making developed in those countries where game or target shooting were popular, as in the great forests of the European Continent and in America.[353]

According to Pridham, "[t]he first use of rifles in warfare appears to have been during the American War of Independence (1776—83) [where] [t]he Kentucky Rifle, used by the Colonists—not as a general issue, but by the Mid-Colonial Militia—was greatly superior to the British Musket, both in accuracy and range,"[354] with General Frasier being killed at the Battle of Saratoga by Colonial rifle fire.[355] Notwithstanding the demonstrable effectiveness of the Pennsylvania Long Rifle, it would be a long time yet before the rifle became the standard infantry weapon. Despite the formation of a Rifle Regiment armed with the Baker Rifle in 1800, it was the smoothbore Brown Bess that was the mainstay of British forces as late as Waterloo.[356] Only with invention of the *minie* ball in 1826 did the rifle—ancient technology from the civilian perspective—began to

---

[351] Harsanyi, 28 – 29.

[352] Pridham, 10.

[353] *Id.*

[354] *Id.*

[355] *Id.* It would appear from Pridham's account that the American Revolutionary War was not the first use of rifles in warfare, but rather the first widespread use – for Pridham himself reports that General Wolfe was killed at Quebec by rifle fire in 1759. Pridham, 10.

[356] Pridham, 10 – 11.

gain serious traction as the standard in military weapons.[357] Only with the Crimean War of 1854, nearly 250 years after Mr. Rostipen got his patent, was the rifle "first generally used" as the standard infantry weapon,[358] and even then it has even been said that it took the influence of Prince Albert himself to persuade the British Army to issue the then new Enfield Rifle to its troops there.[359]

Nor was it just the difficulty of reloading early muzzle loading rifles that inhibited their use; even the paramount importance of accurate fire was ignored by the world's armies long after American frontiersman and European sportsmen had embraced an accurate rifle as a necessity. This is because "[t]he evolution of tactical fighting units on the battlefield was affected as much by control considerations as by developments in weapons technology [because] [o]pen-order tactics tended to be disorderly and inherently prone to desertion."[360] Instead, armies relied upon massed formations deployed in a "firing line and urging volley fire" to "increase the density and improve the control of fire"[361]—"volley" fire being "[t]he simultaneous discharge of a number of cannon, or muskets or any firearms."[362] These tactics have long since given way to decentralized open-order tactics in which soldiers are expected to engage the enemy with accurate, well-aimed fire at discretion.

Civilians embraced the rifled barrel long before soldiers did, with the world's armies adapting the rifled barrel to military requirements literally centuries after its invention by civilian gun makers. In other words, this military technology isn't "military" at all. The pattern of firearms technology developed by civilians later being adopted by military forces has occurred repeatedly. For example,

---

[357] *Id.*, 11.
[358] English, 1.
[359] Pridham, 12.
[360] English, 2.
[361] *Id.*, 4.
[362] War Department, *US Infantry Tactics for the Instruction, Exercise and Manoeuvers of the United States Infantry* (J.B. Lippincott & Co., 1863), 431.

Samuel Colt patented his first percussion revolver in early 1836,[363] and the US Army first formally adopting the percussion revolver in 1848.[364] Other examples include lever action rifles[365] and metallic cartridges.[366] The iconic Colt Model of 1911 in .45 ACP relies upon technology patented by John Browning during the 1890s.[367] On January 4th, 1985, the US military adopted the Beretta 92SB-F as the M9 pistol.[368] The 92SB-F—which later developed into the Beretta 92FS[369]—was a slight variation of the Beretta 92SB, released for commercial sale in 1981,[370] at that time the latest version of the Beretta 92 series pistol first introduced in 1976.[371] Similarly, the M9's replacement—the M17 pistol—was derived from the Sig Sauer P320,[372] introduced by Sig Sauer into the US commercial market in early 2014.[373]

---

[363] Matthew Moss, "How the Colt Single Action Army Revolver Won the West," *Popular Mechanics*, November 3rd, 2016. https://www.popularmechanics.com/military/weapons/a23685/colt-single-action/. Retrieved July 10th, 2019.

[364] Matthew Moss, "The 240-Year Evolution of the Army Sidearm," *Popular Mechanics*, May 25th, 2017, https://www.popularmechanics.com/military/weapons/a26625/us-military-handguns/. Retrieved July 10th, 2019.

[365] See Lucie, 143.

[366] Berkeley R. Lewis. *Small Arms Ammunition at the International Exposition, Philadelphia 1876*, Chapter 1, "Pioneers in Metallic Cartridges." Smithsonian Studies in History and Technology, Number 11 (Smithsonian Institution Press, 1972).

[367] Johnson and Haven, 93.

[368] Angus McClellan. "The Beretta M9: 25 Years of Service." *The American Rifleman*, November 12th, 2009. https://www.americanrifleman.org/articles/2009/11/12/the-beretta-m9-25-years-of-service/. Retrieved April 20th, 2019.

[369] *Id.*

[370] Wood, 171.

[371] *Id.*, 162.

[372] Matthew Cox and Hope Hodge Seck. "Army Picks Sig Sauer's P320 Handgun to Replace M9 Service Pistol," *Military.com*, https://www.military.com/daily-news/2017/01/19/army-picks-sig-sauer-replace-m9-service-pistol.html. Retrieved April 20th, 2019.

[373] "P320 Pistol," *Officer.com*, February 4th, 2014,

Another example of the symbiosis of military and civilian firearms technology is the NATO standard 7.62x51mm rifle round. Although the 7.62x51 cartridge was developed to replace the Army's old 30.06 cartridge of pre-World War I vintage,[374] it became available on the civilian market as a hunting round in 1952, two years *before* coming into service in the US military, and has remained "the most popular short-action, big-game hunting cartridge in the world" ever since.[375]

Little known to either gun control advocates or firearms enthusiasts, the AR-15 rifle itself is a product of the intersection of military and civilian firearms development. The AR-15 was a remarkable rifle when introduced in prototype in 1958,[376] but not for the pistol grip and handguards so disconcerting to firearms prohibitionists. The AR-15 was groundbreaking for two other reasons. One was the "lightweight alloys, plastics, and glass compounds" of which it was constructed—an aspect of the rifle's design so distinctive that in even in 1966, after the Department of Defense's initial bulk purchase of 85,000 XM16E1 rifles, the Army was still poo-pooing the XM16E1's "yet-to-be-confirmed field observations of their wearing qualities and stress resistances."[377] Second, the AR-15 / M16 family of rifles was notable for its adoption of the intermediate-sized 5.56mm cartridge instead of the heavier 30.06 and 7.62x51mm cartridges used by the US military at the time and previously. Both features were influenced by preexisting civilian firearms developments.

---

https://www.officer.com/tactical/firearms/handguns/product/11305415/sig-sauer-inc-p320-pistol. Retrieved April 20th, 2019.

[374] Tom McHale. "7.62 NATO vs.308 Winchester Ammo, What's the Difference?" *Ammoland*, https://www.ammoland.com/2017/06/7-62-nato-vs-308-winchester-ammo-whats-the-difference/#axzz5lhBvIgWA. Retrieved April 20th, 2019.

[375] David Maccar. "The.308 Winchester: A Brief History." *Range365*, July 24th, 2017. https://www.range365.com/308-winchester-762-nato. Retrieved April 20th, 2019.

[376] *FM 23-9*, June 1974, 175.

[377] *FM 23-71*, December 1966, 225.

The development of the AR-15 was set in train when the president of Fairchild Engine and Aircraft Corporation, "avid hunter and gun aficionado" Richard Boutelle, decided to diversify the company by chartering its ArmaLite Division to "develop a line of fine, truly lightweight weapons [using] [m]aterials being used in the aircraft industry [which] were thought to be able to be used in weapons."[378] Although "they deferred commercial work and directed their activities toward military firearms" following the success of their earlier AR-5 survival rifle, ArmaLite's initial plan was "to produce fine sporting arms for the commercial market" under the supervision the Division's chief engineer, the legendary Eugene Stoner.[379]

The other feature which made the AR-15 / M16 remarkable was the round it fired—the 5.56mm cartridge, very similar to the .223 cartridge commonly used in the AR-15. The adoption of this round was groundbreaking in that it was the first time the United States had adopted an intermediate cartridge—that is, a cartridge larger than a pistol cartridge but smaller than a traditional military rifle cartridge like the .303 Enfield or the 30.06.[380] A constituency had long advocated for the adoption of an intermediate cartridge by the US Army: "[s]ince the introduction of firearms into military service, there have been attempts to reduce the size or caliber of bullets used in soldiers' rifles."[381] "Adoption of a small caliber rifle as a standard

---

[378] David R. Hughes. *The History and Development of the M16 Rifle and its Cartridge* (Armory Publications 1990), 254.

[379] *Id.*, 24.

[380] The United States was not the first nation to adopt an intermediate cartridge. Nazi Germany had previously adopted the STG-44 assault rifle, chambered in 7.92mm Kurtz (see Mark Keefe, "Shooting the Sturmgewehr," *American Rifleman*, October 29th, 2014, https://www.americanrifleman.org/articles/2014/10/29/shooting-the-sturmgewehr/. Retrieved July 10th, 2019); and the Soviet Union had long since adopted the M43 7.62x39mm round, which remains one of the most widely used calibers (see "7.62x39 (M43)," Terminal Ballistics Research, https://www.ballisticstudies.com/Knowledgebase/7.62x39+M43.html. Retrieved July 10th, 2019).

[381] Hughes, 376, Introduction, first page (not paginated).

service weapon [was] not a recent requirement,"[382] but "the first written requirement for a small caliber weapon ... began in 1957."[383]

Developing a rifle that would fire an intermediate caliber round was a longstanding interest in some military circles, but the cartridge itself that would become the 5.56mm and .223 Remington rounds was inspired by existing civilian technology:

> The impetus for creating the.223 Remington cartridge came from previous development work at Aberdeen Proving Ground ... However, the .223 cartridge started as the .222 Remington Cartridge, developed particularly for varmint shooters in 1950 by Mike Walker of Remington.[384]

Thus, by dint of the history of its development and of the cartridge it fires the AR-15—as distinguished from the selective fire M16—is not a military weapon. None of its features are exclusively military in character, and those of its features that were most groundbreaking at the time of its development owed their existence, not to the dictates of military procurement officers, but to the innovation of civilian firearms enthusiasts and engineers. The AR-15 is not a "weapon of war." What it is, rather, is a highly versatile general-purpose rifle well suited to most civilian shooting applications, including target shooting, hunting, competition shooting, and defense of the home. Given its history, its uniquely American background, and its kinship with the M16—America's iconic service rifle of the Vietnam era and beyond—the AR-15 is a highly collectible weapon in firearms circles, gun collecting being a pursuit that even Barack Obama recognized as legitimate.[385]

---

[382] *FM 23-9*, June 1974, 175.

[383] *Id.*

[384] Hughes, 23.

[385] President Obama wrote that "[t]he fact is, almost all gun owners in America are highly responsible. They're our friends and neighbors. They buy their guns legally and use them safely, whether for hunting or target

The 4ᵗʰ Circuit Speaks:
Kolbe v. Hogan

A great deal of ink is spilled over whether the AR-15 rifle is a "weapon of war," but no one seems to have set forth a satisfactory definition of what a "weapon of war" is. One of the crudest attempts to answer this question was the majority opinion in *Kolbe v. Hogan*[386], which held that AR-15 rifles are not covered by the Second Amendment at all, the Court seemingly adapting Justice Stewart's much ridiculed test for the detection of "hard core pornography"— that is, "I know it when I see it"[387]—to the task of divining a firearm's status as a "weapon of war." Writing for the majority in *Kolbe*, Judge King wrote that "we are convinced that the banned assault weapons and large capacity magazines are among those arms that are 'like' 'M16 rifles' — 'weapons that are most useful in military service' — which the *Heller* Court singled out as being beyond the Second Amendment's reach,"[388] (leaving aside for the moment the fact that "*Heller* in no way suggests that the military usefulness of a weapon disqualifies it from Second Amendment protection").[389] The Court failed to explain in just what respects an AR-15 is so "like" and M16 as to render it outside the protection of the Second Amendment. Although the Court notes, with a surprising lack of irony, that the version of the AR-15 developed for the Army, that

---

shooting, collection or protection. And that's something that gun-safety advocates need to accept." President Obama held the mistaken view that AR-15s are not suitable for any of these purposes. The collectability of the AR-15 is just one more example of how poorly informed he was about firearms. "Op-ed by President Obama in the *Arizona Daily Star*: We must seek agreement on gun reforms," The White House Office of the Press Secretary, March 13ᵗʰ, 2011. https://obamawhitehouse.archives.gov/the-press-office/2011/03/13/op-ed-president-obama-arizona-daily-star-we-must-seek-agreement-gun-refo. Retrieved April 21ˢᵗ, 2019.

[386] *Kolbe v. Hogan*, 849 F.3d 114 (2017).

[387] *Jacobellis v. Ohio*, 378 US 184 (1964) (Stewart, J. concurring).

[388] *Kolbe.*

[389] *Kolbe* (Traxler, J., dissenting).

would later become the M16, "was designed as a selective fire rifle —
one that can be fired in either automatic mode ... or semiautomatic
mode,"[390] it glosses over this with the almost Orwellian claim that
"[t]he difference between the fully automatic and semiautomatic
versions of those firearms is slight."[391] From the Court's inscrutable
divination, we can infer that a weapon is "like" an "M16" if it looks
like one. The test of the *Kolbe* Court might be called the "All that
Glitters Must be Gold" doctrine (though one might be forgiven if we
suspect, as the dissent warns us, that the Court's real test as to
whether a rifle is "like" whatever the Court or the legislature decides
it is, and that therefore "all semiautomatic firearms — including the
vast majority of semiautomatic handguns — enjoy no Constitutional
protection,"[392] irrespective of its actual features). Like a Carolina dog
fooled by a Scarlet Kingsnake that mimics a Coral Snake,[393] the Court
eschews an ordinary rifle because it resembles an unpalatable
machinegun.

In part, the Court's prejudice against the AR-15 may stem
from that phenomenon of the human mind that resists change and
clings to old paradigms. My wife was once a member of old-
fashioned Baptist Church that forbade listening to what they called
"Contemporary Christian music"—that is, Christian music in the
same style as Pop, Rock, or Adult Contemporary music. Unable to
cite any doctrinal basis for this prejudice, the church justified the
proscription on the dubious ground that the beat of modern music
"deadens the mind." What the congregation really objected to was
change: They wanted the old hymns and were vaguely offended by
any innovation in style or tone of worship, but perceiving that mere
conservatism of taste does not constitute a valid basis for objecting to

---

[390] *Kolbe.*

[391] *Id.*

[392] *Id.*

[393] Eleanor Nelson. "How the Kingsnake Is Still Fooling Predators into
Thinking It's Venomous." *Nova,* August 6th, 2014.
https://www.pbs.org/wgbh/nova/article/mimicry-evolutionary-
momentum/. Retrieved April 21st, 2019.

the new style, they contrived another rationale for their opposition to it. The 4th Circuit's strained objection to the AR-15 is a bird of the same feather. Johnson illustrates the phenomenon as applied to firearms this way:

> Classifications invariably develop from custom and usage. The extent to which ancient forms and established methods dominate military science and tactics is frequently overlooked, yet this phenomenon occurs in all fields. For example, the so-called pistol was at one time a basic weapon of the cavalry, together with the sword, or saber. Horseman, needing one hand for the reins, fired the pistol using one hand only. The functional approach, not the procedure nor the form, dictated the one hand pistol technique. But as time went on, the true reason for one hand pistol shooting was forgotten. Even today we still look askance at the pistol shooter who uses two hands. Sissy stuff.[394]

And further:

> The functional approach is predominant in new types of weapons and vehicles because there are no preconceived notions of how the item should look … But in the field of small arms the ancient forms still cling stubbornly.[395]

The old straight arm one-handed cavalry pistol technique persisted after horse cavalry disappeared. Images depicting shooters using it can be found in books up through the 1920s and 1930s—even works cited in this study. But Lt. Col. Jeff Cooper and Deputy Jack Weaver having won us over to the two-handed grip long since,[396] those old pictures look slightly ridiculous now.

---

[394] Johnson, 3.

[395] *Id*, 4.

[396] Jeff McClellan. "Jeff Cooper, 86; Firearms Expert Set Standard for Pistol

Yet although our pistol technique may have evolved, with rifles "the ancient forms still cling stubbornly" in the mind of the *Kolbe* Court. In the judges' youth, rifles were for hunting and hunting rifles had a wooden stock, a curved pistol grip, and a long wooden forearm. Black rifles were known to them only through grainy television footing depicting our soldiers deployed overseas. Knowing nothing of the ArmaLite Division and its plan to make high-end sporting rifles and shotguns out of plastics, polymers and aluminum alloys, the judges formed the latent opinion that old-fashioned guns with wooden furniture were "good" guns intended for wholesome American sporting pursuits, while those sinister black rifles were strange and frightening because they look like rifles born by soldiers, utterly oblivious to the fact that the rifles carried by those soldiers were selective fire weapons largely impossible for civilians to own while the AR-15 is nothing more than a semiautomatic rifle, the latest in a hundred years of semiautomatic firearms being available to ordinary citizens.

The Court's position on AR-15 rifles seems rather discordant given the actual language of the Amendment itself. Whatever else the Second Amendment stands for—and I believe that it stands for a great deal more than this—it clearly stands for the proposition that the people have the right to bear arms for the defense of the state; that they hold this right directly themselves, and not merely as agents of the state; and that they have the right to possess firearms suitable for the purpose. As Michigan Chief Justice Thomas M. Cooley wrote in 1880:

> It might be supposed from the phraseology of this provision that the right to keep and bear arms was only guaranteed to the militia; but this would be an interpretation not warranted by the intent. The militia, as has been explained, consists of those persons who,

Technique." *Los Angeles Times*, October 1st, 2006. https://www.latimes.com/archives/la-xpm-2006-oct-01-me-cooper1-story.html. Retrieved April 22nd, 2019.

under the law, are liable to the performance of military duty, and are officered and enrolled for service when called upon. But the law may make provision for the enrolment of all who are fit to perform military duty, or of a small number only, or it may wholly omit to make any provision at all; *and if the right were limited to those enrolled, the purpose of the guarantee might be defeated altogether by the action or neglect to act of the government it was meant to hold in check.* The meaning of the provision undoubtedly is, that the people, from whom the militia must be taken, shall have the right to keep and bear arms; and they need no permission or regulation of law for that purpose. But this enables the government to have a well regulated militia; for to bear arms implies something more than the mere keeping; *it implies the learning to handle and use them in a way that makes those who keep them ready for their efficient use; in other words, it implies the right to meet for voluntary discipline in arms*, observing in doing so the laws of public order[397] (emphasis added).

No aspect of the semiautomatic AR-15's capabilities or features render it any more a military arm or "weapon of war"—or any "deadlier"—than any other semiautomatic rifle. However, as a counterpart to the selective fire (and thereby indubitably military) M16, the AR-15 is very well suited to militia use. Having similar (though not necessarily identical)[398] ammunition, the AR-15 is

---

[397] Thomas M. Cooley. *The General Principles of Constitutional Law in the United States of America* (Little, Brown, and Company, 1880), 271.

[398] The M16 family of rifles is chambered in the NATO-standard 5.56mm round. Many (but not all) AR-15s are chambered in the civilian.223 Remington. The two rounds are visually identical on casual inspection and very similar in characteristics, and they are often spoken of as if they are interchangeable. They are not, however, identical. Any rifle chambered in the military 5.56mm round can safely fire the.223 Remington round. The reverse is not necessarily true, however. Due to slight differences in the external dimensions of the case, firing a 5.56mm NATO round from a rifle

particularly well suited to facilitating Americans' "learning to handle and use [arms] in a way that makes those who keep them ready for their efficient [militia] use."[399] The AR-15 rifle is not a military weapon. But given that its layout and configuration are similar to America's current service rifle, it is eminently suited to the purpose of the Second Amendment as set forth by Judge Cooley. This view was reinforced by the United States Supreme Court's prior holding in *United States v. Miller*[400], as procedurally problematic as that case was.[401] In *Miller*, Frank Layton and Jack Miller had been charged with possessing an unregistered short-barreled shotgun in violation of the National Firearms Act. The District Court had "sustained [a] demurrer and quashed the indictment" against Miller and Layton as violating the Second Amendment.[402] The Supreme Court reversed, holding that

> In the absence of any evidence tending to show that possession or use of a 'shotgun having a barrel of less than eighteen inches in length' at this time has some reasonable relationship to the preservation or efficiency of a well regulated militia, we cannot say that the Second Amendment guarantees the right to

---

chambered in.223 Remington produces higher than optimal pressures in the chamber, which can produce problems if a 5.56mm round is fired from a rifle chambered in.223 Remington. For concise review of this issue, see "223 -vs- 5.56: FACTS and MYTHS." Gavintube / Ultimate Reloader, https://www.youtube.com/watch?v=VCS4fXFmCyA. Retrieved January 21st, 2021.

[399] Cooley, 396.

[400] *United States v. Miller*, 307 US 174 (1939).

[401] "As for the 'hundreds of judges' …. who have relied on the view of the Second Amendment Justice STEVENS claims we endorsed in *Miller*: If so, they overread Miller. And their erroneous reliance upon an *uncontested and virtually unreasoned case* cannot nullify the reliance of millions of Americans (as our historical analysis has shown) upon the true meaning of the right to keep and bear arms" (emphasis added). *District of Columbia v. Heller*, 554 US 570 (2008).

[402] *Id.*

101

keep and bear such an instrument. Certainly it is not within judicial notice that this weapon is any part of the ordinary military equipment or that its use could contribute to the common defense.[403]

The 4th Circuit's holding in *Kolbe* is utterly unmoored from Second Amendment's text and history. The AR-15 easily passes muster even under the militia-centric constructions of Justice Cooley and the *Miller* Court. Under these authorities, it would be the very similarity of the AR-15 to the M16 in appearance and layout that would bring it within the protection of the Amendment, as a piece of equipment suitable for militia training and use. But the 4th Circuit turns this precedent upside down by declaring the military utility that that the Court ascribed to the AR-15 as being the very fact that puts it "beyond the Second Amendment's reach."[404] As the *Kolbe* dissent observed,

> [u]nder the majority's analysis, a settler's musket [during the Founding era], the only weapon he would likely own and bring to militia service, would be most useful in military service — undoubtedly a weapon of war — and therefore not protected by the Second Amendment.[405]

The Civilian Marksmanship Program: History and Tradition Contradict the *Kolbe* Court

In response to a question from Senator Cruz about the 9th Amendment during his confirmation hearings, Justice Kavanaugh said

---

[403] *Id.*
[404] *Kolbe*, 385.
[405] *Kolbe*, dissent.

I think that the Ninth Amendment and the Privileges and Immunities Clause and the Supreme Court's doctrine of substantive due process are three roads that someone might take that all really lead to the same destination under the precedent of the Supreme Court, which ... protects certain unenumerated rights so long as the rights, as the Supreme Court said in the *Glucksberg* case, are rooted in history and tradition.[406]

Justice Kavanaugh was referring to *Washington v. Glucksberg*, a 1997 case upholding Washington state's ban on assisted suicide while reaffirming the Court's longstanding position that "the Due Process Clause specially protects those fundamental rights and liberties which are, objectively, deeply rooted in this Nation's history and tradition."[407]

The *Kolbe* Court's cramped view of the Second Amendment is further discredited by its clear conflict with America's history and tradition of firearms ownership. For if a right not expressly enumerated in the Constitution may be entitled to protection from abridgment under the Due Process Clause because of its place in our country's history and traditions, how much stronger must be the protection due to a right that is both expressly set forth in the Constitution's text, and also deeply rooted in our Nation's history and tradition?

The Second Amendment expressly articulates an enumerated right to keep and bear arms, reflecting the deeply rooted and ancient practice in American culture of private gun ownership. Contrary to the implication of the *Kolbe* court, that tradition does not exclude private possession of military-style firearms. In fact, the opposite is

---

[406] Justice Kavanaugh, quoted at Randy Barnett, "Kavanaugh Testimony, Part 3: unenumerated rights and more." The *Volokh Conspiracy*, September 15th, 2018. https://reason.com/2018/09/15/kavanaugh-testimony-part-3-unenumerated/. Retrieved June 28th, 2019.
[407] *Washington v. Glucksberg*, 521 US 702 (1997) (internal quotations and citations omitted).

true: the private possession and use of military arms is a longstanding practice and tradition in American culture. Nothing encapsulates this more than the Civilian Marksmanship Program (CMP).

The CMP was formed in 1903 when the Secretary of War established the National Board for the Promotion of Rifle Practice, which was then chartered and authorized under Title 10 United States Code.[408] The program was a response to "serious problems with mobilization, training, and combat operations [that] surfaced" during the Spanish American War "rais[ing] concern about the adequacy of marksmanship training and the ability of the United States to expand the Army quickly."[409] The National Defense Act of 1916 created the position Director of Civilian Marksmanship, an Army officer that would administer the board's programs,[410] a position which persisted until Congress created the Corporation for the Promotion of Rifle Practice and Firearms Safety in 1996 to supersede the National Board and assume responsibility for the CMP.[411]

> The CMP has a number of functions, including promot[ion] and monitor[ing] generalized rifle training through a system of affiliated clubs and other organizations ... [and] sponsor[ing] marksmanship competitions. As part of these activities, the program sells surplus weapons to affiliated club members, loans surplus weapons to affiliated clubs, and donates

---

[408] *Army's Program for Civilian Marksmanship: Its Practices and Procedures* (General Accounting Office, September 22nd, 1976), 1.

[409] *Army's Civilian Marksmanship Program is of Limited Value* (General Accounting Office, May 1990), 2.

[410] James B. Trefethen and Serven, James E. *Americans and Their Guns: The National Rifle Association and a Century of Service* (Stackpole Books, 1967), 180 – 181.

[411] *Civilian Marksmanship Program: Information on the Sale of Surplus Army Firearms* (United States Government Accountability Office, February 2019), 1.

and/or sells ammunition and other shooting supply items to affiliated clubs.[412]

The surplus weapons sold by the CMP consist largely of former US Army standard weapons; and while the weapons sold are surplus, they have not always been obsolete, and they have certainly not always been devoid of military value. For example, a price list of items for sale issued by the Director of Civilian Marksmanship in approximately 1923 offers a number of obsolete firearms for sale, but it also offered Model 1903 Springfield Rifles, the then US Army standard, along with numerous supplies and accessories for it, as well as ammunition for the Model 1911.45 caliber pistol, then the US Army standard sidearm.[413] The Price List for January 15th, 1937 continued to offer M1903 Springfield Rifles for sale, as well as M1911.45 ammunition;[414] although the Army adopted the M1 Garand in 1936, the M1903 Springfield remained the Army's mainstay for some time thereafter as the M1 was fielded. In fact, the M1903 Springfield was brought back into production and saw service during the Second World War, with production finally being halted in 1945.[415] The Director of Civilian Marksmanship continued to sell M1903 Springfields in both M1903A1 and M1903A3 configurations after World War II,[416] despite the M1903 Springfield continuing in US service until 1957.[417]

---

[412] *Army's Civilian Marksmanship Program is of Limited Value*, 2.

[413] Stodter, C. E., Colonel of Cavalry, Director. *Price List of Supplies Available for Sale to Members of the National Rifle Association*, circa 1923. That this Price List dates from this period is supported by a reference to Colonel Stodter as Director of Civilian Marksmanship in "Annual Rifle Meetings Held," *Arms and the Man*, February 1st, 1921, Vol. LXVIII, No. 12, 5 – 6.

[414] Director of Civilian Marksmanship. *Price List of Supplies Sold to Members of the National Rifle Association of America*, January 15th, 1937.

[415] Rick Hacker. "Classic Guns: The M1903 Springfield Rifle." *Shooting Illustrated*, February 21st, 2019. https://www.shootingillustrated.com/articles/2019/2/21/classic-guns-the-m1903-springfield-rifle/. Retrieved June 28th, 2019.

[416] Director of Civilian Marksmanship. *Price List of Supplies Authorized for Sale on Approval of the Director of Civilian Marksmanship*. May 1st, 1946.

It is likely that the CMP began selling the semiautomatic M1 Garand Rifle in National Match configuration in the mid-1950s, prior to the introduction of the M14 Rifle. By 1960, the Director of Civilian Marksmanship was selling M1 Garands in both National Match and Service Issue configuration.[418] Although the M14 was adopted in 1957, the M1 Garand remained in service, and in large numbers, for years after that due to mismanagement of M14 procurement, with the first production order for a modest 15,669 M14 Rifles not arriving at Springfield Arsenal until April 1958.[419] By June 1961, only 133,000 M14 Rifles existed;[420] later that year, as tensions with communist forces over Berlin increased, it was reported that all the US troops there were equipped with M1 Garand Rifles four years after adoption of the M14.[421] It would take years more to phase the M1 Garand out of service. In 1969, the Army National Guard reported receiving 15,006 M14 rifles;[422] in 1970 the Army National Guard reported that "[t]he allocation of approximately 200,000 M16 rifles, for distribution in FY 1971, and the projected input of additional M14 rifles for service type units [was] expected to be adequate to satisfy ARNG [Army National Guard] requirements and permit turn-in of M1 rifles."[423] The same year the Secretary of Defense issued "52,000 M14/16 rifles" to Guard and Reserve forces and projected "full training allowances of the M14/16 rifles for major combat units" for Fiscal Year 1971.[424]

---

[417] Hacker.

[418] Director of Civilian Marksmanship. *DCM Price List*, July 1st, 1960.

[419] Robert Dale Hinrichs. *Rifle Development, Standardization, and Procurement in the United States Military, 1950-1967* (Master of Arts Thesis, Iowa State University, 2009), 68.

[420] *Id.*, 72.

[421] *Id.*

[422] *Annual Report (63rd) of Chief, National Guard Bureau for Fiscal Year 1969* (National Guard Bureau (Army)), 30 June 1969, 33.

[423] *Annual Report of the Chief, National Guard Bureau for Fiscal Year 1970* (National Guard Bureau (Army)), 30 June 1970, 37.

[424] *Annual Report of the Secretary of Defense on Reserve Forces* (Assistant Secretary of Defense (Manpower and Reserve Affairs), Washington, D. C., 1970), 3.

Thus, until at least 1971, many US Army units were employing the M1 Garand Rifle as their soldiers' primary weapon at the same time the CMP was selling those same rifles, and others, to members of the public. Another popular military weapon distributed by the CMP was the semiautomatic, detachable magazine-fed M1 Carbine.[425] From 1958 to 1975 the CMP sold 519,093 rifles and carbines, and more than 168,000 other firearms;[426] in 1989 the CMP sold approximately 6,000 M1 Garands;[427] in fiscal years 1997 and 1998 the CMP sold 16,326 M1 Garand Rifles to the public;[428] from 2008 to 2017, the CMP sold 203,644 serviceable M1 Garand rifles to the public.[429] Additionally, the CMP received 8,000 M1911 pistols from the Army for sale to the public in 2018, as well as 87,000 M1 Garands from the Philippines and 13,000 from Turkey.[430]

Surplus military firearms have been sold to the public, including sale of models while they were still in use by the US military, for nearly one hundred years; in 1984, the Department of Defense (DoD) declared that "[i]t is DoD policy to encourage actively and support civilian rifle and pistol marksmanship training as an important element of national defense."[431] What's more, the CMP has continued in existence despite substantial criticism over the years.[432]

---

[425] "M1 Carbines Available to NRA Members," *American Rifleman*, May 1963, 36.

[426] *Army's Program For Civilian Marksmanship: Its Practices And Procedures*, 15.

[427] *Evaluation of the Army's Civilian Marksmanship Program: Statement of Richard Davis, Director, Army Issues National Security and International Affairs Division Before the Subcommittee on Readiness Committee on Armed Services House of Representatives* (United States General Accounting Office, March 8th, 1990), 2; General Accounting Office, *The Army's Civilian Marksmanship Program is of Little Value*, May 1990, 4.

[428] *Civilian Marksmanship Program: Corporation Needs to Fully Comply With the Law on Sales of Firearms* (General Accounting Office, January 1999), 6.

[429] *Civilian Marksmanship Program: Information on the Sale of Surplus Army Firearms* (Government Accountability Office, February 2019), 36.

[430] *Id*, 11 and 12.

[431] Department of Defense Directive 1025.1, *SUBJECT: DoD Civilian Rifle and Pistol Marksmanship Training Program*, January 31, 1984, paragraph 3.

The resilience of the CMP in the face of criticism is a testament to the American tradition of arms; to the fact that said tradition includes ownership of military-style firearms by private citizens; and most importantly, to the fact that private ownership of semiautomatic firearms is deeply embedded in and integral to America's historical tradition of arms. In sum, the CMP program constitutes an ongoing contradiction of *Kolbe* Court's findings.

The American history and tradition of marksmanship competition also cuts against *Kolbe*. The competitive shooting tradition in America is closely intertwined with military shooting. The inaugural match at the NRA's Creedmore Range in June 1873 featured fourteen teams from the New York National Guard, two teams from the New Jersey National Guard, and two Regular Army teams.[433] Military participation remained a fixture of competitions at the Creedmore Range. When the NRA transferred its matches to the Sea Girt Range in 1892, the driving force behind those competitions became the New Jersey State Rifle Association, an entity which confined its membership to members of the New Jersey National Guard,[434] and military teams continued to feature prominently in the competition.[435] Likewise, when the NRA commenced its inaugural match at Camp Perry, Ohio on August 19th, 1907,[436] it did so at a facility largely funded and developed by the Ohio National Guard.[437] Indeed, the "promot[ion] … of a system of aiming drill and target firing among the National Guard of New York and the militia of other states" was among the initial objectives of the NRA at its founding in 1871:[438]

---

[432] See, for example, *Evaluation of the Army's Civilian Marksmanship Program: Statement of Richard Davis*, March 8th, 1990.
[433] Trefethen and Serven, 48.
[434] *Id*, 109 – 110.
[435] *Id*, 113.
[436] *Id*, 144.
[437] *Id*, 139.
[438] *Id*, 10.

The NRA instituted the American Military Rifle Championship Match at its annual matches at Creedmoor in 1878, which was won by Sergeant J. S. Barton of the New York National Guard. The name was changed in 1884 to the President's Match for the Military Rifle Championship.[439]

Camp Perry still hosts military marksmanship matches,[440] Small Arms Firing Schools conducted by the Department of Defense for civilian shooters,[441] with military and civilian shooters competing together.[442]

The One Uniquely Military Firearms Technology: Automatic Fire

As the *Kolbe* dissent noted, "*Heller* in no way suggests that the military usefulness of a weapon disqualifies it from Second Amendment protection."[443] As noted above, for most of history there has been no meaningful distinction between "military" and "civilian" firearms technology, except in that military firearms technology often lagged behind civilian arms, and armies often relied upon civilian firearms designers and users for the improvements to firearms that they did adopt. As the *Kolbe* dissent noted,

---

[439] Hap Rocketto. *A Short History of the President's Match and the President's Hundred*, March 19th, 2008, 5.

[440] "Military Matches," TheCMP.org. http://thecmp.org/competitions/military-matches/. Retrieved June 29th, 2019.

[441] "Small Arms Firing Schools," TheCMP.org. http://thecmp.org/competitions/cmp-national-matches/small-arms-firing-schools/. Retrieved June 29th, 2019.

[442] "Service Rifle," TheCMP.org. http://thecmp.org/competitions/service-rifle/. Retrieved June 29th, 2019; see also *CMP Highpower Pistol and Rifle Competition Rules*, 22nd Edition, 2018, Rule 2.6.4 d), 10; and Army Regulation 920-30, *Rules and Regulations for National Matches and other Excellence-in-Competition (EIC) Matches*, 17 August 1990.

[443] *Kolbe* (dissent).

at the time of the Second Amendment's ratification, it was understood that all citizens capable of military service ... would bring the sorts of lawful weapons that they possessed at home to militia duty ... Ordinarily when called for militia service able-bodied men were expected to appear bearing arms supplied by themselves and of the kind in common use at the time.[444]

Nonetheless, the *Kolbe* majority and many other firearms prohibitionists insist on depicting the AR-15 rifle as a "weapon of war" and calling for banning it on that basis. At the end of the 19th Century and the beginning of the 20th, a new technology emerged that would set out a clear line of demarcation between firearms adapted solely to military applications and those useful in other shooting applications—technology that would, for the first time, clearly set apart "weapons of war" from other firearms. That technology was automatic fire: the ability to fire more than one round, whether in a continuous stream or in a burst, with each pull of the trigger. AR-15s are not capable of automatic fire and are not "weapons of war" in the modern sense.[445]

The Basic Aim of Infantry Combat: Fire Superiority

"Crime" as usually understood and "combat" are fundamentally different phenomena. While both are carried out by

---

[444] *Id.*

[445] Of course, bayonet lugs and grenade launchers are military features as well. That the former are of trivial importance to the issue of crime is self-evident. As for the latter, they are useless without the grenades to launch, which are not available to the public and largely obsolete even in military service, so that the chances of any crimes being perpetrated using rifle grenades is vanishingly small; I doubt that such has ever occurred in the United States.

those who seek to impose their will upon others by violence, the two phenomena operate upon entirely different assumptions. The criminal seeks out a victim that is unarmed, unwarned, and unable to offer meaningful resistance; confronted with complicating factors, the criminal is likely to break off his attack and seek another target. Even those most unusual of criminals, the gangland killers and Mafioso that engage in "wars" with their rivals, will not strike their foes on equal terms, but will resort to surprise or subterfuge to strike their enemy at a time and in a manner when the target is more or less helpless. In combat, by contrast, the soldier can never assume that his enemy is helpless. The soldier must presume that his enemy can and will offer meaningful resistance, and must proceed accordingly. Granted, the sophisticated practitioner of maneuver warfare may seek to avoid direct confrontation by "preempt[ing] the enemy, that is, [by] disarm[ing] or neutraliz[ing] him before the fight," and if he cannot do that, he may "seek[] to dislocate enemy forces, i.e., removing the enemy from the decisive point, thus rendering them useless and irrelevant to the fight."[446] But the soldier cannot always avoid the bloody confrontation. For the infantry, the day of reckoning always awaits when they must cross that last hundred yards and "close with the enemy by means of fire and maneuver to defeat or capture him, or to repel his assault by fire, close combat, and counterattack."[447]

In the aftermath of the First World War, British military strategist J.F.C. Fuller "came to believe that no attack in modern war would succeed against an enemy in position unless his resisting power either through surprise or preponderating fire"[448] was reduced. We shall address surprise later. As to achieving "preponderating fire" in the infantry attack, automatic fire—burst or continuous—is the key. To pierce the enemy's defenses and destroy his forces, and

---

[446] Robert R. Leonhard. *The Art of Maneuver: Maneuver-Warfare Theory and Airland Battle* (Presidio Press, 1994), 19 – 21.
[447] *FM 7-8, Infantry Rifle Platoon and Squad* (Department of the Army, 22 April 1992), paragraph 1-1.
[448] English, 38.

conversely, to break an attacking enemy's momentum and prevent him from compromising one's own defenses, an infantry unit must gain *fire superiority*, and it is on this task that automatic weapons—whether full auto or burst—are decisive. In the attack,

> the assaulting force is supported by the support by fire (SBF) element. The SBF element's focus is to gain fire superiority and cover the maneuver of the assaulting force as it gains a foothold onto an objective. Establishing the SBF is as critical to the deliberate attack as conducting the assault. Without the SBF, the assaulting element has to contend with an enemy that is presented with only one problem. When the assault element is covered by the SBF element, the enemy is now presented with a dilemma.[449]

A dilemma, for purposes of infantry combat, is

> a situation in which the enemy is presented with two or more equally bad alternatives. A problem is a situation in which the enemy is presented with only one bad alternative. Creative combinations allow the leader to create a dilemma for the enemy. When presented with a dilemma, an enemy has two reactions. The first reaction is not knowing what to do as he attempts to decide between equally bad options. This effect is commonly termed "fixed." When the enemy is fixed, the leader benefits from freedom of action. The second reaction is to simply choose one of the two equally bad options. Because the enemy's choice is an option in which the friendly

---

[449] SFC Carter H. Conrad and SFC Johnny Tinsley, "The Art of Support by Fire." *Infantry Online*, nd. https://www.benning.army.mil/infantry/magazine/issues/2014/Apr-Jun/ConradTinsley.html, Retrieved April 23rd, 2019.

force has the upper hand, the leader is able to exploit the enemy's decision.[450]

A military unit has achieved fire superiority "if its fires are effective enough to prevent the enemy from returning effective fire of its own."[451] Fire superiority effectuates this

> by fixing the enemy and suppressing the enemy [that is, by] preventing him from withdrawing, repositioning, or counterattacking. We suppress the enemy by gaining fire superiority over him — that is by showering him with such a high volume of effective fire that we thwart his efforts to reply with effective fire of his own. By fixing and suppressing the enemy, we allow our own maneuvering element to accomplish its task relatively unmolested. The support element achieves these effects — fixing and suppressing — in two ways: by inflicting casualties (physical impact), and by convincing enemy soldiers that if they leave their cover to fire or move, they will become casualties (psychological impact).[452]

Automatic fire achieves suppression in part psychologically. Douglas Southall Freeman quaintly illustrates this in his biography of Robert E. Lee: "[I]n one of his brushes in thick woods, [Brigadier General Henry A.] Wise ordered an artillerist to open fire. The officer protested that he could not see the enemy and could do no execution. 'Damn the execution, sir,' Wise was reported to have said, 'it's the noise that we want.'"[453] Another example comes to us from

---

[450] *FM 3-21.8 (FM 7-8), The Infantry Rifle Platoon and Squad* (Headquarters, Department of the Army, March 2007), paragraph 1-103.

[451] Dennis P. Chapman, "An Element of Strength: Reinvigorating Small Unit Training." *Armor*, May-June 2004, 35 – 39.

[452] Dennis P. Chapman, "Tactical Errors in the Dismounted Fight." *Armor*, July – August 2004, 20 – 23.

[453] Douglass Southall Freeman. *Robert E. Lee – A Biography* (Charles Scribner's Sons, 1934). Volume I, 591, note 11, quoting Walter Herron

General Vasily Chuikov, who reportedly sought to paralyze his German opponents at Stalingrad "by trying to make every German soldier feel that he is under the muzzle of Russian gun."[454] As this author has observed elsewhere,

> [w]hether burst or full auto, selective fire serves one function in combat—to gain fire superiority over an enemy force. Fire superiority is achieved when the enemy has been suppressed—which is to say, when one side is placing such a high volume of fire into the enemy's general vicinity that the enemy is forced to seek cover and is thereby prevented from returning effective fire.[455]

Thus, it isn't necessarily the casualty producing effect that gives fully automatic fire its greatest combat value, but its impact on behavior—that is, the effect of impelling the enemy to hide rather than return well-aimed fire, thus degrading his combat effectiveness. To achieve this psychological effect, however, it is not enough that suppressive fire merely be noisily delivered in high volume. It must be delivered with sufficient accuracy to create a real threat of death to enemy occupying or attempting to traverse the "beaten zone"—the cigar-shaped[456] "'... Cone of Misses,' or as it is known today, the deadly beaten zone of falling shot."[457] To the extent that this suppressive fire actually does kill or wound enemy soldiers ensconced in or trying to cross the beaten zone, so much the better. Given their relatively unwieldy physical configuration, fire control, target acquisition, and target engagement by machineguns (except in hasty contacts) is a rather systematic affair often accomplished with the weapon mounted on a tripod and aided by the use of a traversing and

---

Taylor, *Four Years with General Lee*, 34.
[454] English, 223.
[455] Chapman, "The Weapons of War Myth."
[456] *Training Regulation 240-10, Machine Gun. Technique of Machine-gun Fire, Direct Laying* (War Department, December 19th, 1923), 3.
[457] English, 2.

elevating mechanism (commonly known as the T&E).[458] Targets are engaged by increasing the size of the beaten zone by traversing the barrel to the left or right (traversing fire), and by increasing and decreasing the elevation of the barrel (searching fire).[459] On the defense, machineguns employ grazing fire as a defensive barrier to break the momentum of attacking forces and prevent penetration of the defensive position—grazing fire being "fire which is approximately parallel to the ground which does not rise above the height of a man,"[460] or in more contemporary usage, more than one meter above the ground.[461]

The majority in *Kolbe* glosses over the major difference between an AR-15 and M16 – selective fire capability – thus:

> The difference between the fully automatic and semiautomatic versions of those firearms is slight. That is, the automatic firing of all the ammunition in a large capacity thirty-round magazine takes about two seconds, whereas a semiautomatic rifle can empty the same magazine in as little as five seconds … ('[S]emiautomatic weapons can be fired at rates of 300 to 500 rounds per minute, making them virtually indistinguishable in practical effect from machineguns).'[462]

This absurd claim cannot bear even slight scrutiny, falling apart on even a cursory consideration of tactical principles. Although handier than machineguns and therefore not requiring the supplementary equipment such as tripods and traversing and

---

[458] *TR 240-10*, 6; *FM 23-67, Machinegun, 7.62-MM, M60* (Headquarters, Department of the Army, 29 February 1984), 3-2 – 3-7.

[459] *TR 240-10*, 6 – 7; *FM 23-67, Machinegun, 7.62-MM, M60* (Headquarters, Department of the Army, 29 February 1984), 7-4, 9-7; *FM 23-14, M249 Light Machine Gun in the Automatic Role* (Headquarters, Department of the Army, 26 January 1994), 6-5.

[460] *TR 240-30*, 8.

[461] *FM 23-14*, 6-3 and *FM 23-67*, 7-3 and 8-6; see also *FM 23-14*, 6-15.

[462] *Kolbe*.

elevating mechanisms those heavier weapons require,[463] the selective fire capability of an M16 or AK-47 serves the same functions as a machinegun: on the offensive, to suppress enemy personnel to prevent their maneuvering or returning effective fire against the assaulting force; and on the defense, breaking the momentum of an enemy force and disrupting its assault. These functions require a reasonable degree of accuracy even in automatic mode. As already noted, the "noise" of gunfire is not enough to achieve the suppressive effect; the fire must also present a credible threat of "execution"—that is, a material chance that the suppressive fire will cause injury or death to the enemy—if it is to achieve the necessary psychological mastery over them. Semiautomatic fire simply cannot approach the effectiveness of automatic fire in this respect. The huge rate of fire attributed to the AR-15 by the *Kolbe* court is a whimsical fantasy, conceivable perhaps in theory, but impossible in practice. The *Kolbe* dissent points out the first rather obvious flaw in the majority's claim:

> This claim seems counter-intuitive because semiautomatic firearms require that the shooter pull the trigger for each shot fired, while fully automatic weapons—otherwise known as 'machineguns'—do not require a pull of the trigger for each shot and will discharge every round in the magazine as long as the trigger is depressed ... The rate of fire of a semiautomatic firearm is determined simply by how fast the shooter can squeeze the trigger.[464]

A typical shooter would be hard pressed to pull the trigger at such an accelerated rate long enough to effectively replicate fully automatic fire and even if he could, such fire would, as Johnson and Haven have shown us, be unaimed fire, and unaimed fire is ineffective, whether automatic or semiautomatic. The reason for this lies in the fundamentals of marksmanship. One of the most basic

---

[463] Though a bipod is sometimes be attached to the barrel or handguards.
[464] *Kolbe*, dissent.

principles of marksmanship is trigger squeeze. "Any sudden movement of the finger on the trigger can disturb the lay of the rifle and cause the shot to miss the target."[465] Army doctrine explains:

> **Importance of Trigger Squeeze**: Poor shooting is usually caused by the aim being disturbed just before the bullet leaves the barrel and is the result of the firer *jerking the trigger or flinching*. The trigger does not have to be jerked violently to spoil the aim; even a slight sudden pressure of the trigger finger is enough to cause the barrel to waver and ruin the firer's sight alignment ... Correctly applied trigger squeeze causes no movement of the barrel; also, it prevents the rifleman from knowing exactly when the rifle will fire, thus helping him avoid flinching. For these reasons, trigger squeeze is the most important single element in the act of firing the rifle[466] (emphasis is original).

Or, as another source has put it:

> The most important single factor in marksmanship is trigger squeeze. Everything about your position and aim may be perfect, but, unless you squeeze the trigger correctly, your shot will not go where you have aimed ... if you jerk the trigger, you lose control ... jerking the trigger will disturb the sites. Even a slight movement will spoil an otherwise good shot.[467]

The requirement for proper trigger squeeze will frustrate any attempt to replicate fully automatic fire with a semiautomatic weapon as the *Kolbe* court fancifully believes possible. Any shooter but the most skilled world-class expert could not hope to properly squeeze the trigger in such a way as to maintain accuracy when firing at the fantastic speeds envisioned by the Court. A selective fire weapon in

---

[465] *FM 3-22.9*, 2008, paragraph 4-57.
[466] *FM 23-5*, 1958, 110.
[467] *FM 23-7 / AFM 50-4*, January 1952, 157.

automatic or burst mode removes the trigger squeeze problem from the equation by eliminating the need for repeated pulls of the trigger; a crew-served machine gun does this as well, and goes further by the provision of a sturdy tripod and T&E mechanism to provide even further stability. By contrast, anyone attempting to replicate automatic fires with a semiautomatic weapon would be violently jerking the trigger with every shot in order to keep up the rate of fire, spoiling his aim every time. Such a shooter would produce a great sound and fury to be sure, but the substance produced would be in grave doubt. In summary, the selective fire capability of the M16 is superior by orders of magnitude to the firepower of the semiautomatic AR-15.

Other facts show the implausibility the *Kolbe* majority's claim. Once such is the historical development of military firearms in the United States since the Second World War. The US ended World War II with the M1 Garand as its standard infantry rifle – a rifle that continued in that role through the Korean War. Notwithstanding the excellent performance characteristics of the M1 Garand, "it had several perceived or real shortcomings, which included recurring complaints about its weight, the *lack of full automatic capability* and the desire of many users to have a larger capacity, detachable box magazine rather than the M1's eight-round 'en bloc clip'"[468] (emphasis added). Thus, even before the end of the Second World War, the US Army recognized the superiority of a selective fire individual arm for certain infantry applications. The new rifle that finally emerged as the M1's replacement was the "US Rifle, 7.62 mm, M14," introduced in 1957.[469] Per one commentator,

[a]lthough there were obviously differences in the M1 and M14 rifles—including the design of the gas

---

[468] Bruce Canfield. "The M14 Rifle: John Garand's Final Legacy." *American Rifleman,* Thursday, April 28, 2016. https://www.americanrifleman.org/articles/2016/4/28/the-m14-rifle-john-garand-s-final-legacy/. Retrieved April 27th, 2019.
[469] *Id.*

system and the incorporation of a detachable box magazine – there were also many similarities between the two that reflect John Garand's original genius. Although not as long as the M1's receiver (due to the difference in length between the .30-'06 and 7.62 mm NATO cartridges), the M14's receiver design was nearly identical.[470]

A side-by-side comparison makes it obvious that the M14 is a direct descendant of the M1 Garand. Despite the many small differences between the two rifles, the most significant are that the M14 is lighter, it accepts a detachable magazine, *and it is selective fire*.[471] Were there really no difference between selective fire and semiautomatic fire, the US Government could have modified the M1 Garand to accept a detachable magazine, lightened the existing rifle in some way, and been done with it. Obviously the US Army did not agree with the *Kolbe* majority's position.

Further contradiction of the *Kolbe* Court's holding can be found in the policies on selective fire arms of various countries. First, of course, is the United States, where private possession of machineguns, including selective fire rifles, has been tightly regulated since the National Firearms Act of 1934, and even more stringently since 1986; such regulation was expanded with the ban on bump-stocks that took effect on March 29th, 2019.[472] Another example is the former communist regime of Romania. Fearing that Romania could someday fall victim to a Soviet invasion like that of Czechoslovakia in 1968, Nicolae Ceaușescu's regime formed the *Gărzile Patriotice* ("Patriotic Guards") for "territorial defense" that year. As with most Warsaw Pact forces, these paramilitaries were equipped with Kalashnikov (AK-47 or AKM) rifles. Being the profoundly paranoid figure that he was, Ceaușescu likely feared that the Patriotic Guards might someday express their patriotic zeal by bearing their arms against *him*. Undoubtedly as a check on them in

---

[470] *Id.*

[471] *Id.*

[472] *Federal Register*, Vol. 83, No. 246, Wednesday, December 26, 2018.

case of such an eventuality, the Patriotic Guards' weapons, unlike the weapons used by the Romanian Army, were crudely converted to semiautomatic only.[473] The final example is Switzerland, where from

> "the founding of the Swiss Confederation in 1291, every man has been required to be armed and to serve in the militia army. Today, every male when he turns twenty years old is issued a Sturmgewehr military rifle and required to keep it at home. When one is no longer required to serve—typically at age forty-two— he may keep his rifle (*converted from automatic to semiautomatic*)"[474] (emphasis added).

Thus, we have three radically different societies – the cantankerous, right-leaning, authority-distrusting United States; Switzerland, the archetype of middle class probity and rectitude; and Nicolae Ceauşescu's Romania, the most brazen kleptocracy since the Somozas fled Managua, all enacting policies that evince a clear understanding – contrary to the *Kolbe* Court's rather incredible view – that automatic fire is very different indeed from semiautomatic fire.

The *Kolbe* Court's reasoning is as unsound as Huck Finn's counterfeit quarter, "that warn't no good because the brass showed through the silver a little, and it wouldn't pass nohow, even if the brass didn't show, because it was so slick it felt greasy."[475] Like Huck, who hoped to pass off this "bad money" on a magic hairball, as "maybe the hairball would take it, because maybe it wouldn't know the difference,"[476] the Court hopes to pass its shallow reasoning off on the public. Huck Finn hoped to do so by

---

[473] Frank Iannamico. *AK-47: The Grim Reaper* (Chipotle Publishing 2008), 288 – 289.

[474] Stephen P. Halbrook. "Citizens in Arms: The Swiss Experience," *Texas Review of Law & Politics*, vol. 8, Issue 1 (Fall 2003), 146.

[475] Mark Twain, *The Adventures of Huckleberry Finn* (Charles L. Webster and Company, 1891), 37.

[476] *Id.*

split[ing] open a raw Irish potato and stick[ing] the quarter in between and keep it there all night, and next morning you couldn't see no brass, and it wouldn't feel greasy no more, and so anybody in town would take it in a minute, let alone a hairball.[477]

The *Kolbe* Court's "Irish potato" is simply to waive aside the key distinction between and M16 and AR-15 – selective fire – as insignificant. Yet the difference between a brass quarter and a real one would become painfully clear to anyone caught trying to pass the brass one in commerce; likewise, a soldier would rapidly learn just how radically different semiautomatic and automatic fire are were he to find himself grappling at close quarters with an enemy on the verge of overrunning his position while armed only with AR-15 rather than his standard issue M16.

However useful semiautomatic fire may be in military and police applications – as indeed it is, as the *Kolbe* Court notes, and which no one denies – it is equally useful in nearly every conceivable civilian shooting application. As such, no rifle capable of semiautomatic fire only can be fairly characterized exclusively as a "weapon of war."

One question that inevitably arises in discussions like this is whether the protection of the Second Amendment extends beyond semiautomatic rifles with both civilian *and* military utility, to automatic weapons, which are clearly military in character. By the logic of the *Miller* Court, which looked to the potential utility of a firearm for militia service as the criterion conferring protection under the Second Amendment, selective fire weapons and machineguns might conceivably be protected. On the other hand, applying the logic of *Heller*, which found weapons commonly used for lawful purposes to be protected, but implicitly deemed "M-16 rifles and the like"[478] not to be commonly used for lawful purposes, one could

---

[477] *Id.*

conclude the selective fire weapons and machineguns are not protected under the Second Amendment. It is beyond the scope of this book to resolve this dichotomy.[479] But one thing is undeniable: whereas *Miller* and *Heller* may set the conceptual boundaries for consideration of what weapons are protected under the Second Amendment, the *Kolbe* decision is an aberration consistent with neither. AR-15 and other semiautomatic rifles are not military weapons irrespective of how closely they resemble their military counterparts and no matter how many features they have in common with them. Semiautomatic rifles, including those sharing features with their military counterparts, are useful in nearly every non-military shooting application. As such, AR-15s and other semiautomatic firearms fall well within the ambit of the Second Amendment's protection under *Heller*, irrespective of the status of machineguns and selective fire weapons.

---

[478] *Heller I.*

[479] The image of a Venezuelan military or police vehicle deliberately ramming and running down unarmed protesters a few days before I wrote these lines does bring the question into sharper focus, however. See "Warning, graphic video: Government vehicle runs over protesters in Venezuela," *Fox News*, April 30th, 2019, https://video.foxnews.com/v/6031525169001/#sp=show-clips, retrieved May 4th, 2019.

Chapter 7
Civilian Uses of Semiautomatic Rifles: Self-Defense, Shooting Sports, Collecting, and Preparedness

On September 5th, 2018, during the confirmation hearings for Justice Brett Kavanaugh, Senator Dianne Feinstein challenged Justice Kavanaugh for his dissent in *Heller II*,[480] wherein he argued that banning AR-15s as a class of weapons is unconstitutional because they are widely owned. Senator Feinstein castigated him, insisting that "[u]se is an activity – it is not storage or possession, its use. So what you said is these weapons are commonly used. They're not."[481] Senator Feinstein's categorical claim was remarkable for its inaccuracy – so remarkable, in fact, that it was the primary inspiration for the writing of this book. Even granting *arguendo* her premise that storage is not use, Senator Feinstein is still wrong, because gun owners across the United States do much more with their AR-15s and similar rifles every day than just store them. The AR-15 rifle is so versatile and widely accepted in the United States that one commentator was moved to ask, not whether the AR-15 has any practical applications, but whether there is "room for a traditional" – that is, non-AR-15 style – "civilian semi-auto rifle,"[482] prefacing his answer with the acknowledgment that

> [w]e live in a world today that is completely inundated with AR-15 pattern rifles. In 2016, for just five Benjamins – sometimes even less! – you can purchase your very own fantactical [sic] black rifle and rely on it to work when you need to and shoot where you mean to. I won't try to say otherwise: The AR-15 series is a

---

[480] *Heller v. District of Columbia (Heller II)*, 670 F.3d 1244 (D.C. Cir. 2011).

[481] Senator Diane Feinstein to Judge Brett Kavanaugh, video clip hosted at *Mother Jones*, https://www.motherjones.com/politics/2018/09/kavanaugh-defends-opinion-that-assault-weapons-are-common-and-cant-be-banned/. Retrieved May 4th, 2019.

[482] "Is There Room for a Traditional Civilian Semiauto Rifle?" *The Firearms Blog*.

great design, and it deserves its place at the center of the US civilian market.[483]

Senator Feinstein might have known that had she consulted the Bureau of Alcohol, Tobacco and Firearms: In 2017, ATF Associate Deputy Director Ronald Turk wrote:

> Since the sunset of the Assault Weapons Ban in 2004, the use of AR-15s, AK-style, and similar rifles now commonly referred to as 'modern sporting rifles' has increased exponentially in sport shooting. These firearm types are now standard for hunting activities. ATF could re-examine its almost 20-year-old study to bring it up to date with the sport shooting landscape of today, which is vastly different than what it was years ago. Action shooting sports and organizations such as Three Gun and the United States Practical Shooting Association (USPSA) have also drastically expanded in recent years. Restriction on imports serves questionable public safety interests, as these rifles are already generally legally available for manufacture and ownership in the United States.[484]

If Senator Feinstein found Associate Deputy Director Turk's assessment unpersuasive, she or her staff could have tested her hypothesis of the sedentary AR-15 by visiting Sharpshooters, an indoor range in Lorton, Virginia about a half-hour's drive from the Capitol Building. There they would have seen people target shooting and training with a wide variety of handguns and long guns. Among the long guns, the most prevalent on the range, *by far*, would be the AR-15. The AR-15 is the most popular rifle in the United States

---

[483] *Id.*

[484] Ronald Turk. *Options to Reduce or Modify Firearms Regulations* (Bureau of Alcohol, Tobacco, and Firearms, January 20th, 2017). https://d3uwh8jpzww49g.cloudfront.net/sharedmedia/1509466/atf-white-paper-options-to-reduce-or-modify.pdf, retrieved May 4th, 2019.

because it is the most versatile rifle ever made. Every day, thousands of Americans throughout the United States use it for target shooting, competition shooting, hunting, collecting, and self-defense.

Is the AR-15 Fit for Civilian Shooting Applications?

Gun control advocates often assert that AR-15s are not suitable for civilian shooting applications and that civilians are not fit to own them. One good example of this line of reasoning is provided by Dr. Dean Winslow of Stanford University. Dr. Winslow is a retired US Air Force colonel who had been nominated by President Trump to serve as Assistant Secretary of Defense for Health Affairs. At his confirmation hearing, Senator Jeanne Shaheen pressed him about the military discharge of a then-recent mass shooter. In response, Dr. Winslow blurted out that "I'd also like to... just say how insane it is that in the United States of America a civilian can go out and buy a semiautomatic weapon like an AR-15."[485] Not surprisingly, his nomination was put on hold by the administration and subsequently withdrawn. Winslow then published an opinion piece in the *Washington Post*, in which he argued that

> because of their high muzzle velocities, assault weapons are challenging for untrained civilians to control and are not optimal for home defense. A pump action 12-gauge shotgun, with its excellent stopping power, would be far better. Even with imperfect aim, a shotgun will hit its target, while the pellets won't go through a wall to endanger someone

---

[485] Dean L. Winslow. "I spoke my mind on guns. Then my Senate confirmation was put on hold." *The Washington Post*, December 20th, 2017. https://www.washingtonpost.com/opinions/i-spoke-my-mind-on-guns-it-torpedoed-my-appointment-in-the-trump-administration/2017/12/20/8f708f6c-e50d-11e7-833f-155031558ff4_story.html?utm_term=.e104765368fb. Retrieved May 4th, 2019.

in the next room. Assault rifles are also poor hunting weapons due to low accuracy beyond 100 yards.[486]

Nearly everything Dr. Winslow wrote in this passage is wrong, starting with his very first assertion – that such rifles are "challenging for untrained civilians to control." The opposite is true. An AR-15 firing .223 or 5.56mm ammunition produces *zero* felt recoil – that is, nearly all the recoil produced by firing is absorbed by the buffer assembly, transmitting almost none to the shooter's shoulder. Nor is there in any appreciable tendency for the muzzle to rise as is plainly noticeable when firing any handgun. In fact, the AR-15 rifle is extremely easy to use and is really the perfect rifle for a beginning shooter to learn with. Adding an adjustable stock makes an AR-15 even more suitable for women or others of slight stature. Just how easy the AR-15 is to control when firing was clearly demonstrated in a 48-second video posted to YouTube in 2016. In this video, made in response to a claim by *New York Daily News* writer Gersh Kuntzman that when shooting an AR-15 "[t]he recoil bruised [his] shoulder … [and] the explosions [the rounds being fired] — loud like a bomb — gave [him] a temporary form of PTSD,"[487] Christopher Waller grasps an AR-15 by the pistol grip and, holding it with that one hand, places the buttstock against his nose, and proceeds to fire several shots from that position. Mr. Waller than faces the camera, stating that his nose is "not broken, not bleeding, not bruised."[488] I would not recommend repeating this experiment, but it does give the lie to Winslow's claim that AR-15s are difficult to control. Another remarkable illustration is an internet video depicting a father teaching his seven year old daughter to fire an AR-15, which she does safely.[489]

---

[486] *Id.*

[487] Gersh Kuntzman. "What is it like to fire an AR-15? It's horrifying, menacing and very very loud." *New York Daily News*, July 14th, 2016. https://www.nydailynews.com/news/crime/firing-ar-15-horrifying-dangerous-loud-article-1.2673201. Retrieved May 4th, 2019.

[488] Christopher Waller. "AR-15 Recoil Rebuttal." YouTube, June 17th, 2016. https://www.youtube.com/watch?v=8T3qjpZB6ME, retrieved May 4th, 2019.

[489] "7 Year Old's First Time Shooting AR-15." *Haus of Guns*, April 5th, 2014.

Nor are shotguns the panacea that Dr. Winslow makes them out to be. An inexperienced shooter will find an AR-15 much easier to operate than the twelve gauge pump-action shotgun that Dr. Winslow advocates: unlike the AR-15, the twelve gauge really does produce a substantial recoil that will be very palpable to inexperienced shooters; an inexperienced shooter may find the "kick" downright unpleasant and it might cause them to flinch when shooting. Dr. Winslow may have derived his idea of shotgun performance from Hollywood movies, where a shotgun blast covers the body of the target with holes. This is unrealistic. As one commentator noted, "[i]t has been said that 'you cannot miss fast enough to win.' Shotguns also follow this rule; despite offering greatly improved hit probability...*you must still carefully aim a shotgun if you would like to hit your target*"[490] (emphasis added). This is because, at distances within the home, the spread of a shotgun blast will be relatively small, as shown by a study on shotgun ballistics conducted by Brass Fetcher Ballistics Testing. In this study, sixteen 12 gauge shotgun loads were tested; at a maximum range of 10 feet, the average wound diameter produced in ballistic gelatin ranged from .99 to 1.91 inches.[491] These results give the lie to the Hollywood myth about it being nearly impossible to miss with a shotgun. On the other hand, the AR-15 is an extremely accurate weapon, one with which a beginner has a very good chance of hitting home. Furthermore, an AR-15 is a semiautomatic rifle, which means that it automatically chambers the next round after firing. With a pump action shotgun, the shooter must, well, *pump* the action after each shot to bring another round to bear, setting a potential stumbling block for an inexperienced shooter.

---

https://www.youtube.com/watch?v=ttMuvmspa8o. Retrieved June 22nd, 2019.

[490] Brass Fetcher Ballistic Testing. "Shotguns," http://www.brassfetcher.com/Shotguns/Shotguns.html. Retrieved June 22nd, 2019.

[491] Brass Fetcher Ballistic Testing. "12 Gauge Terminal Ballistics," http://www.brassfetcher.com/Shotguns/12%20Gauge%20Shotgun/12%20Gauge%20Terminal%20Ballistics.html. Retrieved June 22nd, 2019.

Accuracy of the AR-15

Winslow's claim that "[a]ssault rifles are also poor hunting weapons due to low accuracy beyond 100 yards"[492] is pure fiction. AR-15s are in fact excellent hunting weapons, as discussed later. As to the matter of *range*, the Department of Justice would appear to disagree with Dr. Winslow if the DEA rifle handbook mentioned previously is any evidence. As that reference points out, the standard rear sight aperture for the AR-15 is configured for two settings: one for targets from 0 to 200 meters away, and another for targets beyond 200 meters, and the manual itself provides instructions for making sight adjustments for ranges out to 500 yards (457.2 meters).[493] Even a cursory examination of US Army marksmanship standards demolishes Winslow's claim. Because the Army conducts marksmanship qualification with the M16 in semiautomatic mode, M16 qualification standards provide a valid basis for evaluating the accuracy of the AR-15. US Army Basic Rifle Marksmanship qualification is conducted on a course of fire in which a soldier has 40 rounds to engage forty targets at varying ranges, as follows: 50 meters, 6 targets; 100 meters, 8 targets; 150 meters, 11 targets; 200 meters, 7 targets; 250 meters, 5 targets; and at 300 meters, 3 targets.[494] The Army has three levels of qualification: to qualify Marksman, a soldier must hit between 23 and 29 of the 40 targets (inclusive); to qualify Sharpshooter, a soldier must hit between 30 and 35 targets; and to qualify Expert, a solder must hit between 36 and 40 targets.[495] Thus, even the worst marksman who barely meets Army standards, must hit at least *nine* targets *beyond* 100 meters to barely squeak by and pass; the average soldier, qualifying as a Sharpshooter, must hit at

---

[492] Winslow.

[493] *Colt M16 Rifle Operation and Field Maintenance Handbook* (US Department of Justice Drug Enforcement Administration, nd), 3-1 and 8-4.

[494] *FM 3-22.9* (April 2003, with changes 1 – 4), Record Fire Scorecard. 6-14, Table 6-11.

[495] *Id.,* 6-14, and Record Fire Scorecard.

least sixteen targets beyond 100 meters; and to be rated an Expert marksman, a soldier must hit at least 22 targets beyond 100 meters.

FM 3-22.9, Rifle Marksmanship, M16/M4 Series Weapons, defines maximum effective range as "[t]he greatest distance at which a soldier may be expected to deliver a target hit."[496] Put differently, maximum effective range is "the maximum range at which a weapon is designed to accurately deliver its destructive force."[497] *FM 3-22.9* specifies the maximum effective range of the M16 series rifles for engaging a point target as between 450 to 550 meters.[498] AR-15 rifles may be expected to have similar accuracy profiles. The accuracy potential of the AR-15 platform is well demonstrated by the course of fire employed in NRA High Power Rifle competitions, which often feature AR-platform rifles. The competitions feature shooting at ranges of 300, 500, and 600 meters.[499] All of this is a far cry from Dr. Winslow's "low accuracy beyond 100 meters."[500]

The ease of use and versatility of the AR-15 is also well demonstrated by the Army's training doctrine regarding the M16. Were the AR-15 and, by extension, the M16 really as difficult and challenging to use as claimed by Dr. Winslow, we might expect Army marksmanship doctrine to account for that by starting soldiers out on marksmanship training using some intermediate, "easier" weapon to handle, and then progress to the more "advanced" M16. But this is not the case. No version of the US Army manual for the M16-series of rifles from the first version published in 1965[501] through the 2012 edition[502] call for such. In fact, it was not until the 1992 edition that conducting any alternative form of live fire marksmanship training

---

[496] *Id.,* Glossary-10.

[497] Captain Tim Zurick. *Army Dictionary and Desk Reference* (Stackpole Books, 1992), 123.

[498] *FM 3-22.9* (April 2003, with changes 1 – 4), 2-1.

[499] *NRA High Power Rifle Rules,* Revised May 2018, 73.

[500] Army findings on hit probabilities at various ranges are discussed further below.

[501] *FM 23-9,* January 1965.

[502] *FM 3-22.9,* August 12th, 2008.

for the M16 was even broached, in the form of the M261 caliber .22 rimfire adapter (RFA).[503] The RFA device is intended "to contribute to a unit's marksmanship program *when 5.56-mm ammunition is not available or when ranges that allow the firing of 5.56-mm ammunition are not available,"* but *"it is not recommended for primary marksmanship training."*[504] Thus, use of the sub-caliber RFA is used not as a set of training wheels to help soldiers learn to shoot before graduating to the M16; rather, it is an expedient training aid for use when circumstances prevent training with live ammunition of the standard caliber.

The US Army trains its soldiers on the M16-series of rifles immediately and expects them to be able to use it competently from the beginning of their service. This is reasonable for, as military historian S.L.A. Marshall observed during the Korean War, "[a]verage Americans, once having received basic training with a weapon, can adjust quickly and naturally to the necessity for arms-bearing when self-protection requires it."[505] All that is needed is a "working knowledge of the arm."[506, 507]

---

[503] *FM 23-9*, July 1989.

[504] *Id.*, C-12; *FM 3-22.9*, 2008, A19.

[505] S.L.A. Marshall. *Commentary on Infantry Operations and Weapons Usage in Korea, Winter of 1950 – 51* (Operations Research Office, The Johns Hopkins University, October 1952), 69.

[506] *Id.*

[507] S.L.A. Marshall was a journalist and prolific military historian who helped pioneer the practice of the after action review (AAR) in the US Army. A controversial figure, he came to national prominence, in part, by his dramatic claim that generally only 15% – 25% at most – of soldiers in contact with the enemy fire their weapons, set forth in his famous book *Men Against Fire: The Problem of Battle Command in Future War* (Infantry Journal and William Morrow, 1947; see pages 50 and 56 – 57 for the quoted figures). For a discussion of Marshall's legacy and the controversy surrounding his claim about low rates of fire, see John Whiteclay Chambers II, "S. L. A. Marshall's *Men Against Fire*: New Evidence Regarding Fire Ratios," *Parameters*, August 2003, 113 – 121. Marshall continued his journalistic work during the Korean War, to include conducting AARs with NCOs and enlisted soldiers after battles. Interestingly, during his work in the Korean War, Marshall observed that a much higher percentage of

My experience confirms the suitability of the AR-15 as a first rifle for beginning shooters. My first significant contact with firearms of any kind was my Plebe summer at West Point, where we went straight to training with the M16A1 and 5.56mm ammunition. I qualified without difficulty. In the late 1990s, I served as an Army Reserve Officers Training Corps (ROTC) instructor at Michigan State University. Among my duties was overseeing marksmanship training for the cadets. We conducted a little premarksmaship training during leadership labs on campus and then lit out to the firing range at Fort Custer for live fire qualification on the M16A2 rifle with 5.56mm ball ammunition. Most cadets would qualify that day.

Neither the AR-15 nor the M16 are hard weapons to master or control. To the extent that controllability has been raised as a problem, it is with selective fire weapons in automatic mode, a consideration not relevant with the semiautomatic AR-15.[508] The AR-15 is an extremely well-designed firearm that is very comfortable and easy to shoot and is well-adapted to shooters of all sizes and

---

soldiers in contact with the enemy fired their weapons than he observed during World War II: more than half in Korea, as compared to 15% to 25% during World War II. *Men Against Fire* had a significant impact on the US Army: "Unquestionably, Marshall's claims that many soldiers were not firing their rifles brought the attention of the public and the Army to this issue. Those claims contributed to analysis and improvements in infantry training designed to increase rates of fire." Marshall's claims about low fire ratios during World War II have come under significant criticism since his death, as Marshall's papers reveal no indication of the statistical data or analysis necessary to support his claim. Thus, it may be that our soldiers in Korea didn't fire their weapons at the enemy more often than they did in World War II, but that Marshall was simply more attentive to this particular aspect of their stories during his Korean War after action reviews than he had been during World War II.

[508] "The US M14 rifle was notoriously uncontrollable in full-automatic mode, though some found its firepower comforting." Canfield, *"The M14 Rifle: John Garand's Final Legacy."*

experience levels. The claim that AR-15s are unsuited to civilian use is without merit.

The Primary Use of All Arms:
Self-Defense

In today's world, where most people need no longer hunt for subsistence, the main practical (as opposed to sporting) civilian application for firearms is self-defense. As gun control advocate James E. Atwood has candidly written, "I've owned hunting guns for over fifty years. Handguns, on the other hand, are not made for sport, but for protection against others, and if need be, to kill them."[509] Atwood's statement rests, in part, on a flawed premise: That the same firearm cannot have both a defensive and a sporting purpose. For the present, however, it is enough to note a point of agreement with him, that defense against attack is a principal purpose of firearms ownership. Per Julian S. Hatcher, a noted firearms writer and expert from the first half of the 20th Century, "[t]here is one vital necessity in the everyday life of the average citizen that is filled by a revolver, and can hardly be filled in any other way. This is the need for an arm of defense. This is the real reason for the existence of the revolver or pistol today."[510] As it happens, Hatcher and Atwood both assumed the handgun to be the weapon of choice for self-defense. Dr. Winslow, quoted above, advocates the pump-action shotgun;[511] President Joe Biden seems to prefer the double-barreled shotgun.[512] On the other hand, some prefer the AR-15 or other semiautomatic

---

[509] James E. Atwood. *Gundamentalism and Where it is Taking America* (Cascade Books, 2017), 63.

[510] Major James S. Hatcher. *Textbook of Pistols and Revolvers* (Small Arms Technical Publishing Co., 1935, reprinted by Wolfe Publishing Co., Inc., 1985), 492.

[511] *Id.*

[512] Steven Nelson. "Joe Biden's Shotgun Advice Could Land Jill Biden in Jail." *US News and World Report*, February 20th, 2013. https://www.usnews.com/news/articles/2013/02/20/joe-biden-shotgun-advice-could-land-jill-biden-in-jail. Retrieved May 5th, 2019.

rifles for this role. For example, on January 20th, 2019 a 20-year old home owner turned the tables on five armed, masked home invaders who had entered his home and demanded money; instead of reaching for cash, he retrieved his loaded AK-47 and engaged the intruders, killing three and driving the others from his home.[513] In 2010, a Harris County, Texas teenager repelled two attempted burglars with his father's AR-15.[514] In February 2018, in Oswego, Illinois, "a witness to [a] stabbing retrieved an AR-15 rifle from his apartment and stopped the knife attack 'with only a threat of force.'"[515] Thus, the AR-15 (and similar firearms) is the defensive weapon of choice for many – and for good reason.

In a sense, however, the efficaciousness of the AR-15 as a weapon of self-defense may be beside the point, as gun prohibitionists have long sought to ban what even they would now acknowledge as the traditional weapon of self-defense, the handgun. As Major Hatcher noted in 1935,

> [t]here are a number of individuals who at the present time are devoting a world of energy to an attempt to regulate the pistol or revolver out of existence by means of drastic laws forbidding the sale or possession of such weapons. They argue that the regularly organized police departments are sufficient protection, and that anyway, the citizen, if held up, should not resist, as someone might get hurt.[516]

---

[513] Katherine Marchand. "5 shot and 3 killed after homeowner opens fire on suspects in east Houston." *ABC Eyewitness News*, Houston TX, January 20th, 2019. https://abc13.com/5-shot-and-3-dead-after-home-invasion-in-east-houston/5097015/. Retrieved May 5th, 2019.

[514] "Investigators: 15-year-old son of deputy shoots burglary suspect." *KHOU 11*. https://www.khou.com/article/news/investigators-15-year-old-son-of-deputy-shoots-burglary-suspect/413200682. Retrieved May 5th, 2019.

[515] Shannon Antinori. "AR-15-Wielding Neighbor Speaks Out, 2 Charged In Stabbing." *Oswego Patch*. https://patch.com/illinois/oswego/ar-15-threat-used-stop-knife-attack-sheriff. Retrieved May 5th, 2019.

Hostility Toward Armed Self-Defense

Hatcher's words point to the true motivation of those denigrating the utility of the AR-15 for self-defense: it is not hostility toward a particular class of weapon that moves them, but hostility to the idea of armed self-defense *at all*. Atwood exemplifies their position, denigrating "[w]ell-intentioned citizens arming themselves" as being as in the thrall of "the hubristic belief that we can actually be in control of our own lives, let alone control other's behavior."[517] He mythologizes firearms, attributing to them supernatural powers over the human psyche:

> A gun may only be a thing, *but it is a thing with a spirit that hungers to be in control.* It is a life-force that captures its owner's thought process, turning his/her values about love and neighborliness upside down. The spirit of the gun does not rest until the owner himself starts believing that which is made to kill is now one's ultimate value providing "life," "security," and "inner peace." Isn't this the work of a god?"[518] (emphasis in original).

Atwood veers wildly between ethical and mystical appeals on the one hand, and appeals to "scientific" authority on the other, as when he asserts that

> there are scientific studies that prove bear spray is more effective in stopping a charging bear than a gun. We don't meet charging bears within our city limits, but what will deter an angry grizzly will stop a human being in his tracks.[519]

---

[516] Hatcher, *Textbook of Pistols and Revolvers*, 492.
[517] Atwood, 74.
[518] *Id.*

At bottom, Atwood preaches a self-defense philosophy of fatalistic submission. "Yes, stuff happens", he writes, but "solid scientific data tells us there is only an infinitesimal possibility that you will be attacked by a violent individual. But, should some scoundrel be intent on harming you, no matter where you are, or who you are, he will likely succeed."[520] He further asserts that

> [h]owever much the culture admires the confident and determined individual, no one can claim the power to control nature or other human beings, let alone the power of evil. Nothing made by human hands or conceived in the human mind can provide the security we all would like to have. *Security is at best a superstition.*[521] (emphasis added).

Should his philosophy of stoic submission to fate be insufficiently appealing, Atwood attempts to bolster it by resort to religious shaming: "What level of stopping power do I want in my ammo? That's simply a euphemistic way of asking what I damage I want my ammo to inflict? WWJHMD [what would Jesus have me do]?"[522] "[A]s you practice shooting, you must decide, "What part of the human body you should aim for? WWJHMD?"[523] "[P]erhaps they should do away with all bull's eye targets on their ranges and replace them with human silhouettes so these young leaders of the church of tomorrow can grow more comfortable shooting people? WWJHMD?"[524]

The Strange Case of *Hines v. Commonwealth of Virginia*

---

[519] *Id.*, 78.
[520] Atwood, 65.
[521] *Id.*, 77.
[522] *Id.*, 69.
[523] *Id.*
[524] *Id.*, 69 – 70.

Open hostility toward personal self-defense can appear among the judiciary as well as the clergy, as it did in the strange case of *Hines v. Commonwealth of Virginia*.[525] In that case, defendant Marvin Hines was confronted in his own home by the drunken, belligerent, and armed Wayne Hudson, longtime partner of Hines' sister, Ruby Strange.[526] "Concerned for his wife and sister" and for his own safety,[527] Hines fired five shots from his gun at Hudson, hitting him three times. Mr. Hudson succumbed to his wounds and Marvin Hines was charged with murder. After a bench trial, the Court convicted him of voluntary manslaughter.[528] In its written ruling, the Court set forth the facts of this case thus:

> When Defendant shot Mr. Hudson in the early hours of May 30, 2013, Mr. Hudson had been drinking since the afternoon of the previous day and was intoxicated. He had become extremely belligerent and argumentative, insisting that Mrs. Hines and neighbor Matt Thomas leave him alone and leave his girlfriend alone. Mr. Hudson's belligerent behavior caused alarm to Mrs. Hines. Mr. Thomas tried without success to get Mr. Hudson to calm down. In the heat of this out-of-control temper tantrum happening in his own house, Defendant confronted Mr. Hudson. Defendant testified that he saw that Mr. Hudson had a gun in his hand.[529]

Although "[t]he Commonwealth hotly contest[ed] Defendant's testimony that the victim was armed and urge[d] the Court to find otherwise,"[530] the court disagreed, noting that

---

[525] *Marvin Hines v. Commonwealth of Virginia*, 791 S.E.2d 563 (2016).
[526] *Commonwealth v. Marvin Hines* (Va. Cir., 2014)(Norfolk).
[527] *Id.*
[528] *Id.*
[529] *Id.*
[530] *Id.*

Defendant's testimony was credible. He was in the presence of an intoxicated, ranting and raving large man with a weapon. He has maintained from his first encounter with law enforcement that the victim had a gun and that he was acting in self-defense.[531]

Notwithstanding the foregoing, the court overruled Hines' plea of self-defense, holding that

it seems the fearful killer is a manslaughterer when his fear is produced by facts insufficient to make him a self-defender, *e.g.*, the deadly response was unnecessary or the fear was unreasonable.[532]

As its basis for convicting Hines of voluntary manslaughter rather than acquitting him outright on the ground of self-defense, the trial court relied on the fact that finding himself confronted with an "intoxicated … belligerent and argumentative," armed with a handgun, "in his own house",[533] Mr. Hines "retreated to an adjacent room, got a weapon of his own, and returned to the room," where he shot Mr. Hines. The court ruled that notwithstanding Hudson's behavior and weapon, Hines had not "carried his burden of proving self-defense" because

[i]f Mr. Hudson's possession of a gun constituted a danger, Defendant had removed himself from that danger when he left the room. Returning to the room with a gun pointed at the victim significantly escalated the danger and undoubtedly caused Mr. Hudson to fear for his own safety. Defendant had the opportunity to retreat and did in fact retreat. He

---

[531] *Id.*

[532] *Id*, quoting Ronald J. Bacigal, *Criminal Offenses & Defenses in Virginia*, 358-9 (2007-08 ed.).

[533] *Commonwealth v. Hines.*

cannot assert any privilege to return to the room with a weapon of his own …[534]

The Court further held that

> [Hines] should have retreated to safety but instead got a gun of his own, and out of fear and impulse, without conscious reflection or malice, he shot the victim.[535]

This is a truly astonishing verdict, given that it is well-established in Virginia law that in a case involving the use of deadly force, "the defendant need not retreat, but is permitted to stand his ground and repel the attack by force, including deadly force, if it is necessary,"[536] and it is even more firmly established that "[a] man is not obliged to retreat if assaulted in his dwelling, but may use such means as are absolutely necessary to repel the assailant from his house or prevent his forcible entry, even to the taking of life."[537] Confronted with its error by the defense via a motion to vacate the verdict, the Court doubled down. While it grudgingly acknowledging its error regarding a duty to retreat, it engaged in mental gymnastics worthy of *Kolbe* majority to uphold its previous verdict:

> The Court acknowledges that the quoted italicized language seems to recognize a duty to that does not exist under Virginia law, in that a homeowner has no duty to retreat if assaulted in his dwelling. The Court retracts the italicized language and clarifies its prior opinion that Defendant was not obliged to retreat; but inasmuch as he was able to leave the room safely and had no reasonable belief that the victim was

---

[534] *Id.*

[535] *Id.*

[536] *Foote v. Commonwealth*, 396 S.E.2d 851, 11 Va.App. 61 (Va. App., 1990) (internal citations and quotations omitted).

[537] *Fortune v. Commonwealth*, 133 Va. 669, 112 S.E. 861 (1922).

going to hurt him or his family, the Court rejects the conclusion that he acted in self-defense when he returned to the room and immediately shot the victim five times.[538]

In doing so, the Court did further violence to Virginia law, for in Virginia, "[a] defendant may always act upon reasonable appearance of danger, and whether the danger is reasonably apparent is always to be determined from the viewpoint of the defendant at the time he acted."[539] Furthermore, Virginia recognizes

'Defense of others' [as] an affirmative defense separate and distinct both legally and factually from the self-defense theories. In considering the theory of defense of others, the Supreme Court has clearly recognized that one is privileged to use force in defense of family members. However, one must reasonably apprehend death or serious bodily harm to another before he or she is privileged to use force in defense of that person. Furthermore, one may avail himself or herself of the defense only where he or she reasonably believes, based on the attendant circumstances, that the person defended is without fault in provoking the fray.[540]

Viewed from Hines' perspective, the situation at hand was fraught with danger both to himself and to his wife and sister – an intoxicated and belligerent Mr. Hudson was confronting Mr. Hines and his female relatives in Mr. Hines' own home *with a firearm*. It is hard to imagine a more reasonable basis for Hines' fear that he, his

---

[538] *Commonwealth v. Hines*, Docket No. CR11-3271, "Opinion and Order Denying Motion to Vacate and Allowing Indictment to be Amended," June 9th, 2014.

[539] *McGhee v. Commonwealth*, 248 S.E.2d 808, 219 Va. 560 (1978).

[540] *Garrard v. Commonwealth* (Va. App., 2010) (internal quotations and citations omitted).

wife, or his sister faced death or great bodily injury, but the Court nonetheless managed to find it unreasonable.

The strangest aspect of the case is what the Court tried to ignore: that when Mr. Hines retreated to retrieve his own firearm, his wife and sister were left alone, unarmed and unprotected in a room with the armed, intoxicated and aggressive Wayne Hudson. It was the Court's bizarre position that Mr. Hines, once having taken himself out of the immediate vicinity of Wayne Hudson, was obliged to leave his wife and sister alone with and subject to the tender mercies of the aggressor, closeting himself away in an adjacent room, in possession of the means of aiding the women, but withholding aid from them. The Court's Orwellian holding that an intoxicated, angry, pistol waiving Wayne Hudson in the house gave rise to "no reasonable belief that [Hudson] was going to hurt [Hines] or his family" is but a fig leaf to cover both its original erroneous holding and its obstinate clinging to that error in the face of all evidence and precedent to the contrary.

Mr. Hines was ultimately vindicated by the Virginia Supreme Court, which held that

> the record in this case demonstrates that Hudson, while in Hines' home, was belligerent, had been drinking and brandished a gun in the presence of Hines, his wife and sister. In an attempt to defuse the situation and protect himself and his family, Hines retrieved his own gun from another room. When reentering the room, Hudson pointed his gun at Hines. Hines, fearing for his life, shot Hudson. These facts support Hines' claim that he shot Hudson in self-defense.[541]

Mr. Hines likely would not have been so fortunate in other common law countries. On October 14th, 2016, Presidential

---

[541] *Hines.*

candidate Hillary Clinton famously (or infamously) said that "certainly the Australia example is worth looking at"[542] with respect to firearms regulation, referring to that country's massive compulsory gun buyback scheme and strict gun control laws enacted in 1996. Clinton's campaign disavowed any suggestion that she supported gun confiscation three days later.[543] Whatever Ms. Clinton's view of it, Australia's hostility to firearms is older and deeper than the 1996 law. As early as 1992, the government of New South Wales proclaimed to its citizens in a series of newspaper public service announcements that "[p]ersonal protection is no reason to have a gun." The announcements went on to state that

> [i]f you own a gun which you keep to protect yourself, your family, or your property, you must dispose of it legally. Under the latest gun laws, ***personal and property protection are no longer considered acceptable reasons to possess any type of firearm***, or to get a license. If you wish to possess any gun, you must have a license and meet the new requirements for safe storage of the weapon and its ammunition. When your current license expires you must reapply if you want to continue to possess or use a gun. Be warned, making a false or misleading statement on your license application could earn you ten years in prison. Act quickly. If you haven't got a license, now is the time to either apply for one, or legally dispose or your gun[544] (emphasis added).

---

[542] Bradford Richardson. "Hillary: Australia-style gun control 'worth looking at.'" *The Hill*, October 15th, 2016. https://thehill.com/blogs/ballot-box/dem-primaries/257172-hillary-australia-style-gun-control-worth-looking-at. Retrieved May 11th, 2019.

[543] Jessie Byrnes. "Clinton aide: Hillary not in favor of gun confiscation." *The Hill*, October 19th, 2016. https://thehill.com/blogs/blog-briefing-room/news/257333-clinton-aide-hillary-not-in-favor-of-gun-confiscation. Retrieved May 11th, 2019.

[544] *The Sydney Morning Herald* (Sydney, New South Wales, Australia). Sunday,

This helpful government notice concluded on the encouraging note that "[p]ossession and use of any firearm for personal or property protection is illegal and will attract severe penalties. No exceptions, no excuses."[545, 546]

Hostility to use of force in self-defense is not limited to firearms. Drastic restrictions on the right to own and use firearms can arise in tandem with equally drastic restrictions on the right to defend oneself in any way, as Dr. Joyce Lee Malcolm showed in her study of English firearms and self-defense law, *Guns and Violence: The English Experience*.[547] Dr. Malcolm charts the path by which

> [t]he right of Englishmen 'to have arms for their defense' has been effectively demolished by a series of ever more stringent parliamentary statutes and bureaucratic regulations. These culminated in a classified 1969 Home Office regulation that barred possession of a firearm for personal protection; the 1988 Firearms Act's tighter controls of shotguns, the last firearm that could be purchased with a simple show of fitness; and the 1997 Firearms Act's nearly complete ban on handguns.[548]

The demolition of the right of self-defense did not stop there:

May 24, 1992, 42.

[545] *Id.*

[546] The question of whether and to what extent one who owns a firearm may lawfully use it in self-defense in New South Wales appears to be in a state of confusion, to say the least. See "NSW Police Claim Self-Defence with a Firearm is Illegal when it isn't," *Firarmsownersunited.com.* https://www.firearmownersunited.com/2017/11/30/nsw-police-claim-self-defence-with-a-firearm-is-illegal-when-it-isnt/. Retrieved May 11th, 2019.

[547] Joyce Lee Malcolm. *Guns and Violence: The English Experience* (Harvard University Press, 2002).

[548] *Id*, 5.

Firearms apart, English law now prohibits civilians from carrying any article for what is termed 'private defense.' Paired with this policy is a much-narrowed legal standard of what force is acceptable for personal protection.[549]

Two statutes – the Prevention of Crime Act of 1953 and the Criminal Law Act of 1967 – have "thrown the law of self-defense [in Britain] into disarray and seriously disadvantaged individual citizens."[550] Dr. Malcolm provides several illuminating examples. In a 1973 case, police stopped a man running on a road carrying several improvised weapons ("a length of polished steel, a two-foot length of bicycle chain, a metal clock weight and a studded glove"). He told the officers that he had been threatened a by a gang, but he was arrested nonetheless. "At his hearing it was determined that on several occasions a group of youths had chased him or threatened him with assault. He had reported these incidents to the police"[551] and was later attacked and beaten.[552] The trial court found that "he had a reasonable excuse for carrying the weapons and did not convict."[553] Unfortunately for the defendant, Britain has a different conception of double jeopardy than ours, under which the Crown may appeal acquittals in certain circumstances. The prosecution did so, and the appellate court reversed and remanded the case to the trial court with an order to convict.[554] Another example cited by Dr. Malcolm is that of 56-year old petrochemicals executive Eric Butler:

> In March 1987 two men assaulted Butler in a London subway car, strangling him and smashing his head against the door. No one in the car came to his aid.

---

[549] *Id.*
[550] *Id*, 182.
[551] *Id.*
[552] *Id.*
[553] *Id.*
[554] *Id.*

Later Butler testified "My air supply was being cut off, my eyes become blurred and I feared for my life." In desperation he unsheathed a sword blade in his walking stick and slashed at one of [his attackers] "as [his] last means of defense" ... The assailants were charged with unlawful wounding but Butler was also tried and convicted of carrying an offensive weapon.[555]

Dr. Malcolm cites further examples: "A tourist who had used her pen knife to protect herself when some men attacked her was convicted of carrying an offensive weapon."[556] Worse,

[m]erely threatening to defend oneself can also prove illegal, as an elderly lady discovered. She succeeded in frightening off a gang of thugs by firing a blank from a toy gun, only to be arrested for the crime of putting someone in fear with an imitation firearm. Use of a toy gun for self-defense during a housebreak is also unacceptable, as a householder found who had detained with an imitation gun two men who were burgling his home. He called the police, but when they arrived, they arrested him for a firearms offense.[557]

The Police – First, Last and Only Hope of the Firearms Prohibitionist

Atwood advocates a fatalistic acceptance that resistance to any criminal assault is hopeless, and the forbearance of any but the most modest means of resistance. The *Hines* trial court sought to prescribe cringing retreat even in the face of armed menace to ones loved ones in their very home, a state of affairs even more debasing than the predicament as described by Christopher Hitchens, of the

---

[555] *Id.,*184.
[556] *Id.,* 185.
[557] *Id.,* 184.

citizen [who] … makes sure to put a "No Radio" sign in his car window (one of the most sickening emblems of capitulation I've ever seen) and to carry a $20-bill when jogging lest the mugger take offense at holding him up for nothing (This piece of servility, too, is usually futile...).[558]

It is not surprising that gun control advocates and others take such views. Some, such as Atwood, have built the criminal offender up in their minds to the status of an insuperable demigod who "will be successful because he will creep up on you on little cat's feet," fretting that "at some terrible moment an assailant with a gun, knife, or club already in hand surprises you, you will not be able to reach for your weapon and protect yourself, even if it is close by."[559], [560]

---

[558] Christopher Hitchens. "The Gun Control Myth." *Scraps from the Loft*, October 2nd, 2017. https://scrapsfromtheloft.com/2017/10/02/the-myth-of-gun-control/. Retrieved May 5th, 2019.

[559] Atwood, 65 – 66.

[560] I myself once shared this view. Sometime in 1993, while serving as an officer with the 10th Mountain Division in the port town of Merka, Somalia during Operation *Restore Hope*, I accompanied an infantry patrol into the city streets one night. The patrol encountered two armed men in the street and disarmed them. The men explained that they had been robbed that evening by bandits and were patrolling the street to prevent further attack. The futility of their action was apparent, the horse having already left the stable, so to speak. In my naiveté I extrapolated their untimely response, in my own mind, into a universal principle: that a criminal will always get the drop, so to speak, on his victim, so that armed self-defense is futile. Experience subsequently disabused me of that notion several years later. On that occasion, I encountered a woman being beaten by her boyfriend outside my apartment building. I gave the woman shelter inside the lobby of the building (which required a key for access), thus temporarily putting her out of the reach of her boyfriend, who charged at the door (it latched, shutting him out, in a nick of time). I then took the woman up to my apartment from whence I called the police. Before the police arrived, however, someone let the boyfriend into the building, and he began to noisily patrol the hallway outside my apartment in search of the woman. While the boyfriend was a towering figure and obviously accustomed to

Others, like retired Virginia police officer Patricia Harman, have taken the position that victims are simply not competent to help themselves with weapons and are likely to make matters worse by trying. In her slim but helpful crime-prevention treatise, *The Danger Zone: How to Protect Yourself from Rape, Robbery, and Assault*, Harman sets forth a great deal of sound, prudent, and practical advice on how to avoid becoming a victim. But she remains skeptical of armed self-defense by private citizens. "I do not recommend weapons as part of your plan," she writes.[561]

> [T]here is a possibility that the attacker will take your weapon and use it on you. In many cases bodily force is the only weapon an attacker may have until he can get control of the victim's weapon. And quite often that is just what happens.[562]

She then ticks off the shortcomings and hazards of various weapons short of firearms. Unlike Atwood, Harman is skeptical of pepper spray: "Mace is by no means fail-safe. In fact, a reported reaction to Mace is anger, not deterrence. You might make matters much worse."[563] She is equally skeptical about stun guns: "Too many things could go wrong with a stun gun. If it is taken away from you

---

violence, I was neither. As a precaution, I made ready a semiautomatic rifle for use – a military surplus SKS carbine of Russian manufacture. As the boyfriend could easily have made mincemeat out of me in a fight had he located us and penetrated the apartment, that rifle would have been all that stood between myself and the woman, and serious bodily harm. Fortunately the police arrived in time and the man fled. The police took no statement from me and neither they nor the woman (so far as I know) ever became aware of my rifle. The experience of numerous others of whom I have heard in the intervening years only confirms what my own experience taught me: criminals are not always quickest on the draw, and many of their would-be victims are able to employ arms in repelling violent attack.

[561] Patricia Harman. *The Danger Zone: How to Protect Yourself from Rape, Robbery, and Assault* (Self-published by Patricia Harman, 1992), 61 – 62.
[562] *Id.*
[563] *Id.*, 62.

or used on you while it is in your hands, you will be left completely defenseless."[564] As to knives, she asks "[i]f you can get to it, will you be able to use it? It takes a great deal of force to effectively stab someone, as well as a strong stomach."[565] [566]

Whatever the merits of these positions, they are vulnerable to a charge leveled by Hitchens in another context, but which is apt nonetheless:

> I respect a person who is a Quaker, for example, and says, 'I would rather do anything, suffer anything than take another human being's life. I'd rather lose my own.' I mean, those who take that view, who are genuine pacifists, I think, hold a ridiculous and masochistic opinion, but I can admire it for its integrity.[567]

However much we might admire that integrity, it is intolerable as a substitute for real security for our persons and property, and gun control proponents know that people quite rightly demand something more efficacious than high-minded platitudes and fatalistic pacifism. The gun control advocates' answer was succinctly stated by James Brady, former press secretary to Ronald Reagan, who was shot and permanently disabled by John Hinckley during latter's attempted assassination of President Reagan. When asked by an interviewer whether "any handguns [are] defensible" Brady replied

---

[564] *Id.*

[565] *Id.*

[566] Harman's book was published before Virginia became a "shall issue" concealed carry state, and reflects affairs as they stood at that time. Accordingly, she dismisses carrying a firearm for self-defense: "It is not legal to carry a gun concealed in any way. Having it strapped to your hip in plain view is not a likely scenario, and may even be illegal in some states." *Id.*, 62.

[567] Christopher Hitchens. *Talk of the Nation*, National Public Radio, October 24th, 2002. https://www.npr.org/programs/totn/transcripts/2002/oct/021024.conan.html. Retrieved May 5th, 2019.

"[f]or target shooting, that's okay … Get a license and go to the range. *For defense of the home, that's why we have police departments*" (emphasis added).[568]

The "English Experience" as reported by Dr. Malcolm shows us that hostility to private self-defense in the face of physical assault crosses temporal and political boundaries. During the Parliamentary debates leading up to the British 1953 Prevention of Crime Act, Northern Ireland MP Lieutenant Colonel H. M. Hyde, understandably skeptical of government assurances that the new law would not be used to harass innocent citizens, related the story

> of a woman employed in the House of Commons whose route home led across a heath where attacks had occurred. She had armed herself with a knitting needle and just a month earlier had been able to drive off a youth who tried to snatch her handbag by jabbing him "on a tender part of his body." Hyde asked whether it was to be regarded as an offense to carry a knitting needle or other object for self-defense. The attorney general, Sir Lionel Heald, was asked to deal with the issue of the innocent person, afraid for his safety, who carried some means of protection. He expressed his belief that if "in a special case" someone "really has justification for carrying a weapon … because he lives on a lonely common and so on … he would be found to have a reasonable excuse" but insisted that "we ought not to mind discouraging members of the general public from going about with offensive weapons in their pockets, even for their own protection." He added: "It is the duty of society to protect them, and they should not have to do that … that argument of self-defense is

---

[568] James Brady. "In Step with James Bradey," *The Daily Oklahoman*, June 26th, 1994, 116. Note: In this piece, James Brady, the former press secretary, was interviewed by another James Brady, the noted columnist.

one to which perhaps we should not attach too much weight."[569]

The upshot is that Great Britain has adopted James Brady's view as both public policy and conventional wisdom:

> Notwithstanding government controls on firearms, the ancient common law notions of self-defense and the actual duty to intervene to protect others remained in force and in mind … [but] the Prevention of Crime Act of 1953 and the 1967 Criminal Law Act[] altered the law behind those traditional concepts, perhaps forever. Repeated government lectures on the foolishness of taking independent action in the face of an assault on oneself or others, of the need to let the experts – the police – handle matters, did the rest.[570, 571]

---

[569] Malcolm, *Guns and Violence*, 176.

[570] *Id.*, 173. It may be that this paternalistic complacency and paralysis has invaded even the public service to some degree in England. The acerbic British commentator and *City Journal* contributing editor Theodore Dalrymple (*non de plume* of Anthony Malcolm Daniels) has written of this from his experience working as a physician and psychiatrist in the British courts and penal system. He relates an episode in which a prison guard extracted a prisoner from his smoke-filled, burning cell, probably saving the prisoner from death by smoke inhalation. When Dalrymple asked the guard whether the prison governor had commended him, the guard replied "[r]eprimanded, more likely," for not following procedure – the correct procedure having been to await the arrival of the fire brigade, notwithstanding that during such interval the prisoner might have died in his cell. "The officer was duly reprimanded," Dalrymple writes, "and a black mark (for disobedience) was put on his record for having saved a prisoner's life in the wrong way, that is to say at risk to himself." In another instance, Dalrymple was asked to investigate a prison hanging. "Asked why he had not rushed into a man's cell to cut him down, an officer replied, 'I could lose my job for saving a man's life." See Theodore Dalrymple, *The Knife Went In: Real-life Murders and Our Culture* (Gibson Square, 2017), 52 – 53.

Gun prohibitionists expect citizens to give up their private means of self-defense in exchange for public security provided by the police, not

> wish[ing] to lend themselves to the support of the proposition that it is right or necessary for the ordinary citizen to arm himself in self-defense. The preservation of the Queen's peace is the function of the police, and ... it would be a great pity if anything were done ... to condone actions which imply the

---

[571] Given that I have quoted Dalrymple here, and elsewhere in this work, it is important to state that it is neither my intention to draft Dr. Dalrymple into my cause nor to imply that he supports my views. Where I quote Dalrymple in this paper, it is because in his penetrating insight and trenchant prose, he brilliantly captures certain modes or methods of thought present in the firearms debate, and not because he agrees with my conclusions on the subject. Rather, it is clear that his views on firearms are quite the opposite of those expressed here and that he would likely reject both my premises and my conclusions. This he makes plain in his book *False Positive*, from which I quote elsewhere in this study, wherein Dalrymple states categorically that the Second Amendment "is now completely obsolete" (p. 197), and otherwise demonstrates his rather pronounced skepticism of American gun culture (see *False Positive* (Encounter Books, 2019), 195 – 198). This is, of course, hardly surprising. Dr. Dalrymple is an Englishman after all, and second only to the National Health Service, there would appear to be nothing in which the British people place more faith than in the efficacy of the disarmament of the populace. Dr. Dalrymple is a dissenter from the modern orthodoxy and his views on many subjects would appear to be fairly compatible with those of American conservative and, to some extent, libertarian intellectuals – but not, however, on the subject of firearms, for however critical he may be of the modern orthodoxy he nonetheless adheres to certain of its tenets. Atheism is one such, and faith in private disarmament is another. My inclusion of quotes from Dalrymple's work is a mark of my admiration for his genius. Therefore, to borrow Dr. Dalrymple's own words, "[h]e will not agree with all [or any of] my conclusions, but I hope he will not be offended by them" (*False Positive*, 251).

inability of the forces of law and order to maintain the Queen's peace.[572]

Indeed, police and prosecutors are absolutely essential to the maintenance of the ordered liberty that all Americans cherish. The work that they perform is essential to public safety. But it does not follow that in fulfilling their role in providing the public's security that the police can be depended upon to secure the safety of each individual citizen: "[A]though society ought to undertake the defense of its law-abiding members,"[573]

nevertheless one has to remember that there are many places where society cannot get, or cannot get there on time. On those occasions a man has to defend himself and those whom he is escorting.[574]

That the police cannot be everywhere is intuitively obvious – we've all heard the old quip, "where's a cop when you need one?" There simply aren't enough law enforcement personnel alive to protect every person all the time. In fact, there aren't even enough police resources available to provide constant surveillance over even those persons facing articulable threats, as Dr. Malcolm's hapless victim who armed himself with a studded glove, a bicycle chain, and a steel bar could attest: he had been attacked despite having reported previous threats to the police.[575] As Hatcher observed,

[t]he theory that the police will always be available for protection in such cases is so ridiculous as scarcely to deserve notice. Even in a city, there are hundreds of

---

[572] Malcolm, *Guns and Violence*, 178, quoting Sir David Maxwell Fyfe, secretary of state for the Home Office, United Kingdom, arguing in favor of passage of the Prevention of Crime Act of 1953.
[573] Malcolm, *Guns and Violence*, 177.
[574] *Id.*, quoting UK MP Ronald Bell, arguing for an amendment to the Prevention of Crime Act of 1953, during the debates leading to the Act's passage.
[575] Malcolm, *Guns and Violence*, 513.

times and places where no policeman is on hand; and in rural districts, the holdup man's chance of encountering the forces of the law are nil.[576, 577]

Worse yet, even where resources are not only available but at hand, help will sometimes be withheld, for however brave, diligent,

---

[576] Hatcher, *Textbook of Pistols and Revolvers*, 492 – 493.

[577] Tragically, it appears that the municipal building in Virginia Beach, Virginia may have been one such place where the police were not able to be immediately at hand when an attacker killed a dozen people there on May 31st, 2019. According to reports, police were temporarily thwarted in confronting the killer "because they didn't have the key cards needed to open doors on the second floor," according to the Associated Press. "Over the radio, they desperately pleaded for the electronic cards and talked of bringing in a sledgehammer, an explosive charge or other means of breaking down the doors. The killer was eventually gunned down, and whether the delay contributed to the toll of 12 victims dead and four wounded is unclear. But the episode last week illustrated how door-lock technology that is supposed to protect people from workplace violence can hamper police and rescue workers in an emergency." Left unstated by this report is the fact that Virginia Beach has a no-guns policy proscribing concealed carry permit-holders from carrying their firearms into the building, and barring other lawful gun owners from open-carrying there, so that any permit holder employed on the second floor inclined to carry would have found himself trapped inside with the killer behind a locked door, and the police locked out on the other side (see Ben Finley and Denise Lavoie, "Police thwarted by electronic doors during Virginia shooting," *Associated Press*, June 5, 2019, https://www.apnews.com/49b0e7e8becb4dcf9a8c3bd77e57d168.
Retrieved July 13th, 2019). Ironically, at least one of the victims had wanted to do just that: "The night before Kate was murdered, she sat Jason down at the table and told him she wanted to take a gun to work because a disgruntled co-worker was being fired and was threatening … That coworker was not the shooter who took the lives of Kate and 11 others, but Kate's intuition of a fateful Friday rang true," "Husband of Virginia Beach mass shooting victim wants open investigation," *Tribune Media Wire* WTVR.com, June 12th, 2019. https://wtvr.com/2019/06/12/husband-of-virginia-mass-shooting-victim-wants-open-investigation/. Retrieved July 13th, 2019.

and dedicated the vast majority of officers are, some will fail in their duty. Major Hatcher relates on such example:

> On the outskirts of a city a woman of my acquaintance called up the police department late one night and complained that a man was trying to get into the house and asked for assistance at once. She was informed that they were sorry but her house was outside the city limits and they could not send a policeman there as it would be off his beat. Fortunately, she had a pistol and was able to frighten the intruder away.[578]

Skeptics might dismiss this as a poor example, it having occurred before 1935; surely police would be more responsive today, and will have made arrangements to deal with jurisdictional conflicts like the one that bedeviled Major Hatcher's female acquaintance. But even now, in our modern world of technological and procedural sophistication, such embarrassments still recur. One such happened on April 20th, 2019, when Angela Valle told police that her ex-boyfriend had forced his way into an apartment and attacked her and her friend Savannah Rivera with an ax. Rivera was nearly decapitated and died, while Valle, wounded by the attacker, was driven from the apartment, leaving her four-year-old daughter asleep inside with the killer. When Valle pleaded with police outside the building to enter and retrieve her daughter, she was rebuffed: 83rd Precinct officers Mary Sobieski and Sean Doohan "ignored the request rather than cross onto the turf of Police Service Area 3 housing cops," according to a witness, even refusing to accompany a Fire Department of New York Emergency Medical Technician into the apartment.[579]

---

[578] Hatcher, *Textbook of Pistols and Revolvers*, 493 – 496.

[579] Tina Moore, Blake Paterson and Aaron Feis. "NYPD cops probed for refusing to enter ax-attack flat: sources." *New York Post*, April 22nd, 2019. https://nypost.com/2019/04/22/nypd-cops-probed-for-refusing-to-enter-ax-attack-flat-sources/. Retrieved May 13th, 2019.

Such failures are not unique to the United States. They can occur even in states with much more pervasive and aggressive security and surveillance regimes than America's, as Chinese student Wang Xiaofei can attest. Xiaofei and her family had been the victims of a severe harassment at the hands of stalker Wang Lei, a co-worker whose amorous advances Xiaofei had spurned. According to Xiaofei, "[h]e asked [her] to be his girlfriend ... but she refused;" Lei "sexually assaulted her the night after she refused him," then "spent a month harassing her at university and at her home."[580] He then "he began a campaign of harassment which escalated to threats that he would kill her, along with her family."[581] Lei "turned up at their home armed with a knife and an electric baton and, on another occasion, broke into their home and stole hundreds of yuan."[582] Throughout this ordeal the family made "numerous complaints to police [yet] *the only advice to the family was to find somewhere else to live*"[583] (emphasis added). Then "Wang Lei turned up at the house for the final time, climbed over the wall into their yard and shouted for them to come out, while also threatening to kill them."[584] A confrontation ensued in which Lei was killed.[585] The police – whose only help to the family to that point had been to advise them, in effect, to abandon their home and flee – then arrested Xiaofei's parents, "against the advice of prosecutors,"[586] "refus[ing] to accept that they acted in self-defense "[587]

---

[580] Mandy Zuo. "Chinese couple accused of killing daughter's stalker await decision in self-defence row," *South China Morning Post*, February 27th, 2019. https://www.scmp.com/news/china/society/article/2187787/chinese-couple-accused-killing-daughters-stalker-await-decision. Retrieved May 13th, 2019.

[581] Zhuang Pinghui. "Chinese family torn apart by stalker killing wins case review after public outcry," *South China Morning Post*, January 23rd, 2019. https://www.scmp.com/news/china/society/article/2183365/self-defence-plea-chinese-family-torn-apart-stalker-killing. Retrieved May 13th, 2019.

[582] *Id.*

[583] *Id.*

[584] *Id.*

[585] *Id.*

[586] *Id.*

because Xiaofei's mother, Zhao Yinzhi "stabbed [Wang Lei] repeatedly after he fell over, which, they said, indicated that she 'had an indulgent attitude toward her action of hurting another person's body.'"[588] Only after a public outcry did the authorities finally relent and drop the charges.[589] The all-pervasive Chinese state – a regime that monitors womens' reproductive status, aggressively regulates family size, interns tens of thousands of religious minorities, imprisons hundreds of dissidents, engages in intrusive surveillance of its citizens at home and aggressive spying abroad – was either too impotent or too apathetic to protect this simple family from attack and then sought to imprison them when they defended themselves.

In the wake of the suicide hijackings of September 11th, 2001 and other terrorist and mass shooting events since, both law enforcement and the public at large are much less likely to take the passive approach to violent crime advocated by some. Nonetheless, as brave and self-sacrificing as the majority of them are, even law enforcement officers can fail in the face of attack, leaving victims to their own powers of self-defense. This is exactly what happened during the atrocity at Marjory Stoneman Douglas High School on February 14, 2018, when Nikolas Cruz shot 34 people,[590] killing 17. An armed officer – Deputy Scot Peterson – was on the campus when

---

[587] *Id.*

[588] Zuo. The police would have been well-served consider Justice Holmes' famous aphorism that "[d]etached reflection cannot be demanded in the presence of an uplifted knife." *Brown v. United States*, 256 US 335, 41 S.Ct. 501, 65 L.Ed. 961, 18 A.L.R. 1276 (1921).

[589] Alice Yan, "Chinese prosecutors forced by public opinion to accept self-defence plea from couple who killed stalker." *South China Morning Post*, March 4th, 2019. https://www.scmp.com/news/china/society/article/2188529/chinese-prosecutors-forced-public-opinion-accept-self-defence. Retrieved May 13th, 2019.

[590] *Initial Report Submitted to the Governor, Speaker of the House of Representatives and Senate President* (Marjory Stoneman Douglas High School Public Safety Commission, January 2nd, 2019), 1 – 2.

Mr. Cruz began his rampage. According to the *Parkland Commission Report*,

> Former Deputy Scot Peterson was derelict in his duty on February 14, 2018, failed to act consistently with his training and fled to a position of personal safety while Cruz shot and killed MSDHS students and staff. Peterson was in a position to engage Cruz and mitigate further harm to others, and he willfully decided not to do so. [] There is overwhelming evidence that Deputy Peterson knew that the gunshots were coming from within or within the immediate area of building twelve. Furthermore, there is no evidence to suggest that Peterson attempted to investigate the source of the gunshots. In fact, the statement of Security Specialist Greenleaf confirms Peterson did not attempt to identify the source of the gunshots, and, by all accounts—including surveillance video—Peterson retreated to an area of safety.[591][592][593]

---

[591] *Id*, 96.

[592] Deputy Peterson was arrested and charged with child endangerment as for his failure to act during the Parkland massacre. This is a highly unusual scenario, however. One commentator stated that "[i]n 25 years of teaching and practicing law he has never seen charges such as these against an officer;" another observed that while he "has never heard of a police officer being prosecuted for not doing his job, he also has never heard of an officer waiting outside during a mass murder." Experts agree that winning a conviction on the charge will be difficult; "[t]o make those charges stick — in a possibly unprecedented case — the state must establish Peterson as a caregiver of the students, prove he exposed them to harm through his inaction and prove he did so as a result of 'reckless disregard for human life,'" a high bar even given his cowardly conduct. Peterson is also charged with perjury, which may be a more viable charge. Lisa J. Huriash and Andrew Boryga, "Legal experts agree that Scot Peterson failed. Whether he can be convicted for it isn't so clear." *South Florida Sun Sentinel*, June 4th, 2019. https://www.sun-sentinel.com/local/broward/parkland/florida-school-shooting/fl-ne-peterson-charges-legality-20190605-

Police and public officials are all too human. Like other people, they do occasionally succumb, not merely to incompetence or cowardice, but also to apathy or even hostility to those whom they are charged to protect. A particularly dreadful example occurred when a "riot and massacre of citizens … white and colored, occurred at and near the hall of the Mechanics Institute … between eleven and twelve o'clock on the morning of July 30," 1866,[594] where Louisiana Republicans were holding a convention to consider adopting a new state constitution that would enfranchise blacks.[595] When the convention was attacked, not only did the New Orleans police fail to protect the assembled delegates, but they actually took part in the riot. According to one witness, "I saw the policemen fire, and when their pistols were unloaded they would take them to citizens for others that were loaded, so that they could fire quick."[596] Another witness testified that "the policemen from the second district came up in a body and commenced firing, and shot every colored man they met."[597]

Firearms prohibitionists would have us rely solely upon the police for our protection. But what recourse have we when, as

---

v2rn5n4dzjbudjyrejucm4qviq-story.html. Retrieved July 14th, 2019.

[593] Even in the unlikely event that Peterson is convicted of the child endangerment charges, such a remedy vindicates the State's interests in the case but does nothing to make the victims whole. "It is not very much consolation that society will come forward a great deal later, pick up the bits, and punish the violent offender." Malcolm, *Guns and Violence,* 177, quoting UK MP Ronald Bell, arguing for an amendment to the Prevention of Crime Act of 1953, during the debates leading to the Act's passage.

[594] *Report of the Select Committee on the New Orleans Riots* (39th Congress, 2d Session, Washington, Government Printing Office, 1867), 5.

[595] Laine Kaplan-Levenson. "An Absolute Massacre: The 1866 Riot at The Mechanics' Institute." *New Orleans Public Radio,* July 14th, 2016. https://www.wwno.org/post/absolute-massacre-1866-riot-mechanics-institute. Retrieved May 18th, 2019.

[596] *Report of the Select Committee on the New Orleans Riots,* testimony of L. J. P. Capla, 120.

[597] *Id.,* testimony of Henry Francis Evans, 196.

sometimes must occur (the police being fully human), they fail to protect us, be it through negligence, incompetence or malice? As victims of the Parkland shooting and other crimes have learned, the answer is *no recourse at all*. In *L.S. v. Peterson*, Parkland survivors sued Deputy Peterson and other defendants on various grounds, including the failure to protect them from Nikolas Cruz's rampage. In response, the defendants moved for dismissal of the claim on the ground that "there is no Constitutional duty to protect students from harm inflicted by third parties."[598] The court agreed, holding that

> [a]s interpreted through case law, the Due Process Clause protects individuals first and foremost from action taken by the state. But, nothing in the language of the Due Process Clause itself requires the state to protect the life, liberty, and property of its citizens against invasion by private actors. The Clause is phrased as a limitation on the state's power to act, not as a guarantee of certain minimal levels of safety and security. It forbids the state itself to deprive individuals of life, liberty, or property without "due process of law," but its language cannot fairly be extended to impose an affirmative obligation on the state that those interests do not come to harm through other means. Indeed, "[i]ts purpose was to protect people from the State, not to ensure that the state protected them from each other."[599]

The *L.S.* court relied, in part, on the holding of another Florida court in yet another homicidal rampage, the 2016 Pulse Nightclub attack at Orlando, Florida. In *Aracena v. Gruler*, plaintiffs "alleg[ed] Constitutional deprivations by the City of Orlando and its officers for not preventing the massacre and not going in quickly enough to 'neutralize' the shooter."[600] The suit rested in part on the

---

[598] *L.S. v. Peterson* (S.D. Fla., 2018).
[599] *Id.,* quoting *DeShaney v. Winnebago Cty. Dept. of Soc. Servs.,* 489 US 189 (1989).

actions of Adam Todd Gruler, a City of Orlando police officer who was on duty providing security at the Pulse that night. According to the Court,

> [a]t some point during his shift, Officer Gruler "abandoned his post." Around 2:00 a.m., an individual (the "shooter") entered Pulse to "look around" and determined he could carry out his plan to murder patrons inside due to the visible absence of security. After scouting the club, the shooter retrieved his weapons—a semiautomatic rifle and semiautomatic pistol—reentered Pulse and opened fire on the patrons inside. When the shooting began, Gruler "immediately became aware an active shooter was shooting patrons in Pulse," but allegedly "stayed outside."[601]

Like the *L.S.* court later, the *Aracena* court denied relief, opining that

> Since this entire circumstance begins and ends with a private actor, Officer Gruler cannot be sued for violating Plaintiff's due process rights. Indeed, Count I boils down to a claim that Gruler initially absconded and then failed to protect Plaintiff after the attack began. Yet, "[t]he affirmative duty of protection that the Supreme Court rejected in *DeShaney* is precisely the duty [Plaintiff] relies on in this case." See [*Pinder v. Johnson*, 54 F.3d 1169 (4th Cir., 1995)]. Officer Gruler's failure to protect Plaintiff "against private violence simply does not constitute a violation of the Due Process Clause." See *DeShaney*, 489 US at 197. The Pulse shooting was a spontaneous act of violence carried out by "a thug with no regard for human life."

---

[600] *Aracena v. Gruler* (M.D. Fla., 2018).
[601] *Id.*, internal citations omitted.

159

With this, Plaintiff's substantive due process claims fail.[602]

The *Aracena* court relied in part on *Pinder v. Johnson*, a 1995 US 4th Circuit Court of Appeals case. In *Pinder*, the Court faced a factual scenario that it conceded to be "genuinely tragic:"[603]

> On the evening of March 10, 1989, Officer Johnson responded to a call reporting a domestic disturbance at the home of Carol Pinder. When he arrived at the scene, Johnson discovered that Pinder's former boyfriend, Don Pittman, had broken into her home. Pinder told Officer Johnson that when Pittman broke in, he was abusive and violent. He pushed her, punched her, and threw various objects at her. Pittman was also screaming and threatening both Pinder and her children, saying he would murder them all. A neighbor, Darnell Taylor, managed to subdue Pittman and restrain him until the police arrived. Officer Johnson questioned Pittman, who was hostile and unresponsive. Johnson then placed Pittman under arrest. After confining Pittman in the squad car, Johnson returned to the house to speak with Pinder again. Pinder explained to Officer Johnson that Pittman had threatened her in the past, and that he had just been released from prison after being convicted of attempted arson at Pinder's residence some ten months earlier. She was naturally afraid for herself and her children, and wanted to know whether it would be safe for her to return to work that evening. Officer Johnson assured her that Pittman would be locked up overnight. He further indicated that Pinder had to wait until the next day to swear out a warrant against Pittman because a county

---

[602] *Id.*

[603] *Pinder v. Johnson*, 54 F.3d 1169 (4th Cir., 1995).

commissioner would not be available to hear the charges before morning. Based on these assurances, Pinder returned to work. That same evening, Johnson brought Pittman before Dorchester County Commissioner George Ames, Jr. for an initial appearance. Johnson only charged Pittman with trespassing and malicious destruction of property having a value of less than three hundred dollars, both of which are misdemeanor offenses. Consequently, Ames simply released Pittman on his own recognizance and warned him to stay away from Pinder's home. Pittman did not heed this warning. Upon his release, he returned to Pinder's house and set fire to it. Pinder was still at work, but her three children were home asleep and died of smoke inhalation. Pittman was later arrested and charged with first degree murder. He was convicted and is currently serving three life sentences without possibility of parole.[604]

Ms. Pinder sued, and as with the courts in *L.S.* and *Aracena*, the *Pinder* court denied relief, holding in part that

[t]he recognition of a broad Constitutional right to affirmative protection from the state would be the first step down the slippery slope of liability. Such a right potentially would be implicated in nearly every instance where a private actor inflicts injuries that the state could have prevented. Every time a police officer incorrectly decided it was not necessary to intervene in a domestic dispute, the victims of the ensuing violence could bring a Sec. 1983 action. Every time a parolee committed a criminal act, the victims could argue the state had an affirmative duty to keep the prisoner incarcerated. Indeed, victims of

[604] *Id.*

virtually every crime could plausibly argue that if the authorities had done their job, they would not have suffered their loss. Broad affirmative duties thus provide a fertile bed for Sec. 1983 litigation, and the resultant governmental liability would wholly defeat the purposes of qualified immunity.[605]

Thus, the 4th Circuit, the same Court that would empower the state to deprive citizens of the use of the most popular rifle in America and presumably other firearms for their defense, would also deprive them of any recourse against that state when the deprivation of their arms results in harm at the hands of stronger criminals.

Violent Crime is an Act of Predation

Bans on the AR-15 and other semiautomatic firearms as "weapons of war" rest on the implicit premise that firearms features useful in combat are also useful in crime, which depends upon the corollary that infantry combat and violent crime are themselves equivalent, or at least strongly related. This is false. In some respects, infantry combat and violent crime take similar form: both involve imposing ones will by the threat or use of physical force against the person of another, often (but not necessarily) with firearms. Because of this gun control advocates often treat them as either identical or substantially similar phenomena. In so doing, they confuse form with content. The Soviet military theoretician Colonel Vasiliy Savkin[606] wrote in 1972 that "[a]s new conditions develop ... [t]he old principles of military art are modified. They change their content (often radically), and sometimes are discarded completely."[607] Even

---

[605] *Pinder*, internal citations and quotations omitted.

[606] "The author, Colonel Vasily Yefisovich Savkin ... served on the faculty of the Frunze Military Academy." American Editor's Comment on the Basic Principles of Operational Art and Tactics, v.

[607] Savkin, V. YE.; and United States Air Force (translator). *The Basic Principles of Operational Art and Tactics*. (Moscow, 1972, and the United States Air Force, n.d., as part of its "Soviet Military Thought" series), 5.

to the extent that infantry combat and violent crime have anything in common conceptually, the entirely different circumstances under which they occur distorts and mutates the content of each phenomenon to that point that they operate under entirely different principles, or any underlying shared principles express themselves radically differently, such that these two forms of violence form entirely separate and fundamentally dissimilar social phenomena.

The content of physical violence at the individual level, as manifested in infantry combat, is fundamentally political, and as Colonel Savkin wrote,

> [t]he political content of war has a deciding influence on the overall character of armed conflict, on the methods and forms of its conduct, and on the employment of particular types of weapons. In other words, the political content of war determines the character of armed violence within it.[608]

As Savkin further noted,

> [t]he laws of armed conflict ... differ from the laws of nature and society, since they characterize an extremely antagonistic process in which there is a constant contest to destroy the enemy's forces and preserve ones own, for the sake of directly opposite military-political goals, according to special plans, and with the help of a special military organization.[609]

And further,

> [t]he laws of armed conflict express the extremely complex and contradictory nature of a special sociopolitical phenomenon – the process of violent

---

[608] *Id.*, 79.
[609] *Id.*, 56.

counteraction of warring sides to achieve diametrically opposed military-political goals for each of them.[610]

While criminal violence may be viewed as a social phenomenon of a peculiar sort, it lacks the political content of warfare (of which infantry combat is one manifestation) and therefore plays out completely differently. This political content creates the circumstances under which individual combatants – the otherwise decent, ordinary folk that find themselves caught up in the extraordinary social, political, and physical drama of war – can be motivated to act contrary to their own physical self-interest and to take actions, and expose themselves to risks, that they might not otherwise take. The combatants engaged in infantry combat are ordinary people caught up in extraordinary social circumstances. As such, they behave socially the way ordinary people do in ordinary circumstances: by cooperating with one another to achieve common goals (including vanquishing the foe). Warfare, including infantry combat, is a hyper-competitive social and political phenomenon in which opposing forces vigorously contend against one another, while the members of each faction energetically cooperate to achieve the shared goal of victory. Ordinary violent crime, even extreme examples such as mass public shootings, rest on a different footing: usually bereft of political content, it is an antisocial, predatory phenomenon. Violent criminals are not the ordinary people serving in the US Army or US Marine Corps infantry. Violent criminals are predators; they behave in a predatory manner, distinctly different from the way soldiers in combat behave. Yet firearms prohibitionists and those opposed to armed self-defense insist upon treating combat and crime as equivalent. Such "identification and mixing is a crude mistake"[611] leading to dangerous and erroneous conclusions, as occurred during the debates leading to passage of the UK 1953 Prevention of Crime Act. There, the Act's proponents argued that "the more the ordinary citizen arms himself, the more excuse is there for the person who intends to perpetrate something unlawful to arm

---

[610] *Id.*, 59.
[611] *Id.*, 121 – 122.

himself so that he can achieve his end."[612] This reasoning is sound in the context of warfare, but it utterly misapprehends the logic of violent crime. The violent criminal is a predator. Like any other predatory animal, a violent criminal does not seek out conflict, he seeks out prey: victims that the predator can fall upon and subdue with the absolute minimum amount of risk of physical injury to himself. A predatory animal seeks out a weak and isolated victim unable to help itself. Likewise, "[c]riminals strike those weaker than themselves. Their edge in strength comes, first, from picking the helpless victims – the crippled, the old. Next, they take weapons, usually bludgeons or knives,"[613] and sometimes guns.

A violent criminal selects his victim with minimization of risk to himself in mind. His thought is not to engage in an arms race with his victim so as to be sure of overpowering her, for such a race implies the specter of single combat with an armed victim – combat that carries with it an enhanced risk of harm to himself. "A criminal is not interested in engaging in [a] … contest of skill and arms. His end state is simple: get paid."[614] The human predator does not wish to engage in combat; the human predator, like his animal counterpart, wishes to achieve an easy kill, at least insofar as risk to himself is concerned. As Massad Ayoob has written,

> A bandit who fears you is unlikely to force you into a situation where you will attempt to harm him. Unless he is suicidal, a criminal who believes he stands a reasonable chance of being killed or injured will give up the attempt.[615]

---

[612] Malcolm, *Guns and Violence,* 178, from T.C. Hansard, *Parliamentary Debates from the Year 1803 to the Present Time.*
[613] Massad Ayoob. *Armed and Alive* (Second Amendment Foundation, 1979., n.p.).
[614] Craig S. Douglas, "The Criminal Assault Paradigm," in Massad Ayoob, editor, *Straight Talk on Armed Defense* (Gun Digest Books, 2017), 94.
[615] Ayoob, *Armed and Alive.*

Even a "suicidal" predator such as a mass shooter will usually avoid armed victims and seek out easy targets. The Pulse Nightclub shooter, for example, reconnoitered the club and confirmed the absence of security before launching his attack.[616]

Although predators often arm themselves to facilitate the domination or destruction of their victims, they will not engage in an arms race to achieve this. Armed or not, the human predator will often *avoid altogether* a victim he deems likely to be armed or likely to resist effectively. As Craig Douglas has noted, "[t]he criminal has no ego investment in who wins or loses. This is mostly economics, and there is probably someone a couple of blocks away and will make a far easier victim."[617] This logic applies to most criminals, whether ordinary street thugs or mass shooters, because all of them carry out their crimes to gratify some need or desire, be it a lust for physical possessions, a craving for drugs, a desire for revenge, or a simple compulsion to kill. As Theodore Dalrymple has observed, criminal predators "can usually control their tempers in the presence of a sufficiently opposing force"[618] capable of thwarting the gratification they seek.

Thus, to the extent that public disarmament has affected any putative public "arms race," its impact is utterly one-sided. As Lord Saltoun noted during the debates on the Prevention of Crime Act in the UK Parliament, "criminals would not pay any attention to this law [mandating compulsory disarmament] … but the law-abiding would be hurt by it," as "the object of a weapon was to assist weakness to cope with strength and it was this ability that the bill was 'framed to destroy.'"[619] The end result of such legislation is to impose

---

[616] See *Aracena v. Gruler* (M.D. Fla., 2018).

[617] Craig, 96.

[618] Theodore Dalrymple. "The Knife Went In: It is a mistake to suppose that all men, or at least all Englishmen, want to be free." *City Journal*, Autumn 1994, https://www.city-journal.org/html/%E2%80%9C-knife-went-in%E2%80%9D-12530.html. Retrieved June 27th, 2019.

[619] Malcolm, *Guns and Violence*, 179.

one-sided, compulsory disarmament upon the potential victims of crime, while leaving the predatory criminals seeking to prey upon them, who already have no respect for law, with an even greater herd of victims to hunt. The impact of such a state of affairs can be expected not to reduce crime but to increase it: In an environment of compulsory disarmament, the predators will be as aware of the prohibition on weapons as everyone else. And while unlikely to honor it themselves, they are also quite aware that their victims *will* honor it. As such, the violent criminal predator can be expected to deduce that the chances of facing effective resistance from his victim are dramatically reduced. The result to be expected– though not intended – can only be to embolden violent criminals to further predation. The logic of the situation was succinctly stated by one of the most notorious criminals of all, former John Gotti associate and government witness Sammy "the Bull" Gravano: "Gun control? It's the best thing you can do for crooks and gangsters. I want you to have nothing. If I'm a bad guy, I'm always gonna have a gun."[620]

The Correlation of Forces in Violent Crime

The predatory and opportunistic nature of violent crime is such that the victim will generally be at a substantial disadvantage vis-à-vis the assailant. As described by Craig Douglas, the victim of a criminal assault generally faces two primary disadvantages.[621] The first, and the one over which the prospective victim may have the most control, is the problem of *"unproportional armament."*[622] A predator's superior physical strength alone may constitute such armament. "More often than not," however, "there is a weapon used to enforce compliance,"[623] which vastly multiplies the assailant's

---

[620] Howard Blum. "The Reluctant Don," *Vanity Fair*, September 8th, 1999. https://www.vanityfair.com/news/1999/09/The-Reluctant-Don. Retrieved January 4th, 2021.

[621] Craig, 92 – 105.

[622] *Id.*, 95.

[623] *Id.*, 101.

superiority over his victim. The second primary disadvantage that the prospective victim faces is *"unequal initiative."*[624]

Unequal Initiative stems from two sources. The first is the criminal himself. As Craig observes,

> [m]ost career criminals are surprisingly adept at laying the groundwork for successful criminal enterprise … a criminal selects a place that is conducive to a crime against a person and carefully assesses people who pass through his hunting grounds for certain characteristics.[625]

The second source of unequal initiative in a criminal attack is our system of laws. "The privilege of striking the first blow is a luxury we must usually grant to our attacker, so in a sense there can be no strategic surprise in the defense."[626] It is axiomatic in American law that, while individuals have a right to use force – even deadly force – to ward off attack, they may only do so when the perceived threat of death or great bodily harm is *imminent*. As the Kansas Supreme Court observed more than a century ago,

> a homicide is justifiable if committed by a person in the lawful defense of himself from an assault, when there shall be reasonable cause to apprehend a design on the part of his assailant to commit a felony or to do some great personal *injury and there shall be immediate danger of such designs being accomplished*[627] (emphasis added).

---

[624] *Id.*, 93.

[625] *Id.*, 94.

[626] Jeff Cooper. *Principles of Personal Defense* (Paladin Press, 1972 (1981 Printing,)), 41.

[627] *State v. Nelson*, 65 Kan. 689 (1902).

The necessity that harm be imminent before a victim can respond unavoidably vests the initiative in the attacker and with it substantial advantages, both psychological and tactical. Psychologically, a surprise attack can be devastating, resulting in the "freeze response," where a victim concludes that he faces a dangerous threat that he can neither defeat nor escape.[628]

It has been theorized that this reaction is an evolutionary response in which our ancient ancestors learned to "play dead" hoping the predator will become disinterested and leave.[629] Such a response may also be adaptive in minimizing the psychological harm inflicted upon the victim of a traumatic event.[630] But the freeze response can also be extremely maladaptive. The victim may be more capable of coping with the impending traumatic event than he or she believes, the "exaggerated fear" engendered by the freeze response may prevent him from acting against the threat.[631] Furthermore, the freeze response is likely to be ineffective against a human predator, who has likely selected his victim in the very hope that she will not be able to resist; as John English has observed, "loss of hope rather than loss of life is the factor that really decides … even the smallest combats."[632]

Initiative also vests the assailant with the tactical benefit of surprise. Surprise does not necessarily mean taking the victim completely unaware. Rather, surprise is achieved when the victim "is unable to counter effectively."[633] A well-known pop-culture reference

---

[628] Leon F. Seltzer, "Trauma and the Freeze Response: Good, Bad, or Both?" *Psychology Today*, July 8th, 2015. https://www.psychologytoday.com/us/blog/evolution-the-self/201507/trauma-and-the-freeze-response-good-bad-or-both. Retrieved May 25th, 2019.

[629] Rachael Sharman, "Why Do We Freeze When We're Scared?" *Popular Science*, October 11, 2017. https://www.popsci.com/why-do-we-freeze-when-frightened. Retrieved May 25th, 2019.

[630] *Id.*; Sharman.

[631] Seltzer.

[632] English, 223.

illustrates this concept well. Toward the end of *Star Wars Episode IV: A New Hope*, during the climactic Rebel aerial assault on the Death Star, the Rebel Alliance sends its X-Wing fighters against a small thermal exhaust port through which missiles can gain access to the station's reactor, causing a devastating chain reaction. Well into the attack, inside the Death Star, a subaltern approaches the station's commander, Grand Moff Tarkin (wonderfully played by Peter Cushing), warns him that they have discovered a weakness in the Death Star's defenses, and asks if Tarkin wants his ship to be kept standing by.[634] In other words, the Empire has ascertained the Rebel's objective – a vulnerable thermal exhaust port into which the Rebel pilots hope to fire missiles – but has identified the threat too late to ward off the attack, with devastating results: The Empire was surprised.

On a more practical level, consider a realistically frightening scenario: a woman, alone at night, traversing a vast, empty parking structure toward her car. She perceives a man in the structure with her, approaching. Though she detects him well before he is within arm's reach and immediately becomes suspicious, there is little she can do to ward off an attack if she is unarmed, notwithstanding her early warning. She, too, has been surprised.

Other things being equal, the party that exercises initiative (in the criminal scenario, this is virtually always the assailant) has a substantial advantage. Writing about naval warfare, Captain Wayne P. Hughes, Jr. wrote that "selecting the time and place of battle bestows an obvious advantage on the attacker"[635] – a truism that he distilled to the aphorism which he called "the great naval maxim of tactics, attack effectively first."[636] Naval warfare is of course a physical, social

---

[633] *FMFM 6-4, Marine Rifle Company/Platoon* (US Marine Corps, 17 February 1978), 17.

[634] *Star Wars: Episode IV – A New Hope*. Written and directed by George Lucas (Lucasfilm, Ltd., 1977).

[635] CAPT (Ret) Wayne P. Hughes, Jr. *Fleet Tactics: Theory and Practice* (Naval Institute Press, 1986), 35.

and political phenomenon even more attenuated from the phenomenon of criminal assault than infantry combat. Nonetheless, with respect to the purely physical interaction between predator and victim and the effect of surprise, Hughes' principle serves to illuminate the advantage enjoyed by the criminal assailant – the "unequal initiative" of which Craig has warned us.[637] This advantage is greatly magnified when coupled with the other factor usually present in a criminal assault, "unproportional armament."[638] Again, while acknowledging the fundamental differences between criminal acts and warfare, certain concepts from military theory can illuminate the predicament in which the victim of a criminal attacker finds himself at the moment of attack. "In 1954 Frederick W. Lanchester introduced his celebrated equations to show the consequences of concentration of force in the modern era ... [which] yielded a square law of effectiveness."[639] Under Lanchester's theory, where two forces of unequal strength concentrate their blows against each other, the weaker force will suffer damage at a geometric rate as compared to the stronger force.[640] Such a disparity of force can be artificially created: consider an attacker of equal strength to his victim who successfully seizes the initiative, lands the first blow, and wounds his victim. The strength of the victim is now unequal to that of the attacker, who will be able to inflict damage upon his victim at an advantageous rate.

The predator in a criminal assault will generally not rely solely on his advantage in "unequal initiative;" he will usually also rely upon superiority of physical force. While that superiority may consist solely of superiority in raw physical strength, the criminal often augments his advantage by employment of a weapon. According to Federal

---

[636] *Id.*, 34 – 35.

[637] Craig, 93.

[638] *Id.*, 95.

[639] Hughes, 34.

[640] *Id.*, 35. Lanchester discussed his theories at William Frederick, Lanchester, "Mathematics in Warfare," in James R., Newman, editor, *The World of Mathematics*, volume 4 (Simon and Schuster, 1956), 2138 – 2157.

Bureau of Investigation (FBI) data, 2017 saw 294,037 robberies, of which 121,577 were strong arm robberies relying on physical superiority alone; more than half – 172,460 – were armed robberies. According to the same data, 748,895 aggravated assaults were perpetrated, of which 189,172 were unarmed, with the remaining 559,723 involving the use of a weapon.[641] The same data reflects 15,129 murders, in only 696 of which were the weapons hands, fists, etc.[642]

Are Semiautomatic Rifles Really Particularly Lethal in Crime?

Of particular interest is the choice of weapon used in the crimes reported in the FBI data. Unsurprisingly, the weapon of choice in most violent crimes is firearms. For 2017, this data only specifies the type of firearm used for murder (not for other crimes), and that data is illuminating. Of these 15,129 murders, 10,982 were perpetrated with firearms: 7,032 with handguns, 403 with rifles, 264 with shotguns, and 3,283 cases in which the type of firearm is not identified.[643] Thus, for murders in which the type of firearm used is specified, only 667 of the murders in 2017 were perpetrated with any kind of long gun: fewer than the number of people killed with hands and fists (696).[644] And this includes *all* long guns, not just semiautomatic rifles. Thus, notwithstanding the consternation by some over the use of AR-15s in high-profile mass killings, the data shows that rifles of any kind pose a threat to public safety only on par with unaided physical strength.

---

[641] "2017: Crime in the United States, Table 15." Federal Bureau of Investigation, https://ucr.fbi.gov/crime-in-the-u.s/2017/crime-in-the-US-2017/tables/table-15. Retrieved May 25th, 2019.
[642] "2017: Crime in the United States, Table 20." Federal Bureau of Investigation, https://ucr.fbi.gov/crime-in-the-u.s/2017/crime-in-the-US-2017/tables/table-20. Retrieved May 25th, 2019.
[643] "2017: Crime in the United States, Table 15."
[644] "2017: Crime in the United States, Table 20."

The rejoinder of firearms prohibitionists will naturally be that AR-15s and similar firearms are more dangerous than other firearms for their capacity to inflict large numbers of casualties in mass shooting scenarios, but this is simply not the case: mass killings can be and have been regularly carried out with a variety of weapons throughout history. Nor are such episodes limited to the United States or even to the West. One such example – from Malay culture – is what John C. Spores called "the curious pattern of amok."[645] The word "amok" – "one of the few Malay words approaching common usage among English-speaking people"[646] – is now used by Westerners and Malays alike to denote "frenzied maniacal behavior in general, often including the connotation that the behavior results in injury or damage to persons or physical objects."[647] In its original meaning, however, the word had a much grimmer connotation, referring to a Malay "suddenly seizing dagger or spear and embarking on a murderous rampage, or 'running amok' as the English corruption would have it."[648] Spores, in the introduction to his work on the subject, vividly describes one such rampage that occurred on February 17th, 1891, in which one Imam Mamat ran amok, killing six people and wounding four others before being captured by colonial authorities.[649] The practice of amok persisted in Malay culture for centuries, with early recorded examples occurring in 1516,[650] 1602,[651] 1720, 1777,[652] 1812,[653] and 1823,[654] among others. According to Spores, the materials he consulted referenced approximately fifty separate instances of solitary amok between 1825 and 1925,[655] with

---

[645] John C. Spores. *Running Amok: An Historical Inquiry* (Ohio University Center for International Studies, 1988), 1.
[646] *Id.*, 6.
[647] *Id.*, 6 – 7.
[648] *Id.*, 1.
[649] *Id.*, 1 – 6.
[650] *Id.*, 32.
[651] *Id.*, 33.
[652] *Id.*, 34.
[653] *Id.*, 36
[654] *Id.* 37.
[655] *Id.*, 40.

no reason to believe this list to be all-inclusive. Most noteworthy for our purposes is the choice of weapons in these attacks: Though firearms existed at the time, the weapon of choice in amoks appear to have been exclusively edged weapons:

> These acts of indiscriminate murder, are called by us mucks … when … raised to a pitch of desperate fury, they sally out with a knife, or other weapon, and kill, without distinction of sex, rank, or age, whoever they meet in the streets…[656]

Such crimes are hardly unknown in the United States, of course. In the early 20th Century, the western US endured a spate of brutal ax murders, including the notorious June 10th, 1912 Villisca, Iowa attack, in which the six members of the Moore family and their two houseguests were bludgeoned to death by ax.[657] Other ax murders occurring around that time included attacks in Ardenwald, Oregon (4 victims) on June 8th, 1911; Rainier, Washington on July 10th, 1911 (2 victims); Colorado Springs, Colorado (6 victims), September 17th, 1911; Monmouth, Illinois (3 victims), September 30th, 1911; Ellsworth, Kansas (5 victims), October 15th, 1911; Mount Pleasant, Iowa (1 victim), October 31st, 1911; Columbia, Missouri (2 victims), December 17th, 1912; Paola, Kansas (2 victims), June 5th, 1912; and Blue Island, Illinois (4 victims), July 6th, 1914.[658]

Nor are mass killings with firearms a new phenomenon or the result of the modern prevalence of semiautomatic weapons, as shown by the 1889 "Jim Jumper Massacre." In that case, Jim Jumper, armed with a lever action Winchester rifle, killed eight people in a half-hour,

---

[656] *Id.*, 34.

[657] Mike Dash. "The Ax Murderer Who Got Away," *Smithsonian.com*, June 8th, 2012. https://www.smithsonianmag.com/history/the-ax-murderer-who-got-away-117037374/. Retrieved May 26th, 2019.

[658] Beth H. Klingensmith, *HI815XA – Research Seminar: 20th Century Topics, Professor Schneider, Emporia State University,* July, 2006, 28. http://freepages.rootsweb.com/~bkling/genealogy/hi815%20moore%20history%20paper.pdf. Retrieved May 26th, 2019.

including at least one person who had attempted to disarm him,[659] after having been rebuffed by the family of a woman whom he wished to marry.[660] Only when another person arrived on the scene with a Winchester of his own and shot and killed Jumper did the massacre end.[661] Another notorious massacre not involving semiautomatic rifles was the Palm Sunday Massacre in which Christopher Thomas shot "two women and eight children dead [by] point-blank gunshot wounds to the head."[662] When found by the police, "the victims were seated or reclined in a gruesome still-life, a few lounged in front of a television, another in the bedroom had been napping, and one woman held a tin of pudding and a spoon."[663] Thomas' weapons of choice: a .22 pistol and a .38 revolver.[664]

Even hideous school massacres that have so bedeviled our country in recent decades are not a new phenomenon. One of the deadliest occurred about a dozen miles from my childhood home in 1927, when school board member Andrew P. Kehoe bombed the Bath Consolidated School at Bath, Michigan, killing 45 people (including himself and his wife, whom he murdered at their home) and injuring 58.[665] It remains among America's deadliest school disasters.[666]

---

[659] "Victims of an Insane Indian," *New York Times*, March 3rd, 1889.

[660] Jim Robison, "Seminole Deaths Traced to Failed Courtship." *Orlando Sentinel*, April 12th, 1998. https://www.orlandosentinel.com/news/os-xpm-1998-04-12-9804110474-story.html. Retrieved May 26th, 2019.

[661] *Id.*

[662] "The Courtroom Sketches of Ida Libby Dengrove." University of Virginia Law School Library, https://archives.law.virginia.edu/dengrove/writeup/palm-sunday-massacre. Retrieved May 26th, 2019.

[663] *Id.*

[664] John M. Doyle. "Man Convicted of Manslaughter In Slayings of 10 Women and Children." *Associated Press*, July 19th, 1985. https://www.apnews.com/d920ee8e21aaae989de9bacc36258373. Retrieved May 26th, 2019.

[665] See M. J. Ellsworth, *The Bath School Disaster* (np, 1927); and Arnie Bernstein, *Bath Massacre: America's First School Bombing* (University of

The question remains, however: are semiautomatic rifles sharing features with military weapons (i.e., AR-15s and semiautomatic Kalashnikov rifles) really more dangerous, from a violent crime perspective, than other firearms? The data suggests not – even when that data is presented by researchers who claim the opposite. Because the key attribute of an AR-15 rifle is that it is a semiautomatic firearm, useful insight may be had from examining the data as it pertains to other semiautomatic firearms much more commonly used in crimes: semiautomatic handguns. One such study, conducted by D.C. Reedy and C.S. Koper in 2003, found that

> *evidence linking the spread of semiautomatic weaponry to higher levels of gun deaths and injuries is limited and equivocal.* A few studies made indirect links between the growing use of semiautomatics and rising levels of gun homicide and injuries in some cities during the late 1980s and early 1990s. However, other studies failed to demonstrate convincing links between city level trends in the use of semiautomatics and lethal gun violence. National data also present mixed signs as to whether gun attacks have become more injurious and lethal as semiautomatics have become more prevalent (emphasis added).[667]

This ambiguity was reflected in their own findings, which included the following data points: First, "assailants using [semiautomatic] pistols attacked victims [e.g., shot them or attempted

---

Michigan Press, 2009).

[666] Lorraine Boissoneault. "The 1927 Bombing That Remains America's Deadliest School Massacre." *Smithsonian.com.* https://www.smithsonianmag.com/history/1927-bombing-remains-americas-deadliest-school-massacre-180963355/#wxszhoqXfePC1JwO.99. Retrieved May 31st, 2019.

[667] D.C. Reedy and C.S. Koper. "Impact of handgun types on gun assault outcomes: a comparison of gun assaults involving semiautomatic pistols and revolvers." *Injury Prevention*, 2003: 9, 151.

to shoot them] in virtually the same proportion of cases as assailants using revolvers (69.0% and 68.3%, respectively)."[668] Second, crimes involving semiautomatic pistols "were not significantly more likely to result in injuries (fatal or nonfatal) than were revolver cases. Attackers killed or injured victims in 57.6% of gunfire cases involving [semiautomatic] pistols and 56.3% of gunfire incidents involving revolvers."[669] Third, "gunshot injury incidents involving [semiautomatic] pistols were less likely to produce a death than were those involving revolvers (15.8% to 25.0%)."[670] Another finding was that "[a]lthough a higher percentage of pistol victims sustained multiple wounds (24.3% to 20% for pistol and revolver victims, respectively), the average number of wounds for pistol victims (1.44) was actually lower than that for revolver victims (1.50)."[671]

The primary objection of firearms prohibitionists to semiautomatic firearms is, of course, that they accept detachable magazines, allegedly allowing assailants to fire a greater number of shots. As Wake Forest Sociology Professor David Yamane sarcastically put it, "[o]f course we all know that a benefit of semi-autos over revolvers is that you can just rain bullets down on people with semi-autos."[672] So, does Reedy and Koper's work show that assailants armed with semiautomatic pistols really do "rain bullets down on people?" They do not:

> Given that the gun was fired, the average number of shots in pistol cases ranged from 3.23 to 3.68, based on minimum and maximum estimates (table 1). In contrast, the average number of shots in revolver cases ranged from 2.30 to 2.58. Using both minimum

---

[668] *Id.*, 152.

[669] *Id.*, 153.

[670] *Id.*

[671] *Id.*

[672] David Yamane. "Revolvers Kill! (May Be Even More Lethal Than Semiautomatic Handguns)." *Gun Culture 2.0*, October 24th, 2017. https://gunculture2point0.wordpress.com/2017/10/24/revolvers-kill-may-be-even-more-lethal-than-semiautomatic-handguns/. Retrieved May 26th, 2019.

and maximum shots fired estimates, pistol cases averaged about one more shot than did revolver cases...[673]

Summarizing Reedy and Koper's findings, we find that assailants armed with semiautomatic pistols were about as likely as those armed with revolvers to shoot or attempt to shoot their victims. In other words, notwithstanding the greater potential rate of fire of semiautomatic pistols and their generally larger magazine capacity, assailants armed with semiautomatic handguns fire, on average, only one more shot during attacks than do assailants armed with revolvers, and they were only slightly more likely to injure their victims than those armed with revolvers. Furthermore, their findings show that assailants armed with revolvers were significantly more likely to kill their victims than those armed with semiautomatic pistols. Notwithstanding this inflated fatality rate when revolvers were the weapon of choice, Reedy and Koper conclude that "that the overall number of wounded victims would have been reduced by 9.4% had revolvers been used in all of the attacks,"[674] to which Yamane reasonably objects: "The number of victims would have been 9% lower, but the fatality rate of revolvers is 58% higher (25% vs. 15.79%). So that is an acceptable trade-off?"[675] Reedy and Koper seem to rest this conclusion on two considerations: The first is that attacks with semiautomatic pistols resulted, on average, in 1.15 victims, while those with revolvers resulted in a single victim per incident.[676] They deem this difference statistically significant,[677] to which Yamane replies "[t]he difference is statistically significant, but is it substantively significant?"[678]

---

[673] Reedy and Koper, 152.

[674] *Id.*, 153.

[675] Yamane.

[676] Reedy and Koper, 153.

[677] *Id.*

[678] Yamane.

The real manner in which Reedy and Koper support their conclusion that a world with only revolvers would result in fewer gunshot injuries, however, is by simply assuming away the higher fatality rate that they found for revolvers, asserting that "we would not expect victims shot with pistols to die more frequently than victims shot with revolvers, holding gun caliber, wound location, the victim's physical condition, and other relevant factors constant,"[679] simply ignoring their own finding of substantially more fatalities in revolver incidents than in semiautomatic pistol incidents.

Thus, notwithstanding Reedy and Koper's conclusions, their work actually demonstrates that the mere introduction of a weapon with a semiautomatic firing action into a criminal assault simply does not result in a vast increase in shots fired, persons wounded, or victims killed. What effect does introduction of a so-called "assault weapon" have when introduced into a criminal assault scenario? Koper, in the company of several other researchers, has examined this question as well, in "Criminal Use of Assault Weapons and High Capacity Semiautomatic Firearms: an Updated Examination of Local and National Sources," *Journal of Urban Health* (2017).[680] As with other studies on so-called "assault weapons," Koper's 2018 study rests upon the assumption that "assault weapons" have features "that *appear* useful in military and criminal applications but unnecessary in shooting sports or self-defense" (emphasis added).[681] To support this assumption, Koper cites the 2004 "Report to the National Institute of Justice,"[682] a source that itself *assumes* this conclusion without testing it. Koper's 2018 report further asserts that "[p]rior research has shown that AWs [assault weapons] and LCM firearms are used in a higher share of these crimes [murders of police officers and mass murder incidents]."[683] Koper cites two sources for this assertion: A

---

[679] Reedy and Koper, 153.

[680] Koper, *et. al.* "Criminal Use of Assault Weapons and High-Capacity Semiautomatic Firearms," 313–321.

[681] *Id.*, 314.

[682] *Id.*, note 2.

[683] *Id.*, 315.

1995 report by Handgun Control, Inc., a pressure-group avowedly committed to a great degree of firearms prohibition,[684] and once again, the 2004 "Report to the National Institute of Justice." Koper's reliance on the 2004 report is problematic in a number of respects. First, the 2004 report candidly admits that "the estimates consistently show that AWs are used in a small fraction of gun crimes. Even the highest estimates, which correspond to particularly rare events such mass murders and police murders, are no higher than 13%."[685]

Second, the usefulness of the 2004 report with respect to evaluating the utility of AR-15s and similar semiautomatic rifles in crime is substantially limited by what it includes in the scope of the term "Assault Weapon [AW]:"

> Note also that the majority of AWs used in crime are assault pistols (APs) rather than assault rifles []. Among AWs reported by police to ATF during 1992 and 1993, for example, APs outnumbered ARs by a ratio of 3 to 1.[686]

Finally, it states in a conclusory fashion that "AWs account for a larger share of guns used in mass murders and murders of police, crimes for which weapons with greater firepower would *seem* particularly useful"[687] (emphasis added).
Turning to the 2017 report, the abstract asserts that

> Assault weapons *and other high capacity semiautomatics* together generally account for 22 to 36% of crime guns, with some estimates upwards of 40% for cases involving serious violence including murders of

---

[684] W.C. Adler; F. Bielke; D.J. Doi; and J.F. Kennedy. *Cops Under Fire: Law Enforcement Officers Killed with Assault Weapons or Guns with High Capacity Magazines* (Handgun Control, Inc, 1995).

[685] Koper, *Updated Assessment of the Federal Assault Weapons Ban,* 15 – 16.

[686] *Id.,* 19.

[687] *Id.,* 87.

police. Assault weapons *and other high capacity semiautomatics appear* to be used in a higher share of firearm mass murders (*up to 57% in total*), *though data on this issue are very limited*[688] (emphasis added).

This is deceiving in the first instance in conflating rifles such as AR-15s with other semiautomatic weapons, such as the Beretta 92 series pistols, which are considered high capacity by the definitional terms of the article.[689] More importantly, however, the data in the report paint a much *less* grim picture of so-called "assault weapon" crime than the summary implies. The report's data analysis at the national level reveals the following significant findings:

AW prevalence was approximated in the national ATF tracing data for 2012 and 2013 (n = 481,632) based on traces of guns in calibers .223, 5.56, and 7.62 mm. These are common calibers for AW-type semiautomatic rifles, though not all firearms in these calibers are AWs, and not all AWs fall into these calibers. *This method nonetheless yielded an estimate of 5%, which is within the range of estimates provided by the local analyses*[690] (emphasis added).

With respect to murders of police, the report found that from 2009 to 2013, so-called assault weapons "accounted for an estimated 13.2% of the firearms used in these crimes overall and varied between 8 and 18% from year to year."[691] Unlike the 2004 report, "[v]irtually all of the [assault weapons] (97%) were assault rifles. Semiautomatic rifles overall accounted for 15.5% of the firearms used in these cases and ranged from 5 to 23% annually."[692] With

---

[688] Koper, *et. al.* "Criminal Use of Assault Weapons and High-Capacity Semiautomatic Firearms," 2018, abstract.
[689] *Id.*, 314.
[690] *Id.*, 317.
[691] *Id.*
[692] *Id.*

respect to mass murder, among the "42 incidents [between 2009 –
2013 that] had sufficiently detailed information to make a definitive
determination regarding [assault weapon] use … 35.7% involved
[assault weapon] use."[693] Large capacity magazines were used in
between 18.6% to 57% of such instances.[694]

Koper, *et al.* conclude that data sources suggest that AWs are
used in between 2 and 9% of gun crimes in general with most
estimates being less than 7%. Upper bound estimates of AW use
based on semiautomatic rifles range from 4 to 12% in most data
sources and are typically less than 9%. These estimates are broadly
similar to those generated in the early 1990s prior to the Federal AW
ban, though they are perhaps somewhat higher on average.[695] They
also found that

> LCM firearms, which include AWs as well as other
> high capacity semiautomatics, appear to account for
> 22 to 36% of crime guns in most places, with some
> estimates upwards of 40% for cases involving serious
> violence. These estimates are comparable to or higher
> than earlier estimates of LCM use. However, the
> higher-end estimates may overstate LCM use
> somewhat as most are based on measurement of
> LCM-compatible guns that may not all have been
> equipped with LCMs.[696]

Finally Koper and his colleagues conclude that

> LCM firearms, which include AWs as well as other
> high capacity semiautomatics, appear to account for
> 22 to 36% of crime guns in most places, with some
> estimates upwards of 40% for cases involving serious

---

[693] *Id.*
[694] *Id.*, 317 and Table 2.
[695] *Id.*, 318.
[696] *Id.*, 319.

violence. These estimates are comparable to or higher than earlier estimates of LCM use. *However, the higher-end estimates may overstate LCM use somewhat as most are based on measurement of LCM-compatible guns that may not all have been equipped with LCMs ...* Estimates for firearm mass murders are very imprecise due to lack of on the guns and magazines used but available information suggests that AWs and other high capacity magazine semiautomatics are involved in *as many as* 57% of such incidents"[697] (emphasis added).

The data above demonstrates that by most estimates so called "assault weapons" are the weapon of choice in a distinct minority of gun crimes of all types, including mass shootings, with even the highest figures still showing a very large proportion of attacks being perpetrated with other weapons. Thus, there is simply no basis upon which to conclude that semiautomatic rifles like the AR-15 are more deadly as instrumentalities of crime than are other firearms.

Do Large Capacity Magazines Contribute to Deadlier Outcomes in Crime?

One of the most controversial firearms technologies today is the detachable box magazine, particularly the so-called "large capacity" magazine (LCM), usually defined as a magazine capable of holding more than ten rounds.[698] Firearms prohibitionists advocate the ban such magazines on the ground that "semiautomatic weapons with LCMs enable offenders to fire high numbers of shots rapidly, thereby potentially increasing both the number of persons wounded ... and the number of gunshot victims suffering multiple wounds,"[699]

---

[697] *Id.*

[698] *Id.*, 314; and Gary Kleck, "Large-Capacity Magazines and the Casualty Counts in Mass Shootings: The Plausibility of Linkages." *Justice Research and Policy*, 2016, Vol. 17(I), 29.

[699] Gary Kleck. "Large-Capacity Magazines and the Casualty Counts in Mass Shootings: The Plausibility of Linkages." *Justice Research and Policy*,

and that lower capacity magazines would force potential mass shooters to change magazines more often, creating windows of opportunity during which victims and bystanders can either escape or tackle the shooter.[700]

In 2014, Roy Hayes and Reginald Hayes tested these assumptions, publishing their results in the *Journal of Artificial Societies and Social Simulation*. About so-called "assault weapons" bans, they found that

> [u]sing the simulation we examined the assault weapons ban proposed by Senator Feinstein. In its current configuration the ban does not limit the rate of fire (Assault Weapons Ban 2013). The ban would allow for detachable magazines as well as semiautomatic pistols, shotguns, and rifles. In the best possible case, the Assault Weapons Ban may make firearms slightly less accurate by disallowing forward grips and barrel shrouds. However, wearing a heat resistant glove would serve the same purpose as a barrel shroud. Additionally, the simulation illustrates that in crowded mass shooting events, lowering a weapon's accuracy may actually increase the number of people shot. As the crowd becomes denser, such as when people are going through a door, a gunman can widen his shooting area generating a deadlier impact. As the crowd assembles to get through a door, the crowd becomes significantly wider than it is deep. Thus, there are fewer people in front of a civilian than beside him, making the gunman more likely to hit somebody if he widens his target area. *Therefore, we conclude that the assault weapons ban will not have any effect*

2016, Vol. 17(I), 29, quoting Koper, *Updated Assessment of the Federal Assault Weapons Ban*, 80.
[700] Kleck. "Large-Capacity Magazines and the Casualty Counts in Mass Shootings: The Plausibility of Linkages,"30 – 31.

on the number of people shot during mass shootings (emphasis added).[701]

They further conclude that

> [e]xcluding adding armed guards, of the parameters tested limiting a weapon's rate of fire, making it impractical to fire a weapon more than a defined number of times in a finite period, is the best way to decrease the number of people shot. The ban on high capacity magazines seeks to accomplish this by forcing a shooter to reload more often. For example, if forcing a shooter to reload lowers the shooter's rate of fire by 0.2 bullets per second, this lowers the rate of fire by twelve bullets per minute. More extreme proposals could include banning semiautomatic weapons, which would lower the rate of fire because it would require the operator to perform an additional task when firing. Additionally, banning detachable magazines and requiring that magazines only allow for bullets to be individually loaded (i.e., revolver design) would lower the rate of fire because it would take longer to reload the weapon.[702]

Hayes and Hayes' conclusions about magazine capacity are problematic, in that their simulation parameters assumed a rate of fire of one round per second.[703] This assumption is unsound for at least two reasons. First, as the authors themselves note, the maximum effective rate of fire of an AR-15 is 45 rounds per minute or 0.75 rounds per second, so that their simulation parameters already credit a mass shooter with a 25% premium in his rate of fire.

---

[701] Roy Hayes and Reginald Hayes. "Agent-Based Simulation of Mass Shootings: Determining How to Limit the Scale of a Tragedy." *Journal of Artificial Societies and Social Simulation* 17 (2) 5 (2014), paragraphs 5.1 and 5.2.
[702] *Id.*, paragraph 5.3.
[703] *Id.*, paragraph 3.19.

Much more important are Gary Kleck's findings, showing that a rate of fire of one round per second assumed by Hayes and Hayes exaggerates the actual rates of fire in mass shootings. Rather than rates of fire measured in rounds per second as often assumed, Kleck's analysis shows that actual rates of fire in mass shooting events is measurable in *seconds per round* – sometimes many seconds. In a 2016 paper Kleck explored the hypothesis that lower magazine capacity would reduce mass shooting casualties by forcing shooters to change magazines more often. He defined "[a] mass shooting … as one in which more than six people were shot, either fatally or non-fatally, in a single incident,"[704] explaining that

> [t]he six-victim cutoff was used because an offender could shoot as many as six persons using a typical old-fashioned six-shot revolver of the sort that has been around since the 19th century, and our goal was to identify all incidents in which it was plausible that use of an LCM (always used in connection with modern semiautomatic firearms) affected the number of casualties.[705]

Using these criteria, Kleck "identified 23 total incidents in which more than six people were shot at a single time and place in the United States from 1994 through 2013 and that were known to involve use of any magazines with capacities over 10 rounds."[706] He identified three instances during this period in which bystanders were reported to have attempted to tackle a mass shooter. In one, the shooter's weapon was a shotgun which had to be reloaded by inserting one round at a time through the loading gate; in another, the bystanders tackled the shooter, not while reloading, but while he was switching guns. In only one case was the mass shooter tackled

---

[704] Kleck. "Large-Capacity Magazines and the Casualty Counts in Mass Shootings: The Plausibility of Linkages," 33.
[705] *Id.*
[706] *Id.*, 37.

while attempting to change out a detachable box magazine: Jared Loughner's attempted assassination of Representative Gabrielle Giffords in 2011.[707] According to Kleck,

> The bystander intervention in the Giffords shooting was, however, unique, and occurred only because there were extraordinarily courageous and quick-thinking bystanders willing and able to tackle the shooter. Over a 20-year period in the United States, the Tucson incident appears to be the only known instance of a mass shooter using a semiautomatic firearm and detachable magazines in which the shooter was stopped by bystanders while the shooter may have been trying to reload such a magazine. *All other mass shootings have instead stopped only when the shooter chose to stop and left the scene, the shooter committed suicide, or armed police arrived and forced the shooter to stop*[708] (emphasis added).

Even this case provides only equivocal support for the theory that bystanders might exploit the interval in which a mass shooter changes magazines, as it was reported that Loughner's fire may have been interrupted by a gun or magazine malfunction.[709] Kleck cites only one other potential example – a report of six children escaping while the shooter reloaded during the attack on Sandy Hook Elementary School in 2012. However, that story "went on to concede that this was just a speculation by an unnamed source, and that it was also possible that some children simply escaped when the killer was shooting other children."[710] Thus, there appears to be little if any evidence that reducing magazine capacity would materially reduce injury fatality rates for gun crime.

---

[707] Kleck. "Large-Capacity Magazines and the Casualty Counts in Mass Shootings: The Plausibility of Linkages," 39.
[708] *Id.*, 40.
[709] *Id.*
[710] *Id.*, 42.

Kleck posits two reasons for this. The first is that magazine capacity is frankly irrelevant in most crime scenarios. As Kleck points out,

> [p]ossession of LCMs is largely irrelevant to ordinary gun crimes, that is, those with fewer victims than mass shootings, because it is extremely rare that the offenders in such attacks fire more rounds than can be fired from guns with ordinary ammunition capacities. For example, only 2.5% of handgun crimes in Jersey City, NJ, in 1992–1996 involved over 10 rounds being fired. Even among those crimes in which semiautomatic pistols were used, and some of the shooters were therefore likely to possess magazines holding more than ten rounds, only 3.6% of the incidents involved over 10 rounds fired. Thus, if LCMs have any effect on the outcomes of violent crimes, it is more likely to be found among mass shootings with many victims, which involve unusually large numbers of rounds being fired.[711]

The other reason is that detachable magazines can be changed very quickly, and that mass shooters rarely achieve rates of fire even close to the theoretical maximum rate of fire of their weapons, so that magazine changes do not actually slow the shooter's *effective* rate of fire. Kleck writes:

> Skilled shooters can change detachable magazines in 2 seconds or less, and even relatively unskilled persons can, with minimal practice, do so in 4 seconds (for a demonstration, see the video at https://www.youtube.com/watch?v=ZRCjY-GtROY which shows a 2-seconds magazine change by an

---

[711] Kleck. "Large-Capacity Magazines and the Casualty Counts in Mass Shootings: The Plausibility of Linkages," 29, citing Reedy and Koper, 154.

experienced shooter). Certainly, additional magazine changes do not increase the time needed to fire a given number of rounds by much.[712]

Kleck then reviewed 25 mass shooting incidents from 1994 through 2013 in which rates of fire could be calculated. Of this sample, in only three cases was the average number of seconds per shot less than two, and in only five instances was it less than four seconds per shot:[713]

> In sum, in nearly all LCM-involved mass shootings, the time it takes to insert a new detachable magazine is no greater than the average time between shots that the shooter takes anyway when not reloading. Consequently, there is no affirmative evidence that reloading detachable magazines slows mass shooters' rates of fire, and thus no affirmative evidence that the number of victims who could escape the killers due to additional pauses in the shooting is increased by the shooter's need to change magazines.[714]

Aggravating this fact, from the killer's perspective, is the reality of marksmanship fundamentals: As discussed above, the faster the shooter fires, the more likely he is to jerk the trigger, throwing off his aim. Thus, even if a mass shooter did fire rounds fast enough that a pause to change magazines would effect a reduction of rate of fire, the accuracy of his shots would likely be less, reducing the chance of hitting his targets. Kleck concludes:

---

[712] Kleck. "Large-Capacity Magazines and the Casualty Counts in Mass Shootings: The Plausibility of Linkages," 30, citing Doug Koenig, "Speed Reload: Handgun Technique | Competitive Shooting Tips with Doug Koenig," (National Sports Shooting Foundation, 2011). https://www.youtube.com/watch?v=ZRCjY-GtROY. Retrieved January 5th, 2021.
[713] Kleck. "Large-Capacity Magazines and the Casualty Counts in Mass Shootings: The Plausibility of Linkages," 43, Table 3.
[714] Id., 44.

In light of the foregoing information, it is unlikely that the larger number of rounds fired in the average LCM-linked mass shooting found by Koper (2004) was in any sense caused by the use of LCMs. In all but one of such cases in the period from 1994 through 2013, there was nothing impossible or even difficult about the shooter firing equally large numbers of rounds even if he had possessed only smaller capacity magazines, since the same number of rounds could easily have been fired with smaller detachable magazines of the sort that would remain legally available under LCM bans. Instead, the larger number of rounds fired by LCM-using shooters is more likely to reflect the more lethal intentions prevailing among such shooters.[715]

Considering the foregoing in toto, one is forced to conclude that, notwithstanding their prevalence in the marketplace, semiautomatic firearms, so-called "large capacity" magazines, and so-called "assault weapons" have not produced a spike in either gun violence or gun fatalities. Nor have they wholly, or even disproportionately, displaced other firearms deemed less threatening by firearms prohibitionists as implements of crime.

Koper, *et al.* assert that "[t]rend analysis … indicate that high capacity semiautomatics have grown from 33 to 112% as a share of crime guns since the expiration of the Federal ban – a trend that has coincided with recent growth in shootings nationwide."[716] One interpretation of this could be that this growth is attributable to criminals seeking out such weapons as more useful in the pursuit of their criminal enterprises than other arms, but a simpler explanation is indicated, one hinted at by the circumstances of the early 20th Century ax murders alluded to above:

---

[715] *Id.*, 44.

[716] Koper, *et. al.* "Criminal Use of Assault Weapons and High-Capacity Semiautomatic Firearms," 313.

The use of an ax in almost every case was perhaps not so remarkable in itself; while there certainly was an unusual concentration of ax killings in the Midwest at this time, almost every family in rural districts owned such an implement, and often left it lying in their yard; as such, it might be considered a weapon of convenience.[717]

In other words, the perpetrators of the early 20th Century ax murders resorted to axes as the weapon of choice because they were commonly owned, not the reverse. As Koper and Reedy state,

During recent decades, there has been a shift away from production of revolvers to production of semiautomatic pistols in the civilian handgun market. Pistols grew from 28% of handgun production in 1973 to 46% by 1985 and to 80% by 1993. This trend is also apparent in criminal weaponry, as pistols have overtaken revolvers as the predominant type of handgun used in crime.[718]

In 2017, Koper *et al.* stated that "[s]emi-automatic weapons and LCMs and/or other military-style features are common among models produced in the contemporary gun market."[719] Only a small fraction of these, or any, firearms are ever used in criminal attacks. Likewise, only a tiny fraction of legal gun owners use their firearms, of whatever type, unlawfully. As to those few who do use firearms unlawfully, there is no more reason to believe that these offenders would have killed fewer people had they been forced to resort to other weapons than there is to believe that the ax murders discussed above were provoked to kill by the existence or presence of axes. The

---

[717] Dash, 657.
[718] Reedy and Koper, 151.
[719] Koper *et. al.*, "Criminal Use of Assault Weapons and High-Capacity Semiautomatic Firearms," 314.

perpetrators of both groups were men determined to kill who, in carrying out their intention, resorted to a familiar implement ready to hand, be it an ax or a commonly owned firearm.

That those determined to kill will not be deterred by proscription of firearms, but will simply resort to other available instruments as their weapon of choice, appears to be confirmed by the experience of another society about as different from the United States politically and culturally as can be: the former Soviet Union. In a 2007 article in the *Harvard Journal of Law and Public Policy*, Don B. Kates and Gary Mauser noted that

> Since at least 1965, the false assertion that the United States has the industrialized world's highest murder rate has been an artifact of politically motivated Soviet minimization designed to hide the true homicide rates. Since well before that date, the Soviet Union possessed extremely stringent gun controls that were effectuated by a police state apparatus providing stringent enforcement. So successful was that regime that few Russian civilians now have firearms and very few murders involve them. Yet, manifest success in keeping its people disarmed did not prevent the Soviet Union from having far and away the highest murder rate in the developed world! In the 1960s and early 1970s, the gunless Soviet Union's murder rates paralleled or generally exceeded those of gun-ridden America. While American rates stabilized and then steeply declined, however, Russian murder increased so drastically that by the early 1990s the Russian rate was three times higher than that of the United States.[720]

---

[720] Don B. Kates and Gary Mauser. "Would Banning Firearms Reduce Murder and Suicide? A Review of International and Some Domestic Evidence." *Harvard Journal of Law and Public Policy*, Volume 30 Number 2, Spring 2007, 650 – 651.

Based upon analysis of data made available following the dissolution of the USSR, William Pridemore observed in 2001 that

> the annual homicide victimization rate in Russia has been comparable with or greater than the rate in the United States for at least the past three and a half decades. The US rate was slightly higher from 1965 to 1975, and the Russian rate was then higher until 1985. However, with the exception of a slight dip in US rates in the mid-1970s, the homicide victimization rates in both countries followed remarkably similar patterns from the mid-1960s until the dramatic changes in Russia in the mid- to late-1980s.[721]

Russia's experience seems to bear out Gary Kleck's observation that "where guns are scarce other weapons are substituted in killings."[722] Thus it is very likely that to the extent that semiautomatic weapons, "large capacity" magazines, and AR-15 style rifles have become more prevalent as weapons in criminal assaults, such increase is simply because these weapons are more popular in the culture at large, exist in larger numbers, and happen therefore more often to be the weapon at hand, and that had such firearms *not* been available, the killers would have resorted to implements.

Surplus to Requirements: Why So-Called High Capacity Magazines and Other "Assault Weapon" Features are Irrelevant in Crime – Even Mass Shootings

A few years ago a satirical television ad spoofed high-end luxury watches. In it, the narrator recited a litany of the watches' advanced features suitable for various high-adventure applications.

---

[721] William Alex Pridemore. "Using Newly Available Homicide Data to Debunk Two Myths About Violence in an International Context." *Homicide Studies*, Vol. 5 No. 3, August 2001, 271.

[722] Gary Kleck, *Targeting Guns: Firearms and their Control* (Aldine De Gruyter, 1997), 20.

Building to a crescendo, he then rhetorically asked, "what will you do with it [the watch]?" Answering his own question, the narrator then delivered the punch line: *probably just tell time*. The advertisement was using this tongue-in-cheek approach as a lead-in to an offer of financial management services (don't waste your money, invest it instead). But as with most humor, the advertisement contained a germ of truth, as attested by luxury watch blogger Ariel Adams, who wrote that owners of high-end watches don't actually much use their most beloved "complications."[723]

Much the same applies to criminals who use firearms for violent purposes – even mass shooters. Criminals simply do not need the features that gun prohibitionists find so frightening to carry out their wicked intentions, while gun owners using their firearms for legitimate applications do use them.

One commentator recently observed that "[b]ased on recent history, it doesn't make a difference if a mass shooter is using a rifle or handgun … 'You can cause severe damage with any kind of gun.'"[724]

Not only a firearm, but nearly any weapon, in the hands of an attacker who confronts an *unarmed* victim enjoys a correlation of force so one-sidedly in favor of the assailant as to be nearly insuperable. Consider the example of the Malay *amokers*, armed only with edged weapons, where those who attempted to disarm them were slain or grievously wounded themselves. A firearm enables a latter-day *amoker* to multiply victims, to be sure. But the type of firearm is largely irrelevant, so long as it is a reasonably modern repeating arm of some kind. Essentially, the criminal on a rampage shoots fish in a barrel: his victims are at close range and helpless, so

---

[723] Ariel Adams. "Top Five Ironies Of High-End Watches." *Forbes*, August 15th, 2013. https://www.forbes.com/sites/arieladams/2013/08/15/top-five-ironies-of-high-end-watches/#3aa2f94956cc. Retrieved July 13th, 2019.

[724] Alvarado, quoting David VanDriel, co-founder of Miami-based Direct Action Industries. "https://news.vice.com/en_us/article/gy9nj4/glock-pistol-omar-mateen-orlando-mass-shooting. Retrieved July 13th, 2019.

that he employs only the most basic capabilities of his weapons. The advanced "complications" of his gun lie fallow in his hands even as he slays his victims. He is as deadly with an uncontroversial shotgun or a venerable revolver as he would be with an AR-15 with its 20 or 30 round magazines, and he would kill as many with a featureless New York compliant AR-15 as one in its original configuration. As Herman Melville was able to observe about much less advanced firearms even in 1850, "Colt's patent revolvers, which, though furnished with but one tube, multiply the fatal bullets, as the naval cat-o'-nine-tails, with a cannibal cruelty, in one blow nine times multiplies a culprit's lashes."[725]

The reverse, however, is not the case: The innocent person confronted with an armed attacker requires the most powerful and effective weapon available if she is to wrest the initiative away from her assailant and either escape or overpower him. Capabilities irrelevant to the criminal, who seeks out a helpless victim unable to resist, are absolutely essential to victim hoping to turn the tables on their attacker. Restrictions on firearms capability do nothing to deter predators, while harming only the innocent.

Firearms Are Essential to Any Victim Who Hopes to Resist and Escape Unharmed, and are Often Used For that Purpose

A weapon – any weapon, be it a knife, sword, club, or gun – gives an attacker a huge advantage over an unarmed victim. Examples of the likely outcome of a contest between combatants armed with edged weapons and unarmed opponents include some of the Malay amok incidents noted above: In the case of Imam Mamat, Mamat attacked the family of Bilal Abu, who "rushed to the rescue, and received for his trouble a deep puncture wound in the region of the heart and a superficial wound on the right side: he fell never to rise again."[726] Later in the same incident another victim, Uda Majid,

---

[725] Herman Melville. *White Jacket* (Quality Paperback Book Club, 1996), 155 – 156. *White Jacket* was originally published in 1850.

"wrested the spear from [Imat] but before he could do anything received a stab in the left lung and another in the windpipe, upon which he fell."[727] A third victim, Ngah Lassam, succeeded with the assistance of his son in getting the spear away from Mamat, but at the cost of enduring a knife wound to the face.[728] A more famous example occurred during Abraham Lincoln's assassination. After John Wilkes Booth expended the single round from his pistol into the President, Major Henry Rathbone "sprang forward and tried to catch" Booth as the assassin prepared to leap to the stage below. Rathbone failed, receiving for his trouble a severe wound from Booth's secondary weapon, a knife.[729]

A victim who hopes to escape uninjured requires a weapon to counterbalance her attacker's superiority. A knife, club, or similar weapon is insufficient: at *best*, these weapons only put the victim on a level of parity with her attacker, and given a stronger or more skilled assailant, she will remain at a profound disadvantage. Even if she achieves true parity, she remains in severe danger, as any physical altercation involving cudgels or edged weapons poses a grave risk of injury to both combatants.

In short, when facing the threat of death or serious bodily injury, there is no substitute for a firearm as an instrument of self-defense. Only a firearm vests the victim with sufficient physical power to seize and retain the initiative and to overpower his attacker while minimizing the risk to himself. True, use of a firearm in self-defense carries challenges of its own, not least of which being the requirement for the fortitude and confidence necessary to actually use it. In words reminiscent of Harman's doubts noted above, Lt. Col.

---

[726] Spores, 3, quoting "Report of a case of Amok, Pulau Tiga, Lower Perak."

[727] *Id.*

[728] *Id*, 4.

[729] T.M. Harris. *The Assassination of Lincoln: A History of the Great Conspiracy* (American Citizen Company, 1892), 39. See also James L., Swanson. *Manhunt: The 12-Day Chase for Lincoln's Killer* (William Morrow, 2006), 46.

Baron De Berenger articulated this concern in his 1835 treatise on self-defense and personal safety:

> [W]hen you have procured the best pistols possible, there are two other points deserving of your grave consideration ... Say to yourself, 1ˢᵗ, On being attacked, may I rely on having sufficient firmness and self-possession to use them? 2d, If this should be the case, do I possess sufficient skill to use them to the purpose? On failing to use arms, and which robbers most likely will discover about you, additional ill-treatment may fall to your lot, on grounds of your hostile intentions, and your want of nerve to carry them into effect.[730]

Yet, many Americans *do* possess the "firmness and self-possession" to use arms for their own defense, and often do so. Just how often defensive gun uses occur is probably unknowable. For that reason, and given the passion surrounding guns in America, the issue of defensive gun use is controversial. Yet efforts have been made to ascertain how often it occurs. Among the most notable are those of Gary Kleck. In *Armed: New Perspectives on Gun Control*, he and Don B. Kates examined various surveys addressing defensive gun use. By Kleck's interpretation, all of these early surveys "imply at least 700,000 annual defensive gun uses."[731] Kleck's own research not only supports this conclusion, but shows that the early surveys understated defensive gun uses. His National Self-Defense Survey, conducted from February through April 1993, "indicate[d] that each year in the US there are about 2.2 to 2.5 million DGUs of all types by civilians against humans, with about 1.5 to 1.9 million of the incidents involving use of handguns."[732]

---

[730] Lt. Col. Baron De Berenger. *Helps and Hints how to Protect Life and Property*, (T Hurst, 1835), 125.

[731] Gary Kleck and Don B. Kates. *Armed: New Perspectives on Gun Control* (Prometheus Books, 2001), 215.

[732] Gary Kleck and Mark Gertz. "Armed Resistance to Crime: The

Kleck's results are controversial and often criticized, with some criticism going so far as to accuse gun owners of exaggerating defensive gun uses by incorporating instances from outside the survey period in their responses or even of lying outright:

> First, there is the social desirability bias. Respondents will falsely claim that their gun has been used for its intended purpose—to ward off a criminal—in order to validate their initial purchase. A respondent may also exaggerate facts to appear heroic to the interviewer. Second, there's the problem of gun owners responding strategically. Given that there are around 3 million members of the National Rifle Association (NRA) in the United States, ostensibly all aware of the debate surrounding defensive gun use, Hemenway suggested that some gun advocates will lie to help bias estimates upwards by either blatantly fabricating incidents or embellishing situations that should not actually qualify as defensive gun use. Third is the risk of false positives from 'telescoping,' where respondents may recall an actual self-defense use that is outside the question's time frame.[733]

Other critics cite competing research, such as the National Crime Victimization Survey (NCVS), characterized by some as "the gold standard of criminal victimization surveys."[734] One paper critical of Kleck that relies on the NCVS was produced by David McDowall and Brian Wiersema in 1994. By their analysis, "there were an

---

Prevalence and Nature of Self-Defense with a Gun," *Journal of Criminal Law and Criminology*, Volume 86, Issue 1, Fall 1995, 160 – 164.

[733] Evan Defilippis and Devin Hughes, "The Myth Behind Defensive Gun Ownership," *Politico*, January 14th, 2015, https://www.politico.com/magazine/story/2015/01/defensive-gun-ownership-myth-114262_full.html#.VOhWtPnF-Sp. Retrieved June 9th, 2019.

[734] *Id.*

estimated 258,460 incidents of firearm resistance" from 1987 through 1990, yielding "a mean of 64,615 annually." Correcting for police officers defensively employing their firearms in the course of their duty included in the NCVS data, McDowall and Wiersema estimated average annual civilian DGUs at 51,959.[735] However, just a few years later, "Dr. McDowall published a follow-up study in 1998 using data from the 1992 and 1994 waves of the NCVS, in which the estimate of yearly DGU was adjusted upwards to 116,000."[736]

Kleck countered this criticism in a June 2018 paper analyzing data on defensive gun uses produced for the Centers for Disease Control (CDC) Behavioral Risk Factor Surveillance System Surveys for the years 1996, 1997, and 1998 – the only years CDC seems to have gathered such data. Kleck writes:

> These three DGU counts average 1,138,534 per year for the period 1996-1998. This puts the CDC results squarely within the range of DGU estimates typically produced by the many private surveys (Kleck 2001b). This figure, however, is eighteen times larger than the number of DGUs supposedly implied by the NCVS (McDowall and Wiersema 1994). Thus, even other Federal Government surveys indicate that the NCVS "estimate" of DGU prevalence is grossly inaccurate.[737]

---

[735] David McDowall and Brian Wiersema. "The Incidence of Defensive Firearm Use by US Crime Victims, 1987 through 1990." Public Health Briefs, *American Journal of Public Health*, December 1994, Vol. 84, No. 12.

[736] Hugh Jim Bissell. "Defensive Gun Use (Part III) - The National Crime Victimization Study." *The Daily Kos*, October 3rd, 2013, citing McDowall, D., C. Loftin, and B. Wiersema, "Estimates of the Frequency of Firearm Self-Defense from the Redesigned National Crime Victimization Survey," Violence Research Group Discussion Paper 20, 1998 (unpublished report). https://www.dailykos.com/stories/2013/10/03/1242310/-Defensive-Gun-Use-Part-III-The-National-Crime-Victimization-Study. Retrieved June 9th, 2019.

[737] Gary Kleck. "What Do CDC's Surveys Say About the Frequency of Defensive Gun Uses?" (July 11, 2018), 13.

Kleck is not alone in his estimation of the scale of defensive gun usage in America. In their 1996 report *Guns in America: Results of a Comprehensive National Survey on Firearms Ownership and Use*, Philip J. Cook and Jens Ludwig wrote that "[t]he NSPOF data indicate that in 1994 at least 1.5 million adults used a gun defensively against another person, a figure that is much closer to Kleck and Gertz's 2.5 million figure than to the NCVS-based estimates."[738] Also noteworthy is a 2017 Pew Research Center survey that found "[o]ne-in-six gun owners have used a gun to defend themselves," explaining that while

> "[o]nly 1% of non-gun owners who have never owned a gun say they have used a gun to defend themselves[,] [r]oughly one-in-ten (9%) of those who have owned a gun in the past but no longer do, say they have done this. Among current gun owners, 17% say they have used a gun to defend themselves."[739]

What Does a Citizen Need in a Defensive Firearm?

Irrespective of the specific figures one accepts, large numbers of have Americans used firearms in self-defense. Given that the *Heller* decision has enshrined the right to bear arms as a Constitutionally protected individual right, firearms prohibitionists have had to concede a right to the possession of some type of gun. Nonetheless,

---

https://ssrn.com/abstract=3194685   or http://dx.doi.org/10.2139/ssrn.3194685. Retrieved July 15th, 2019.

[738] Philip Ludwig and Jens Ludwig. *Guns in America: Results of a Comprehensive National Survey on Firearms Ownership and Use* (Police Foundation, 1996), 57.

[739] Kim Parker, Juliana Menasce Horowitz, Ruth Igielnik, J. Baxter Oliphant and Anna Brown. "America's Complex Relationship With Guns," Part 2, "Guns and daily life: Identity, experiences, activities and involvement," (Pew Research Center, 2017). https://www.pewsocialtrends.org/2017/06/22/guns-and-daily-life-identity-experiences-activities-and-involvement/. Retrieved June 9th, 2019.

they continue to press for significant limitations on what arms citizens may possess for their defense. As Parkland survivor Cameron Kasky tweeted:

> "I think responsible ownership of a *small weapon* is not something that should be revoked. It should be much more difficult to get a gun than a car and there should be frequent psychological checkups, *but some weapons can protect a home. Assault weapons are not those*"[740] (emphasis added).

In a similar vein, author Stephen King opined that "[i]f you can't kill a burglar with ten shots, you need to go back to the shooting range."[741]

Are commenters such as Kasky and King correct? Are powerful firearms or those with "large" magazine capacities as unnecessary to the defensive requirements of law-abiding citizens as they are to the criminal requirements of predators? The answer is an emphatic *no*. However good a shot one is at the range, and however relentlessly Hollywood promotes "the myth of the single shot kill,"[742] the fact is that when a citizen is forced to defend herself with a firearm, the chances are good that the first shot will not hit her attacker, and further, that the first shot that does strike home will not immediately incapacitate the assailant. Multiple shots are likely to be required – all the more so when she faces multiple attackers.

---

[740] Cameron Kasky, March 27th, 2018. https://twitter.com/cameron_kasky/status/978627390493650944. Retrieved June 6th, 2019.

[741] Stephen King. "Stephen King: why the US must introduce limited gun controls." *The Guardian*, February 1st, 2013. https://www.theguardian.com/books/2013/feb/01/stephen-king-pulled-book-gun-controls. Retrieved June 9th, 2019.

[742] Dr. Jim Kornberg. "The Myth of the Single Shot Kill." *TrueWest*, July 17th, 2019. https://truewestmagazine.com/the-myth-of-the-single-shot-kill/. Retrieved June 9th, 2019.

So-Called "High Capacity" Magazines are Critical to Effective Self-Defense with a Firearm

A 2014 study published in the *International Journal of Police Science & Management* analyzed the firearms accuracy of expert, intermediate, and novice shooters drawn from among various police training programs. Their skill was tested at various distances under controlled circumstances at a firing range. The study found that novice shooters had a 75% rate of accuracy at 3 to 15 feet, while intermediate and expert shooters achieved an average accuracy of 84% and 88%, respectively, at those ranges; at 18 – 45 feet the rates were 37.95%, 40.85%, and 27.60%; and at 60 – 75 feet accuracy rates were 14.06%, 12.68%, and 5.56%.[743] Overall average rates of accuracy for expert shooters was 49.26%, 48.20% for intermediate shooters, and 39.91% for novice shooters. Thus, even under the controlled, low-stress circumstances of this firing range study, shooters of all skill levels miss the target a substantial portion of the time.

Army marksmanship research shows that soldiers firing rifles are more proficient marksmen than these police cadets presumably firing pistols, but even military marksmanship falls short of theoretical estimates. The Army opines that "[t]esting and development indicates that the soldier should hit at least 39 of 40 targets if he applies the marksmanship fundamentals correctly (assuming that target mechanisms have been checked and are functioning)."[744] Thus, under ideal conditions, for a soldier applying marksmanship fundamentals correctly with each shot, the probability of hitting a target at 200 meters would be .99; it would be .95 at 250 meters; and it would be .90 at 300 meters.[745] Obviously,

---

[743] William J. Lewinski, Ron Avery, Jennifer Dysterheft, Nathan D. Dicks, and Jacob Bushy. "The real risks during deadly police shootouts: Accuracy of the naïve shooter." *International Journal of Police Science & Management*, 2015, Vol. 17(2), 121.

[744] *FM 3-22.9*, (April 2003, with changes 1 – 4), 6-11.

[745] *Id.*, 6-11 – 6-12, Table 6-1.

marksmanship qualification in the real world does not occur under ideal conditions and soldiers will not properly apply marksmanship fundamentals all of the time; recognizing this, the Army has found that where "an adequate unit training program is conducted,"[746] a soldier with an average Probability of Hit, has a hit probability at 150 meters of .90, at 200 meters of .70, at 250 meters of .60, and at 300 meters of .50; while for soldiers with a high Probability of Hit, hit probabilities are .95 at 150 meters, .90 at 200 meters, .85 at 250 meters, and .80 at 300 meters.[747]

Self-defense shootings do not occur in the antiseptic, low-stress conditions of the firing range, and in real world defensive shootings, accuracy suffers, as the authors of the police cadet study attest:

> a majority of gunfights and critical situations will likely involve multiple shots being fired in close proximity, usually within only 3-15 ft of the suspect … A study of officer-involved shootings in Philadelphia revealed that the average distance between the suspect and officer during a shooting incident was a mere 3.52 ft … Additional research supports this lack of accuracy, indicating that when police officers use deadly force, they more often they miss the target than actually hit the target … Although hit rates across different police agencies vary, officer hit rates often do not exceed 50% during officer-involved shootings … In a national survey completed by the Dallas Police Department (1992), hit rates were recorded as low as 25% in some locations. A study examining officer-involved shootings found that as the distance between suspects and officers increased beyond 3 ft, noninjurious

---

[746] *Id.*, 6-12.
[747] *Id.*, 6-12, Table 6-2.

shooting (to the suspect) increased from 9% to over 45% (in the 4-20 ft range) ...[748]

In aggregating the results of a number of studies, Koper produced similar results, reporting that

> a study of handgun assaults in one city revealed a 31% hit rate per shot, based on the sum totals of all shots fired and wounds inflicted ... Other studies have yielded hit rates per shot ranging from 8% in gunfights with police ... to 50% in mass murders ... Even police officers, who are presumably certified and regularly re-certified as proficient marksman and who are almost certainly better shooters than are average gun offenders, hit their targets with only 22% to 39% of their shots. [749]

Firearms expert Massad Ayoob gives us a striking illustration of just how difficult it can be to hit and disable an assailant when firing under conditions of extreme stress:

> An illustrative, real world example is the case of Susan Gonzalez. She and her husband were attacked by two intruders within their home one night. The attackers shot both of them multiple times, but she was able to escape to their bedroom where she located her husband's semiautomatic pistol, while her husband bravely physically fought the attackers off into the front room. She entered the room where the attackers were struggling with her husband, and, not wanting to shoot her husband, discharged three warning shots in the air, hoping the attackers would flee. They did not. One attacker charged toward her, causing her to flee back to the bedroom. From an opening in the

---

[748] Lewinski, *et. al.*, 118.
[749] Koper, *Updated Assessment of the Federal Assault Weapons Ban*, 83.

bedroom she could see the attacker lying in wait for her in the kitchen. So she used her knowledge of the house to exit the bedroom from [sic] and approach the attacker from behind via another door leading to the kitchen. She pointed the pistol at the attacker and discharged seven rounds in his direction, gravely wounding him, but not immediately killing him. The wounded attacker was still able to exit the house aided by his accomplice. The other attacker reentered the house and demanded Mr. Gonzalez give him keys to an automobile to escape. During his search for keys in the bedroom he located Mrs. Gonzalez who was out of ammunition. He put the gun to her temple and demanded the keys, which she gave him. Fortunately, the attacker decided to spare Mrs. Gonzalez's life, but he could have just as easily pulled the trigger. Had she had more rounds in her magazine, maybe she would not have had to leave her fate to chance. It is impossible to say how many more cases where victims lost (or almost lost, as in Mrs. Gonzalez's case), due to having an insufficient amount of ammunition readily available in a self-defense firearm. The published account of this shooting has Mrs. Gonzalez firing three shots into the ceiling, then seven at the homicidal intruder, and then running dry. This would indicate only ten cartridges at her disposal. The gunfight occurred during the ten-year period when the Federal "high capacity magazine ban" was in force. The Ruger 9mm pistol she used, designed to hold fifteen cartridges in the magazine and one more in the firing chamber, was sold during that ten year period of that ban with magazines which could only hold ten rounds. In such a situation, five more shots can make the difference between neutralizing the murderous threat, and being rendered helpless with an empty gun at the hands of a law-breaking, homicidal, heavily armed felon.[750]

As Mrs. Gonzales' experience makes clear, it is only law abiding citizens that are disadvantaged by arbitrary limitations on magazine capacity. She needed every one of the fifteen rounds that her firearm was designed to hold; the arbitrary 10-round limit imposed by law could easily have killed her, and only the caprice of her attacker saved her. Granted, had she not fired the three warning shots into the ceiling of her home, she would have had those rounds to fire at the second attacker when he came for her car keys, but "[d]etached reflection cannot be demanded in the presence of" a pair of violent home invaders any more than it can be expected in the face of an "uplifted knife."[751] As Ayoob observes,

> [t]he loss of time for a magazine change is generally of little consequence for the attacker. This is because it is the attacker who gets to choose when, where, how, and whom to attack. So the attacker is not burdened by the surprise and shock factor that the victim is.[752]

Having chosen the time and place of his attack with an eye toward minimizing the chance of resistance, the attacker likely need not fire numerous rounds to accomplish his aim. By contrast, Ms. Gonzales' terrifying experience establishes that the innocent person on the receiving end of such an attack faces a much more difficult task: *she must use her own firearm to wrest the initiative from her attacker and then overpower him – and she must do so under the extreme emotional and psychological stress of a surprise attack.*

---

[750] Declaration of Massad Ayoob in Support of Motion for Preliminary Injunction, *San Francisco Veteran Police Officers Association, et al., v. The City and County of San Francisco, et al.*, US District Court for the Northern District of California, San Francisco Division, Case No. 13-CV-13-5351, Document 17, filed December 27th, 2013, paragraphs 5 – 9.
[751] *Brown v. United States*, 256 US 335, 41 S.Ct. 501, 65 L.Ed. 961, 18 A.L.R. 1276 (1921).
[752] Ayoob. *Declaration*, paragraph 28.

Limiting magazine capacity may substantially impair the ability of the defender to overcome her assailants' advantages in initiative and armament, but it will do nothing to impede the criminal, even in mass shooting scenarios. As Kleck explains,

> there is considerable evidence that people who commit large-scale shootings, unlike most ordinary aggressors, devote considerable advance planning to their crimes. Part of their preparations entails cumulating multiple guns, multiple magazines, and many rounds of ammunition. The significance of this is that, in cases where the shooter has more than one loaded gun, he can continue firing, without significant pause, even without LCMs, simply by switching to a loaded gun. Alternatively, if he has multiple small magazines rather than LCMs, the shooter can continue firing many rounds with only a 2- to 4-[second] pause between shots for switching magazines.[753]

Ayoob concurs, pointing out that

> [c]riminals bent on causing harm ... even assuming they were impeded from obtaining magazines holding over ten rounds ... could simply arm themselves with multiple weapons, and often do.   Criminals have time to assess and plan shootings, whereas victims do not. Whitman, the Texas Tower mass murderer, literally brought a large box of rifles, handguns, a shotgun and ammunition to his sniper perch. Harris and Klebold had four firearms between them at Columbine. Holmes in Aurora brought a rifle, shotgun, and pistol into the theater. Hassan was armed with a pistol and a revolver at the Fort Hood

---

[753] Kleck. "Large-Capacity Magazines and the Casualty Counts in Mass Shootings: The Plausibility of Linkages," 41.

[sic]. Lanza entered the elementary school in Newtown, Connecticut, armed with a rifle and two pistols, leaving a shotgun in his car. The mass murderer Cho entered Virginia Tech armed with two pistols and a backpack full of magazines. None of these murderers' victims had planned to repel an attack by a perpetrator with multiple firearms. The likelihood of the mass murderer arriving on scene with multiple firearms also largely negates the theory that with fewer rounds in the gun, the killer could be more easily disarmed and subdued by unarmed citizens when he first ran empty, before he could reload. Hassan, Holmes, Lanza, or Cho simply could have drawn a second (or third) gun that they had on their persons and shot whoever attempted to grab the empty one.[754]

Ayoob also contrasts the advantages that the attacker enjoys with the plight of the assailant's victims:

The homeowner who keeps a defensive firearm and is awakened in the night by an intruder is most unlikely to have time to gather spare ammunition. The sudden and unpredictable nature of such attacks, and their occurring in relatively confined spaces, generally do not permit gathering multiple firearms or magazines. Ideally, one hand would be occupied with the handgun itself, and the other, with a telephone to call the police. And, assuming they even had time for a magazine change, most people do not sleep wearing clothing that would allow them to stow spare magazines, etc. on their person. They would have only what was in the gun … The virtuous citizen, by contrast, cannot practically be expected to have accessible that many guns or that much ammunition

---

[754] Ayoob. *Declaration*, paragraphs 19 – 22, internal citations omitted.

at a moment's notice. The victimized citizen is the one who is, therefore, most deleteriously impacted by the magazine capacity limitation. If he or she must use the gun to protect self and family, they will most likely have only the ammunition in the gun with which to fend off determined, perhaps multiple, attackers. Virtuous citizens buy their guns to protect themselves from the same criminals police carry guns to protect the citizens, the public, and themselves from. Therefore, armed citizens have historically modeled their choice of firearms on what police carry. The vast majority of California law enforcement agencies, including those in the Bay Area, carry pistols with double-stack magazines whose capacities exceed those of the San Francisco ordinance.[755]

There is evidence that higher magazine capacity may correlate to higher rates of survivability for victims fending off attack. Dr. J. Eric Dietz of the Purdue Homeland Security Institute has begun modeling the impact of various magazine capacities on victim survivability in these scenarios, with preliminary results indicating that higher capacity magazines do correlate to higher survival probability. According to Dr. Deitz, in a home defense scenario involving a home owner confronted by two armed home invaders,

> we found that magazine capacity does have a significant effect on the survivability of the homeowner who is facing this kind of an event … at a seven round magazine we saw that the homeowner was at just under 30% survivability … but if we expand the magazine capacity to 30 rounds we observed that the homeowner [had] a survivability of just over 60%.[756]

---

[755] *Id.*, paragraphs 15 – 17, 23.
[756] J. Eric Dietz, PhD, PE, Director, Purdue Homeland Security Institute & Professor, Computer and Information Technology, Purdue University.

Regarding magazine capacity, "[c]urrent [and proposed] restrictions on 'high capacity' magazines are not only ineffective but dangerous. *Standard magazines designed for the weapon in question are the most effective tools for lawful defense*" (emphasis added).[757]

A Powerful Firearm is Necessary for Effective Self-Defense

Next we turn to Kasky's assertion, above, that a "small weapon," but not an "assault weapon," can be useful in defending a home.[758] Addressing the advisable means to respond to an assault, Lt. Col. De Berenger observed that "as no one can foresee what may follow such a beginning, the quest must ever be the best way of putting a stop to it; for such reasons do I advise your inflicting a very determined, a very severe blow."[759] Stopping an attack as early in its progress as possible is of critical importance. For although criminals generally seek out weak victims unlikely to resist, and while many criminals may be deterred and retreat when faced with the prospect of firm resistance, both Harman and De Berenger – not to mention the harrowing experience of Mrs. Gonzales, discussed above – warn us that such will not always case. Some criminals, once engaged, may not withdraw. Therefore, when appealing to a firearm for defense, it is critical that it be powerful enough to end the attack.

Any firearm can inflict injury on a human being – comparatively little power is required for that. According *Wound*

"High-Capacity Save Lives," NRATV, *Cam & Co*, S15, E103. June 6th, 2019, 1:25 – 2:36. https://www.nratv.com/videos/cam-and-company-2019-j-eric-dietz-research-suggests-high-capacity-magazines-save-lives?utm_source=nratv&utm_campaign=daily_20190608&utm_medium=email&utm_content=body. Retrieved June 14th, 2019.

[757] Matthew Larosiere. *Losing Count: The Empty Case for "High-Capacity" Magazine Restrictions* CATO Center for Constitutional Studies, Legal Policy Bulletin, July 17, 2018, Number 3, 13.

[758] Kasky.

[759] De Berenger, 164.

Ballistics, an extensive report prepared by the Surgeon General of the Army based upon injury data accumulated during the Second World War and the Korean War,

> [t]he designer of a shell or bomb … has adopted an arbitrary criterion of 58 ft-lb of kinetic energy as determining a fragment which is capable of producing a human casualty … So far, the arbitrary criterion of 58 ft-lb of energy for an effective wound-producing missile has proved to be reasonable. It provides the basis upon which the relative effectiveness of antipersonnel agents may be compared.[760]

The science of wound ballistics has advanced considerably since then, of course.[761] Nonetheless, the 58 ft-lb rule is reasonable for our purposes. Various estimates for the kinetic energy of a .22 LR (long rifle) projectile range from 50 ft-lbs[762], to 93 ft-lbs (standard velocity) or 100 ft-lbs (high velocity) fired from a pistol[763] to 85 and

---

[760] James C. Beyer, Major MC (Editor). *Wound Ballistics* (Office of the Surgeon General, Department of the Army, 1962), page 107.

[761] According to a 1991 report by the Ballistic Research Laboratory, Aberdeen Proving Ground, Maryland, "[p]rior to about 1960, various simple rules for predicting casualties existed. Probably the best known and most widely misused casualty criterion is the so-called 58 ft-lb rule. This rule of thumb, established around the turn of the century, states that missiles having at least 58 ft-lbs of kinetic energy will produce a casualty. In the years since about 1960, correlations have been established between P(I/H) for a standard set of fragments and various ballistic parameters (mas, velocity, etc.). Due to the complex behavior exhibited by bullets, estimates of bullet incapacitation have been obtained by firing the bullet of interest into a gelatin tissue simulant and then relating the kinetic energy deposited to some previously determined empirical relationship between energy deposit in gelatin …" David N. Neades and Russell N. Prather. *The Modelling and Application of Small Arms Wound Ballistics*, (Ballistic Research Laboratory, Aberdeen Proving Ground, Maryland, August 1991), 5 – 6.

[762] Hatcher. *Textbook of Pistols and Revolvers*, 322.

[763] *NRA Fact Book*, 261.

92 ft-lbs (standard and high velocity, respectively) fired from a rifle.[764] It is well known that a .22LR bullet can produce a casualty; a victim shot with a .22LR round will be gravely injured and may die. But can the .22LR round, when fired defensively by the victim at his attacker, be relied upon to consistently produce a significant enough injury to incapacitate an attacker quickly enough to prevent the assailant from further injuring his victim? This question was effectively answered *in the negative* by Colonel Louis A. LaGarde, US Army Medical Department, more than 100 years ago. In his classic treatise *Gunshot Injuries,* Colonel LaGarde addressed the incapacitating effects of small arms bullets, basing his comments upon both experimental observations and anecdotes from the war in the Philippines and elsewhere. Repeating the experiences of British and American officers, Colonel LaGarde shows how arms much more powerful than the .22LR can fail to immediately incapacitate an adversary. Relating experiences reported by the British in the Wizirestan Chitral Expeditions of 1895, he writes that "'[m]any of the enemy in these two campaigns continued to advance and fight after receipt of from one to six wounds by Lee-Metford bullets.' These bullets were only effective upon striking vital parts or parts concerned in bodily activity."[765] Turning to American experiences in the Philippines, LaGarde reports that

> [o]ur own officers have repeatedly reported in a
> similar way against the effectiveness of the Krag-
> Jorgensen bullet in the Philippine Campaigns. Colonel
> Winter and Captain McAndrew, Medical Corps, USA,
> have related the following incident … In 1907 a Moro
> charged the guard at Jolo P.I. When he was within
> 100 yards, the entire guard opened fire on him. When
> he had reached within 5 yards of the firing party he
> stumbled and fell and while in the prone position a
> trumpeter killed him by shooting through the head

---

[764] *Id.,* 264.

[765] Colonel Louis A. LaGarde *Gunshot Wounds: How they are Inflicted, their Complications and Treatment.* (William Wood and Company, 1914), 66.

with a .45 caliber Colt's revolver. There were ten wounds in his body from the service rifle. Three of the wounds were located in the chest, one in the abdomen, and the remainder had taken effect in the extremities. There were no bones broken.[766]

As Colonel LaGarde dryly observed, "[t]he stopping power of firearms is of vital importance on certain occasions ... *For personal encounters in self-defense, it is useless to carry anything but an effective weapon*"[767] (emphasis added). "Because the stopping power of our .38-caliber Colt's revolver [the standard US Army sidearm at that time] had failed us on numerous occasions in the Philippines and elsewhere," Colonel LaGarde writes, "the War Department constituted a board in 1904 composed of Col. John T. Thompson and [Colonel LaGarde] as medical member, to conduct a series of tests with bullets of different size, weight and other characteristics, to determine upon a bullet that should have the stopping power and shock effect at short ranges, necessary for the military service."[768] Tests consisted of firing into ten cadavers suspended by the neck, sixteen beeves and two horses.[769] The tests against living animals revealed that

> [a]s one might suppose, all shots against vital parts from whatever arm showed an immediate stopping power. [However], [f]or shots in non-vital parts like lungs, liver, intestines, etc. ... the shock or stopping power increased with the sectional area of the missile and it was notably less with smaller sectional area projectiles although they possessed far more energy."[770]

Comparing the .45 Colt, 9mm Parabellum, and other pistol rounds then in use, LaGarde found that "[t]he animals invariably

---

[766] *Id.*, 66 – 67.
[767] *Id.*, 62 – 66.
[768] *Id.*, 67.
[769] *Id.*, 68.
[770] *Id.*, 69.

dropped to the ground when shot from three to five times with the larger caliber Colt's revolver bullets and they failed in every instance to drop when as many as ten shots of the smaller jacketed bullets from the Colt's automatic and Luger pistol bullets had been delivered against the lungs and abdomen."[771] LaGarde's findings clearly show that stopping power varies widely from round to round and that a single shot cannot necessarily be relied upon to bring down a target. Nonetheless, his work has its limitations, which Evan P. Marshall and Edwin J. Sanow point out in their 1992 book *Handgun Stopping Power: The Definitive Study*:

> The Thompson-LaGarde study was seriously flawed. Thompson and LaGarde based their conclusion[s] on the results of shooting live steers and human cadavers ... The resistance of dead human flesh, of course, differs substantially from that of live human tissue. As a result, any attempt to evaluate penetration and/or tissue damage from dead human flesh is largely invalid ... The shooting of live steers was also of extremely limited value. First, steers of varying weights and sexes were included in the testing. Second, multiple shots were included. This meant that the study evaluated the effectiveness of two rounds of one load versus three rounds of another. Third, the steers were incapable of understanding what was happening and articulating their concerns, which meant that one could not effectively measure the results of individual shots on the steers (That statement may sound strange, but some of our best insights into the incapacitating effect of nonlethal gunfire has come from debriefing police officers who were shot and later recovered). Fourth, steers are much harder to kill than humans, so applying the results of shooting animals to how particular handgun

---

[771] *Id.*, 72.

loads would work against humans was a hopeless task.[772]

To address these shortcomings, Marshall and Sanow carried out their own study. Focusing only on pistol ammunition, they sought to ascertain how effective various combinations of loads, calibers and projectiles were in stopping an assailant with a single shot. Their data set consisted entirely of real world shootings meeting a raft of stringent requirements, including, among others, the following:

> 1. Only torso shots were used. I didn't think it was a fair indication of any round's stopping power to include shootings where the victim was hit in the hand and continued to pursue his antisocial activities, and then log this as a failure.
> 2. Multiple hits were also discarded. Again, I didn't consider it a true indication of any rounds performance to include instances where the victim took three hollowpoints to the chest and collapsed. How could we include these along with cases where one round was effective? If I included multiple hits, then this study could legitimately be attacked on the grounds that multiple hits are not a reliable indicator as to any round's stopping power.
> 3. A stop is defined as follows: if the victim was assaulting someone, he collapsed without being able to fire another shot or strike another blow. If he was fleeing, he collapsed within 10 feet.
> ...
> 5. A minimum of five shootings were required before a handgun load was included in this study. Fortunately, in most instances I was able to obtain much more than that, and the actual number of

---

[772] Evan P. Marshall and Edwin J. Sanow. *Handgun Stopping Power: The Definitive Study* (Paladin Press 1992), 13.

shootings using each load (at the time of publication) is listed in the results.[773]

The results of their study are illuminating. For the two loads of the diminutive .32 Auto analyzed, the rounds achieved a first shot stop 50% of the time (full metal jacket – FMJ – round), and 59% of the time (hollow point), respectively.[774] Their analysis of the results of various loads of .380 FMJ and hollow point rounds showed first shot stops achieved from 54.21% to 63.82% of the time;[775].38 Special +P and +P+ rounds including many hollow point projectiles achieved first shot stops between 52.28% and 72.78% percent of the time;[776] 9mm +P and +P+ rounds, again including many hollow points, achieved first shot stops from 60.81% - to 89.28% of the time;[777] the first shot stop rate for .357 magnum with various projectiles ranged from 67.60% - 96.05%;[778].44 Magnum achieved first shot stop rates of 73.58% - 87.87%; and.45 Auto and +P achieved first shot stop rates ranging from 60.72% - 88.37%.[779] Examining the efficacy of strictly non-hollow point rounds, they found first shot stop rates ranging as follows: .380 Auto, 51.25% - 57.14%;.38 Special and +P, 52.28% - 58.06%; 9mm, 60.81% – 82.35%; .357 Magnum, 67.60% - 73.39%; and .45 Auto, 60.72% - 64.02%.[780]

Overall, Marshall and Sanow's study shows that for handgun calibers, a substantial portion of assailants will not be stopped on the first hit, but that more powerful rounds have a greater chance of stopping an assailant on the first shot than lesser powered rounds.

---

[773] *Id.*, 43 and 44.
[774] *Id*, 48.
[775] *Id.*, 50.
[776] *Id.*, 55.
[777] *Id.*, 62.
[778] *Id.*, 75.
[779] *Id.*, 92.
[780] *Id.*, 115.

Implications for the AR-15 as a Defensive Weapon

The implications of the foregoing for the use of the AR-15 as a home defense weapon are profound. First, it is clear from the data reviewed above that armed resistance plays an important role in limiting the damage done by armed assailants. Koper has noted that

> studies have yielded hit rates per shot ranging from 8% in gunfights with police to 50% in mass murders. Even police officers, who are presumably certified and regularly re-certified as proficient marksman and who are almost certainly better shooters than are average gun offenders, hit their targets with only 22% to 39% of their shots.[781]

The remarkable disparity in hit rates for mass killers (50%) compared to police (8% or 22% to 39%) reflects the impact of armed opposition on shooting accuracy. Mass shooters (and other criminals) expect to do their killing unopposed, having selected targets and victims unlikely to present them with vigorous armed resistance to their onslaught from the outset, and can, therefore, shoot at their leisure, taking as good aim as they care to. By contrast, unfortunate and sensationalized aberrations notwithstanding, police do not make a habit of seeking out unarmed and helpless victims for the purpose of shooting them down. When police fire their weapons, they usually do so in the face of armed opposition, resulting in the lower hit rates cited. *But the impact goes both ways*: The criminal assailants themselves will hit their targets at lower rates as well in the face of armed resistance, reducing the number of casualties they may inflict. Also noteworthy is one of the findings of Hayes and Hayes, who wrote that "increasing the number of security guards greatly decreases the number of people shot. There is a large reduction in the number of people wounded or killed when the first security guard is added to

---

[781] Koper. *Updated Assessment of the Federal Assault Weapons Ban*, 83.

the simulation."[782] Reflecting Craig's concept of *Unequal Initiative* discussed above, Hayes and Hayes do add that

> "there is a smaller reduction in the number of people shot for every new security guard added. This is because the gunman acts first and is likely to shoot somebody on his first turn. Even if a guard is close by, the gunman has the element of surprise and is able to shoot somebody before the guard can react."[783]

Hayes and Hayes try hard to minimize the implications of their own findings, cautioning that

> [t]he results of the model cannot be used to promote adding security guards. There are numerous factors that determine a security guard's effectiveness, from training to combat experience. Therefore, a prototypical 'highly trained' guard was simulated to examine the nonlinear effects that arise as guards are added to the simulation. *Although the model determines adding security guards is the number one way of decreasing casualties*, it does not take into account the varying skills that security guards will have. Therefore, this finding cannot be used to promote adding additional security guards[784] (emphasis added).

Notwithstanding this disclaimer, Hayes and Hayes' results, like Dietz's preliminary findings on magazine capacity, provide a tantalizing indication as to the efficacy of armed resistance in limiting the lethality of criminal attacks.

The data indicate that a large percentage of shots will fail to hit their targets – particularly shots fired in the face of armed opposition. The data also shows that of those assailants that are hit, a

---

[782] Hayes and Hayes, paragraph 4.2
[783] *Id.*
[784] *Id*, paragraph 5.4

substantial portion will not be stopped on the first hit. But while magazine capacity has no demonstrable impact on the number of injuries that an attacker will inflict, it does seem to improve the defender's chances of repulsing the attack; for whereas the attacker is likely to have brought additional magazines or firearms, the defender likely has easy access to the ammunition in the magazine inserted in his weapon and no more. Together with the degrading impact facing an armed attacker has on the defender's own hit ratio, this places the defender at a profound disadvantage – a disadvantage that can be offset by the defender's use of so-called "high capacity" magazines. This likely explains Dietz's preliminary finding of a doubling of survivability rates for defenders equipped with 30 round magazines vice seven round magazines.[785] Thus, larger magazine capacity likely does nothing to either limit or enhance the attacker's lethality, but likely does enable a defender to continue to resist for a longer period. Likewise, more powerful ammunition provides a material increase in the chances of disabling the attacker early in the encounter.

These findings have major implications for the effectiveness of the AR-15 rifle as a defensive weapon. Contrary to the claims of gun control activists, three attributes of the AR-15 render it admirably suited to this role: The first is superior accuracy. The contrast between the shooting accuracy of soldiers equipped with rifles as compared to police cadets, presumably firing handguns, indicates that a homeowner equipped with AR-15 is much more likely to hit his attacker when firing defensively than someone defending themselves with a handgun. Second, an AR-15 or semiautomatic AK-47 equipped with a standard 30 round magazine gives a defender two or three times as many shots as a handgun equipped with a standard 7, 15 or 17 round magazine (depending on the handgun model); given the high miss-rates when shooting in the face of armed opposition, these extra rounds are decisively important to a citizen defending his home. Finally, as LaGarde, Evans and Sanow and others have shown, more powerful rounds are much more likely to stop an attacker on the first hit, again giving a defender

---

[785] Dietz.

equipped with an AR-15 chambered in .223 Remington or 5.56mm, or an AK-47 chambered in 7.62x39mm a much greater chance of quickly disabling his assailant than he would have with a handgun chambered in a standard pistol caliber.

The Unusual Case of Unlawful Combatants

Heretofore we have set out certain general principles that set *violent crime* apart as a phenomenon separate and distinct from *infantry combat*, in particular the principle that the typical criminal is not so much interested in achieving fire superiority over an opposing force as he is finding victims who cannot offer meaningful resistance of any kind, so that from the perspective of the criminal virtually any weapon will serve his purpose, and especially any firearm.

We all know that exceptions exist to every general rule. We have already noted one such exception pertaining to violent criminals: while criminals ordinarily seek helpless victims and will usually avoid potential targets that might fight back, this calculus sometimes changes once the attacker has initiated contact with his victim and found the victim to armed. While many criminals will attempt to break contact and withdraw in this scenario, some will choose to carry the assault through to the end once the battle is joined – hence the need of the law abiding citizen for a powerful and effective weapon with which to break the attacker's momentum and regain the initiative.

Another exception to the general rule is the case of "unlawful combatants" – actors willing to wage war on the state or on other powerful armed competitors. The typical criminal has no political motive and no desire to cross swords with those able to overpower him; he attacks simply to gratify whatever desire animates his actions. The unlawful combatant, however, proceeds from a different point of reference: he is animated by a strong political motive and pursues his agenda – which could range from compelling a discrete change of government policy all the way to the destruction of the state itself – by armed force. The existence of such unlawful combatants – real or imagined – is sometimes cited as a rationale for gun control. As recently as March 2021 Senator Dianne Feinstein invoked this "threat" in support of her "Assault Weapons Ban of 2021," alleging that "[w]e're now seeing a rise in domestic terrorism, and military-style assault weapons are increasingly becoming the guns of choice for these dangerous groups."[786]

Senator Feinstein's hyperbolic claim notwithstanding, there is no evidence of any burgeoning domestic terrorist movement embracing the AR-15 or any other semiautomatic rifle as its weapon of choice. But even if there were such a dangerous movement at large in the land, attempting to curb its activities by prohibiting law-abiding citizens from owning the semiautomatic firearms of their choice would be a misguided approach at best, for several reasons.

One reason is related to Robert Leonhard's concept of *dislocation* discussed previously. No matter how many firearms are present in the country, those in the hands of law-abiding citizens are useless to insurgents or terrorists, their inaccessibility to the insurgents rendering them irrelevant to the conflict. An interesting illustration of this comes to us from Jahanara Imam's account of the 1971 Bangladesh Liberation War. Imam describes an incident in which Pakistani soldiers – against whom the people of Bangladesh were struggling for their independence – came to her neighborhood and confiscated privately owned weapons:

---

[786] Steven Nelson, "35 Senate Democrats introduce AR-15 gun ban, cite 'domestic terrorism.'" *New York Post*, March 12th, 2021. https://nypost.com/2021/03/12/35-senate-dems-introduce-ar-15-gun-ban-cite-domestic-terrorism/. Retrieved May 16th, 2021.

At around 9 o'clock … we heard a voice on the mike in front of our house. People are being called upon to surrender their guns, rifles, and pistols along with the licenses … We have a 12 bore [gauge] shot-gun, a 22 bore [caliber] rifle and an Astra pistol. Sharif and Jami took these weapons out on the main road. Our neighbors also carried out their weapons. Sharif and Jami returned at 4 o'clock in the afternoon without the weapons. They surrendered them and got a receipt.[787]

That the occupying forces of a government struggling to stamp out a vigorous secession movement would confiscate privately owned firearms is unremarkable. More noteworthy are the surrounding circumstances. Bangladesh's War of Independence began in late March 1971; per Imam, this confiscation of privately owned firearms was not carried out until November 17th, 1971, more than eight months later. Imam's family sympathized with the independence struggle and her son Rumi had joined the insurgents the previous May. Yet never since the beginning of the war had Rumi or anyone else in the family contemplated using these weapons against the Pakistani forces (as will be seen below, the insurgents would acquire their arms from other sources). The weapons seized from Imam's family were utterly irrelevant to the ongoing struggle and their confiscation accomplished nothing more than depriving the family of the means of defending themselves against any predatory elements in the society that might have found themselves emboldened by the ongoing chaos triggered by the civil war. If these firearms in the hands of citizens strongly sympathetic to the

---

[787] Jahanara Imam and Mustafizur Rahman (trans.). *Of Blood and Fire: The Untold Story of Bangladesh's War of Independence* (The University Press Limited, second edition, second printing, 2007), 222 – 223.

insurgency in their country's civil war were completely irrelevant to that struggle, then the vast majority of privately owned firearms of law abiding American citizens are utterly useless to anyone contemplating such a movement here.

The presence of an insurgency or other unlawful combatants within a community do not alter the basic realities of life: criminals still seek to satisfy their lusts by attacking helpless members of the community, and law abiding citizens still require the means to repel such attacks. In fact, the existence of unlawful combatants within the community rather aggravates the situation, for insurgents often engage in robbery, extortion and terrorism against the wider population to fund their operations and to coerce the compliance of the citizenry, so that the ordinary law abiding person needs to defend himself and his family against both the ordinary criminal and the insurgent. Attempting to limit the access of unlawful combatants to semiautomatic weapons by prohibiting the population *in toto* from owning them will only exacerbate the vulnerability of ordinary citizens to predation, both criminal and political, due to the disproportionate impact that such a ban would have on law abiding citizens as compared to criminals and unlawful combatants. As Sammy "The Bull" Gravano has already told us, "[i]f I'm a bad guy, I'm always gonna have a gun."[788] If a mere criminal is so strongly motivated to acquire arms, how much more will an ideologically motivated terrorist or insurgent be? Very much so, we can presume. What's more, as even the most cursory examination of the daily news will reveal, there is no shortage of actors on the world stage ready and willing to feed the unlawful combatant's appetite for firepower. In the Bengali example, the independence fighters got their weapons via locally recruited units of the Pakistani Army that defected to the insurgents; by capture from the enemy; and from India.[789]

---

[788] Blum, "The Reluctant Don."

Notwithstanding the employment of End User Certificates to prevent diversion of arms from legitimate to illegitimate channels, terrorists or other unlawful combatants can still acquire access to arms.[790] As a sympathizer of the Irish Republican Army observed in 1986,

> While I have no information as the sources of the IRA's armaments, I suspect that they will employ any weapons that are available to them ... Weapons sales are a multi-billion dollar industry worldwide and any person or organization who has the financial resources can purchase enough arms, tanks, airplanes, and weaponry to equip a large army.[791]

None of this should be read as opposing efforts to keep firearms out of the hands of criminals and unlawful combatants. Such efforts should be made and can impact the capabilities of such actors. What it does mean, however, is that depriving the law abiding and peaceable citizen of access to the semiautomatic firearms of his or her choice is the wrong approach. Ordinary citizens complying with such an edict would be stripped of their firearms, but the same would not be true of the bad actors we are discussing. While such a ban might impede their acquisition of firearms, it would not block it off altogether. The net result would be to put violent actors in a position of greater advantage over peaceable citizens.

---

[789] For a discussion of the development of the Bangladeshi forces in the War for Independence, see Sarwar Hossain. *Liberation War of Bangladesh-1971: A Study on the Armed Struggle: 25 March to 16 December* (University of Dhaka Doctoral Dissertation, 2016).

[790] For a discussion of the End User Certificate system, see Mark Bromley and Hugh Griffiths, *End-User Certificates: Improving Standards to Prevent Diversion* (SIPRI Insights on Peace and Security, No. 2010/3, March 2010).

[791] Robert Emmet Connolly. *Armalite and Ballot Box: An Irish-American Republican Primer* (Cuchullain Publications, 1985), 35 – 36.

Sporting Uses of the AR-15 and
Similar Rifles

A few years ago I encountered on odd work entitled *The Lawn: A History of an American Obsession,* by Victoria Scott Jenkins. In the introduction, Jenkins writes that she

> grew up in a house in Connecticut with a front lawn, but the American aesthetic of the lawn as a 'green velvety carpet' was not part of my childhood ... My mother ... was far more interested in her garden than in the grass in the front yard.[792]

"[T]he aesthetic that a velvety green carpet was necessary in front of our house ... [has never been important] to me as an adult," she continues:

> I can remember the first time I visited Ohio and saw people riding mowers over acres of front lawn. I was amazed and wanted to know why they were willing to spend so much time, energy and money on what appeared to be unused space.[793]

Jenkins seems skeptical of Americans' love of their lawns, observing that while "[s]ome European immigrants to the New World may have been familiar with lawns ... peasants and city dwellers were not. Lawns were not part of the cultural baggage of South American, African, and Asian immigrants."[794] Lawns having not figured significantly in her own upbringing, she does not appear to be able to conceive of their utility to others, seemingly viewing them with bemusement at best, and mild derision at worst.

---

[792] Virginia Scott Jenkins. *The Lawn: A History of an American Obsession* (Smithsonian Institution Press, 1994), 1.
[793] *Id.*
[794] *Id.,* 3.

Yet Jenkins' understanding of the lawn may be incomplete. My family and I, for example, use our lawn extensively. It is the playground for my children and those of our neighbors; the hunting ground of our cat; the sovereign domain of our golden retriever; the *souq*, bazaar and flee market for my wife's approximately annual yard sales; and the social center for the adults of our neighborhood, who gather at our little front yard gravel patio for block parties and evening drinks in good weather.

Senator Feinstein's attitude toward AR-15 rifles is not dissimilar to Jenkins' toward lawns: Having neither experience with, interest in, nor affinity for such rifles herself, the senator extrapolates from her own limited experience that no one else uses them either; that they have no practical purpose in themselves; and that there is no legitimate justification for the interest in them that others feel. Author Stephen King offers a similar view, observing that

> I have nothing against gun owners, sport shooters, or hunters, but semiautomatic weapons have only two purposes. One is so that owners can take them to the shooting range once in a while, yell yeehaw and get all horny at the rapid fire and the burning vapor spurting from the end of the barrel. Their other use – their only other use – is to kill people.[795]

King dismisses the owners and users of semiautomatic rifles – objects which hold no appeal or interest for *him* – in vulgar, crude terms; and, like Senator Feinstein, having no use for or experience with these firearms himself, he cannot conceive of anyone else putting them to any practical use, either. Nonetheless, Senator Feinstein, Mr. King, and other gun control advocates are wrong about the utility of the AR-15 rifle.

---

[795] Stephen King. "Stephen King: why the US must introduce limited gun controls." *The Guardian*, February 1st, 2013. https://www.theguardian.com/books/2013/feb/01/stephen-king-pulled-book-gun-controls. Retrieved June 15th, 2019.

In *District of Columbia v. Heller*, the late Justice Anthony Scalia wrote that *Miller* "say[s] only that the Second Amendment does not protect those weapons not typically possessed by law abiding citizens for lawful purposes, such as short-barreled shotguns."[796] Attempting to square this circle regarding AR-15s, Senator Feinstein hectored now-Justice Brett Kavanaugh that while such firearms might be commonly possessed or stored, they are not commonly used. Even leaving aside Senator Feinstein's dubious dismissal of the possibility that passive uses of firearms may exist, her claim that AR-15s are not commonly used in a more active sense is simply wrong: The AR-15 and similar rifles are frequently employed in a variety of practical applications.

Even as late as 2018 Koper persisted in the claim that "military-style features [of the AR-15 and similar rifles] ... appear useful in military and criminal applications but unnecessary in shooting sports or self-defense."[797] We have already seen that, Koper's assumption notwithstanding, people do use AR-15s and other semiautomatic rifles in self-defense, and their principal features (rounds more powerful and magazines of larger capacity than those used with pistols) are very useful in that capacity. But Koper's error does not end there, for AR-15 rifles are also commonly used in sporting applications as well.

Target Shooting

Probably the most the most common active use to which AR-15s are put is target shooting. I enjoy target shooting and, in my experience, the AR-15 is far and away the most common rifle that I see appearing on the ranges that I frequent. Many ranges rent firearms to shooters as well as allowing shooters to bring their own. At the range I most often use, the AR-15 rifle is a frequent rental

---

[796] *Heller I,* citing *United States v. Miller,* 307 U. S. 174 (1939).
[797] Koper, et. al. *"Criminal Use of Assault Weapons and High-Capacity Semiautomatic Firearms,* 314.

selection, with semiautomatic Kalashnikov rifles being on offer as well.

One useful proxy by which we might glean some sense of the scale of practical use to which AR-15s and similar rifles are put is the marketing of the supplies and equipment necessary for such use. One such is ammunition: a search that I conducted on the popular firearms retail site *Gunbroker.com* for .223 Remington ammunition – most commonly used in AR-15 rifles – produced 2159 listings from 27 manufacturers (the category "other manufacturer" being counted as one manufacturer), in increments ranging from 10 to 2000 rounds. A similar search for the term "5.56" – another common AR-15 caliber – produced 248 listings of ammunition from seventeen manufacturers. A search for the term "7.62x39" – the most common Kalashnikov caliber – produced 331 listings from 23 manufacturers. A search for the term ".223" under the category "Gun Cleaning Kits & Gun Cleaning Supplies" produced approximately 1,076 results, while a search for the term "AR-15" under "Gunsmithing Tools & Gunsmith Supplies" produced 310 results, and a generic search under the category "AR-15 Parts" resulted in "Over 10000 Items Found." A search for ".223" under "Ammunition Reloading" produced 1,929 results, including the empty brass, bullets, and tools necessary for hobbyists to reload their own .223 cartridges.

Similar searches on the website for the popular retailer Brownells produced 122 results for .223 Remington ammunition, 51 results for 5.56mm ammunition, and 208 results for .223 reloading supplies. For the retailer Midway USA, searches produced 116 results for .223 ammunition and 44 for 5.56mm ammunition; 21 results for 7.62x39 ammunition, and 121 results for AR-15 gunsmithing items. Sales of such items are not limited to firearms oriented retailers: A search on Walmart's website for term ".223" produced 87 results, while a minimal amount of searching on Amazon.com produced huge numbers of items relating to AR-15 and similar rifles – for example, a search for the term "AR-15" under "Gun Parts and Accessories" produced 816 results.

These results are hardly scientific of course, and likely include errors such as incorrect categorization of items and ambiguity in the search terms. However, the results are not merely over inclusive. They are also under inclusive, in that they are derived from only a cursory review of a few huge online retailers. These numbers do not begin to account for the vast network of other small, medium and large retailers both online and at traditional brick-and-mortar stores trading in supplies for AR-15 and other semiautomatic rifles. In sum, the market for the ammunition, tools, parts, accessories and supplies necessary to create, use and maintain these rifles is huge, and the brisk trade in these products can only be reasonably understood as indicative of a very strong culture of actively using them, with the simplest expression of that culture being target shooting.

Hunting

Former *Wired* editor Jon Stokes has written that "I've owned an AR-15 for four years, and I use it for varmint control on my 17-acre Texas estate,"[798] showing that contrary to the misconceptions of some, AR-15s are used in hunting. In fact, Colt originally marketed the AR-15 for just that purpose, promoting as a "superb hunting partner … Colt's new AR-15 Sporter" in 1964.[799] As an example, an acquaintance of mine has recently gone boar hunting twice in the Carolinas, bagging three between himself and his daughter, his weapon of choice on these hunts being the AR-10, a version of the AR-15 rifle chambered in the more powerful 7.62x51mm round[800] (similar but not identical to the commercial .308 Winchester cartridge).[801]

---

[798] Stokes.

[799] *American Rifleman*, April, 1964. Perhaps the most interesting aspect of this advertisement is the price of the rifle – $189.50. How times change.

[800] Elwood Shelton. "The Rise and Fall of the AR-10." *GunDigest*, September 5th, 2018. https://gundigest.com/military-firearms/the-fall-and-rise-of-the-ar-10. Retrieved June 22nd, 2019.

[801] Tom McHale. "7.62 NATO vs.308 Winchester Ammo, What's The Difference?" *Ammoland.com*, October 12, 2020. https://www.ammoland.com/2020/10/7-62-nato-vs-308-winchester-

Will Drabold of *Time* profiled six hunters who use the AR-15 or AR-10 in 2016, quoting Eric Mayer of *AR-15Hunter.com* as saying of the AR-15 that "[i]t's the most capable tool for the job at this time, bar none. Period. It is."[802] The first hunter profiled was Jay Perreira, who hunts feral goats on the Hawaiian island of Kauai. According to Drabold, Perreira's "favorite feature of the AR-15 is how easily it can be disassembled. The gun can be taken apart and carried several miles in a backpack through Kauai's mountains to goat sanctuaries."[803] Texas resident Jonathan Owen uses an AR-15 to kill wild boar. According to Drabold,

> A west Texas pig sighting is not a cute barnyard encounter; it's a reason to grab a rifle. Across the southern United States, wild pigs cause $1.5 billion in annual property damage. Boar can weigh up to 300 pounds, run up to 30 miles per hour and in Jonathan Owen's experience, quickly turn violent.[804]

While an AR-15 is not necessary to hunt boar, Drabold quotes Owen as saying that "the practical benefits of being able to engage a lot of pigs at a time, safely, is a big win."[805] Drabold elaborates, writing that "[t]he semiautomatic and large capacity magazine features allow Owen to take several shots at multiple pigs in a few seconds. When engaging a pack of wild pigs in west Texas' shrubbery, Owen says these features ensure his safety" when pursuing such dangerous game.[806] Pursuing game at the other end of the spectrum is Eric Mayer of Arizona, who uses an AR-15 to hunt antelope jackrabbits. "Antelope jackrabbits dart up to 30 miles per

---

ammo-whats-the-difference/. Retrieved January 23rd, 2021.

[802] Will Drabold. "Here Are 7 Animals Hunters Kill Using an AR-15." *Time*, July 6th, 2016. https://time.com/4390506/gun-control-ar-15-semiautomatic-rifles/. Retrieved June 22nd, 2019.

[803] *Id.*

[804] *Id.*

[805] *Id.*

[806] *Id.*

hour between bunches of upright dead sticks that could generously be called bushes," Drabold writes. "For skilled shooters, hunting these northern Arizona sprinters is a challenge," and according to Mayer, "it's nearly impossible without an AR-15."[807]

"While [bolt action] rifles, as well as shotguns, remain popular with hunters, semiautomatic guns have become popular because they can take multiple shots without losing sight of an animal"[808] when chambering another round, Drabold observes. But such a consideration is of little importance to an offender using such a firearm as the instrument of his crimes. People are not as fast or agile as animals and are easier to kill; victimizing human beings is like shooting fish in a barrel, or perhaps more accurately, like walking through a barnyard or a zoo and shooting the captive animals inside their enclosures. Wild animals in their habitat, however, are another thing altogether, and a hunter needs every advantage he can get to overcome the physical superiority of his prey in terms of speed, agility, and alertness. Montana elk hunter Gary Marbut, according to Drabold, uses an AR-10. "Many hunters say the ... AR-15 is preferable for hunting smaller animals." But "for Marbut to successfully hunt elk that weigh at least 500 pounds, the larger [7.62x51] bullet [of the AR-10] is a must ... After stalking elk for hours through forested mountainous terrain in western Montana, Marbut says he needs a gun he can trust to hit its mark. That gun is his AR."[809] Marbut remarks that "The last two elk I've taken, I took at about 300 yards ... They were both headshots"[810] (compare to Winslow's opinion about AR-15s being unsuitable for hunting, noted above). Drabold next profiles George Sodergren, who hunts coyotes in Maine. According to Drabold, Sodergren "does not believe a semiautomatic rifle is necessary for all animals. But for coyotes, he makes an exception."[811] Because coyotes can approach in packs, Drabold writes, "the AR-15 gives [Sodergren] the chance to land

---

[807] *Id.*

[808] *Id.*

[809] Drabold.

[810] *Id.*

[811] *Id.*

more than one shot … 'if you've got multiple animals or you miss, you've got a quick follow-up shot.'"[812] The final AR-15 hunter that Drabold profiles is deer hunter Will Chambers. "While the AR-15 is preferable for smaller game," Chambers customizes his AR-15 "with a larger caliber receiver" enabling him to fire larger .277 caliber rounds. "That small difference can mean killing an adult deer in one shot or condemning the animal to a slow death. There are hundreds of ways to customize and accessorize the AR-15."[813]

At their website, *AR-15Hunter.com*, Mayer and Chambers write that "[t]he AR-15 is the most versatile firearm platform in the world, and there are millions of them in the hands of American sportsmen and women today. Using it as the hunting tool of this generation only makes sense."[814] They provide a wealth of information on the use of the AR-15 platform as a hunting weapon, including reports on various AR-15 hunting expeditions. These include hunting antelope in Wyoming with AR-15s in caliber .22 Nosler and .224 Valkyrie;[815] hunting mule deer in Nevada with an AR-15 in caliber 6.8mm Remington SPC;[816] hunting bobcat in California with an AR-15;[817] hunting wild boar with an AR-15;[818] Nebraska deer hunting with an AR-10;[819] hunting prairie dogs in

---

[812] *Id.*

[813] *Id.*

[814] *AR-15Hunter.com.* http://AR-15hunter.com/about-us/. Retrieved June 22nd, 2019.

[815] *AR-15Hunter.com.* http://AR-15hunter.com/wyoming-antelope-hunt-with-the-22-nosler-and-224-valkyrie-video/#more-2731. Retrieved June 22nd, 2019.

[816] *AR-15Hunter.com.* http://AR-15hunter.com/nevada-mule-deer-hunt-ar/#more-2368. Retrieved June 22nd, 2019.

[817] *AR-15Hunter.com,* http://AR-15hunter.com/hunting-california-bobcat-AR-15/#more-2061. Retrieved June 22nd, 2019.

[818] *AR-15Hunter.com*http://AR-15hunter.com/first-hunt-with-the-hornady-6-8spc-100-grain-gmx-full-boar-ammo/#more-1589. Retrieved June 22nd, 2019.

[819] *AR-15Hunter.com*-take-friend-ar-10/#more-935. Retrieved June 22nd, 2019.

Northern Arizona with an AR-15 in .223 Remington or squirrel in Nebraska;[820] and hunting groundhogs with an AR-15.[821]

Notwithstanding the belief persistent in some quarters to the contrary, the AR-15 rifle is a versatile and effective hunting platform used by many. Nor is hunting limited to the AR-15. According to one analysis,

> [w]hile the AK-47 and SKS were primarily designed for military use, vast numbers of these weapons have been exported and sold to Western civilian markets as cheap alternatives to sporting rifles. Both rifles are particularly popular with military match shooting enthusiasts as well as hunters involved in culling operations while the cheaper SKS has found favor with hunters on a strictly limited budget. In its home territory, the AK-47 is often used as a basic hunting tool, employed throughout the vast expanses of Russia, Kazakhstan, and Mongolia. [822]

While it may not appear obvious to older sportsmen who pursued hunting in their youth or to those whose knowledge of hunting is cursory or derived from hackneyed depictions in popular media, semiautomatic rifles such as the AR-15, civilian variants of the AK-47, and other rifles are not only capable of being usefully employed in hunting, they actually *are* so employed, and widely.

Competition Shooting

---

[820] *AR-15Hunter.com.* http://AR-15hunter.com/squirrel-hunt-tennessee-arms-polymer-lower/#more-137. Retrieved June 22nd, 2019.

[821] *AR-15Hunter.com.* http://AR-15hunter.com/hunting-ground-hogs-AR-15-helping-farmers-one-shot-time/#more-126. Retrieved June 22nd, 2019.

[822] "7.62x39 (M43)," Terminal Ballistics Research, https://www.ballisticstudies.com/Knowledgebase/7.62x39+M43.html. Retrieved July 10th, 2019.

Competitive shooting has a long history in the United States, Britain, Canada, and Europe. The sport was standardized and put on a regular footing in the United States to a large extent through the efforts of the NRA, with the first shots being fired at its famous Creedmore Range on April 25th, 1873.[823] "Informal shooting matches were being held all over the country" before that, of course,

> but, for each match, rules were made on the spot … the common method of scoring was by 'string length,' the aggregate distance of all shots from a common center, but there was no standardization of the number of shots that might be fired.[824]

To remedy this, the NRA adopted as standard the British scoring system, by which "the performance of American shooters could be measured against that of Scot Highlanders or of Sikh warriors guarding the Khyber Pass."[825] The center of gravity of US marksmanship competition shifted to the Sea Girt Range in New Jersey in 1889;[826] on August 19th, 1907, it shifted again when the NRA commenced its first shooting competition at Camp Perry, Ohio, which remains an important host to numerous high-level shooting events to this day.[827]

Competitive shooting sports continue to thrive in the United States today in many forms. These include Action Handgun Sports, Bullseye, Three-Gun, Cowboy Action Shooting, and Long Range Shooting.[828] Others include High Power Rifle Competition, Small Bore Rifle Competition, Conventional Pistol Competition, Shotgun

---

[823] Trefethen and Serven, 47.

[824] *Id.*, 46.

[825] *Id.*

[826] *Id.*, 108.

[827] *Id.*, 144.

[828] Tom McHale. "NRACompetitive Shooting Series, Part 1: Is It for You?" *Outdoor Hub.* http://www.outdoorhub.com/how-to/2016/09/23/competitive-shooting-is-it-for-you/. Retrieved June 23rd, 2019.

Competitions, Airgun Shooting, Black Powder Competition, Silhouette Competition,[829] and finally Service Rifle Competition.

The AR-15 rifle features prominently in both Service Rifle and High Powered Rifle competition. "Service Rifle is one of the most popular forms of rifle competition in the country,"[830] and while M1A1s (the semiautomatic only, civilian version of the M14 Rifle), M1 Garands, and even bolt action 1903 Springfield rifles still appear at Service Rifle competitions, "[t]he most popular rifle is of course the AR-15."[831] Likewise, "[t]he AR-15 is the most popular rifle across the course competition" in High Power Rifle Competition.[832] While

> "[t]hose who want to shoot a larger caliber such as .30-06 can use an M1 Garand ... most use the AR-platform, as it is more accurate and has less recoil. This has made it easier and more enjoyable for many people to shoot high power—specifically women. It has also made the sport more inclusive, as anyone who can safely use the rifle can learn to shoot high power."[833]

---

[829] Tom McHale. "NRA Competitive Shooting Series, Part 2: The Disciplines." NRABlog, December 22nd, 2016. https://www.nrablog.com/articles/2016/12/nra-competitive-shooting-series-part-2-the-disciplines/. Retrieved June 23rd, 2019.

[830] Frank Melloni. "Intro to Service Rifle," NRA Shooting Sports USA, June 5th, 2019. https://www.ssusa.org/articles/2019/6/5/intro-to-service-rifle. Retrieved June 23rd, 2019.

[831] Id.

[832] SSUSA Staff. "10 Essential Items You Need To Get Started In High Power Rifle" (photo caption). NRA Shooting Sports USA, September 20th, 2017. https://www.ssusa.org/articles/2017/9/20/10-essential-items-you-need-to-get-started-in-high-power-rifle. Retrieved June 23rd, 2019.

[833] Serena Juchnowski. "Why Shoot High Power Service Rifle?" NRA Shooting Sports USA, November 19th, 2018. https://www.ssusa.org/articles/2018/11/19/why-shoot-high-power-service-rifle/. Retrieved June 23rd, 2019.

Getting started in High Power Rifle shooting competition "is easy," requiring only an "AR-15 in any configuration" and a few basic accessories.[834]

That the AR-15-style rifle is integral to competition shooting is shown by the rules promulgated by two of the major sponsors of marksmanship competitions: the CMP and the NRA. Pertinent CMP Highpower Rifle Competition Rules provisions include:

M16/AR-15-Type service rifle. The rifle must be an M16 U. S. Service Rifle or a similar AR-15-type commercial rifle that is derived from the M16 service rifle design. Rifles must exhibit the general overall external appearance of the M-16 rifle or carbine. *Visible barrel profiles, handguards or quad rails, receivers, pistol grips, carry handles or rails and fixed or collapsible stocks must appear essentially the same as the M16 service rifle*

…

…

The following specific rules apply to this rifle:
a) *Cartridge. Must be chambered for the 5.56 x 45 mm NATO (.223) cartridge.*
b) Action. *Must be designed or modified so that only semiautomatic fire is possible.* The gas operating system must be fully operable and adhere to the original M16 rifle design (i.e. Stoner design, gas impingement system) or have a piston-operated gas system.

…

Handguard. The receiver and handguard must be machined as separate

---

[834] Dennis Santiago. "What You Need To Know About High Power Rifle Competition." *NRA* *Shooting* *Sports* *USA.* https://www.ssusa.org/articles/2018/9/18/what-you-need-to-know-about-high-power-rifle-competition/. Retrieved June 23rd, 2019.

*parts. Standard M16-type service handguards … may be used
or military design or aftermarket free floating rail
systems may be used,*

…

f) Buttstocks. Buttstocks may vary in length and be either fixed or adjustable. Adjustable length buttstocks may be changed during an event, but buttstocks that allow other adjustments such as the cheek-piece height or buttplate location are not permitted. *Only standard A1 or A2 type pistol grips are permitted.*

g) Magazines. Metal or synthetic (polymer) magazines, standard issue or commercial equivalent, straight or curved, must be attached during the firing of all courses and in all positions. *Allowable magazines must have external dimensions that are similar to the standard service 20 or 30-round box magazines,* but may vary slightly in length and curvature, provided they do not exceed 7 ¾ inches, from top to bottom, as measured along the back of the spline. Magazines must not have any additional pads, extensions or other support features. A 10-round magazine with external dimensions at least as long as a standard service 20-round box magazine, but not longer than a 30-round box magazine, may be used. A dummy magazine with a ramp for single shot loading may be used if this magazine has external dimensions at least as long as a standard service 20-round box magazine, but not longer than a 30-round box magazine"[835][836] (emphasis added).

---

[835] *CMP Highpower Rifle Competition Rules*, 23rd Edition—2019, 33 – 35.
[836] The CMP rules provide for an "Alternative CMP Rifle," stating that "Residents of states where the ownership of a Service Rifle that complies with Rule 4.1.1 is prohibited by law may use a CMP Alternative Rifle that

The *NRA High Power Rifle Rules* similarly provide for the use of the AR-15 platform as a competition rifle. For the Service Rifle category, the rules provide, *inter alia*, as follows:

3.1 Service Rifle—As issued by the US Armed Forces, *or the same type and caliber of commercially manufactured rifle*

…

…

US Service Rifle 5.56 mm M-16 series—
• Must be chambered for the 5.56 x 45 mm NATO (.223) cartridge.
• The gas operating system must be fully operable and adhere to the original M-16 rifle design (i.e. Stoner design, gas impingement system) or have a piston-operated gas system.

…

• Metal or synthetic (polymer) magazines, standard issue or commercial equivalent, *with standard service 20 or 30- round box magazine dimensions must be attached during the firing of all courses and in all positions.* A 10-round magazine with the extra external dimensions as a standard service 20-round box magazine may be used. A dummy magazine with a ramp for single shot loading may be used if this magazine has the same external dimensions as the standard service 20-round box magazine.

….

• *Buttstocks may vary in length and be either fixed or collapsible.* Collapsible or adjustable length stocks may be adjusted during an event, but buttstocks that allow for other adjustments such as the cheek-piece height or buttplate location may not be used.
• *Only standard A1 or A2 type pistol grips may be used.*

---

complies with the … requirements" further set forth in the rules. *CMP Highpower Rifle Competition Rules*, 23rd Edition – 2019, 36.

• Quad rails or similar handguards may be used"[837] (emphasis added).

...

The NRA Rules further contain AR-15 specific provisions, such as:

MID- RANGE COMPETITION FOR TACTICAL RIFLES ON THE 'AR-PLATFORM'

Conceptually, this new NRA Mid-Range (Prone) Tactical Rifle (AR) program will be designed to provide civilian, military, and police shooters with an opportunity to shoot NRA Mid-Range Prone competition alongside of other Mid-Range Prone shooters *in matches using semiautomatic rifles built on an 'AR-Platform'* and equipment generally thought of as being "tactical" in design and use. These rifles will be configured so as to replicate as closely as possible the tactical rifles (semiautomatic) and equipment used by the United States Military and America's Law Enforcement Community in "mid-range" tactical applications. These semiautomatic rifles will be more "off the rack" or "stock" than "competition" in nature. They will be more of a "tactical design" than "match design" and therefore less expensive than the vast majority of mid-range prone rifles currently in use. *These rifles will be of the 'AR-Platform' variety, semiautomatic, chambered in any caliber from.223 cal./5.56mm up to and including.308 cal./7.62mm.* The courses of fire will be the same courses of fire currently used for other NRA Mid-Range (Prone) High Power Competition (300, 500 & 600 yards) and are designed to be fired concurrently with other

---

[837] *NRA High Power Rifle Rules*, 7 – 8.

forms of Mid-Range competition"[838] (emphasis added).

AR-15, Kalashnikov and other military-style carbines also feature prominently in shooting competitions sponsored by the USPSA, including 3-Gun, Multigun and Pistol Caliber Carbine competitions.[839] Nor is this a new feature of their competitions, as such firearms have frequently graced the cover of *Frontsight*, the association's official journal, since at least July 1989.[840]

As Mr. Turk of the ATF has previously acknowledged, AR-15s and similar semiautomatic rifles are thoroughly entrenched in American competitive shooting.

Passive Uses: Preparedness

---

[838] *Id.*, 73.

[839] For example, see images and/or text in the following: John B. Holbrook, "John Wick 3-Gun," *Frontsight*, Official Journal of the United States Practical Shooting Association / IPSC, Vol 36, July-August 2019, 56 – 60; Aaron Bright, "Review: A Couple of Carbines from Palmetto State Armory," *Frontsight*, Vol 36, July-August 2019, 42 – 48; Troy McManus, "Coaching Steel Challenge," *Frontsight*, Vol 36, July-August 2019, 9; Manny Bragg and Carole Bryant, "The Glock 2018 Area 6 Championship," *Frontsight*, July/August 2018, Vol. 35, no. 4, 11; Jessica Nietzel, "Multigun Nationals: What a Blast," *Frontsight*, July/August 2018, Vol. 35, no. 4, 16, 18, 20, and 22; Kristine Hayes, "The Science of Competition: is Knowing How to Fail the Secret to Winning?" *Frontsight*, July/August 2017, Vol. 34 No. 4, 18; Cora Maglaya, "2017 USPSA Armscore Rock Island Multigun National Championship," *Frontsight*, July/August 2017, Vol. 34 No. 4, 22 – 26.

[840] *Frontsight*, July/August 1989, Vol. 6, No. 3; March/April 1990 Vol. 7, No. 2; September/October 1991, Vol. 8, No. 5; July/August1 Vol. 18, No. 4; July/August 2002 Vol. 19, No. 4; May/June 2005, Vol. 22, No. 3; January/February 2006 Vol. 23, No. 1; March/April 2010, Vol. 27, No. 2; November/December 2010, Vol. 27, No. 6; September/October 2014 VOL. 31, NO. 5; July/August 2015 VOL. 32, NO. 4; July/August 2016 Vol. 33, NO. 4; May/June 2017 VOL. 34, NO. 3; July/August 2017 VOL. 34, NO. 4; July/August 2018, Vol. 35, No. 4;

and Collecting

Even if Senator Feinstein's belief that AR-15s are merely stored but not commonly "used" were true in the sense of their not being fired often, it would still be a highly dubious proposition, for one common use of many things is to retain them against some future contingency. Everyone legally on the roads has automobile insurance though (unlike myself, to my embarrassment) many people never have occasion to call upon their insurer to reimburse a claim. Fire extinguishers, ground fault circuit interrupters, automobile air bags, and numerous other precautionary appliances and services pervade modern life. Yet in the vast majority of instances, no contingency will ever arise throughout the life cycle of a particular example of a given device requiring that it be put to the use for which it was intended. For decades as a soldier I carried a field dressing in a small nylon pouch attached to my load bearing equipment, yet never was I called upon to dress a wound (I think I still have that field dressing). While serving in Iraq, my team of military advisors and I carried thousands of rounds of ammunition of various types and calibers on our persons and in our vehicles, yet we never exchanged fire with the enemy.[841] Does this render all of these items useless? Of course not. Nor does it follow that those possessing them are merely storing or hoarding them, but not using them. For procuring and retaining supplies and equipment against the eventuality of an emergency would certainly seem not only a justifiable but a prudent *use* of ones' resources. Other forms of passive use exist as well. Return, for example, to Jenkins' remarks, cited earlier, about Ohio suburbanites expending time and resources maintaining lawns that they allegedly do not use. Even assuming that they make no active use of their lawns as my family does, this does not preclude passive use: A lawn is, after all, a ground covering, the functions of which include to holding the soil in place, thereby preventing erosion; to

---

[841] The enemy did have occasion to attack *us*. My vehicle – with myself and the rest of its crew inside – was destroyed by an improvised explosive device in Baghdad in April 2007. Circumstances precluded us from returning fire.

reducing dust; and to keeping the dirt held down by the roots from being tracked into ones' home.

A firearm not actively used by its owner, in the sense of being taken out and fired regularly, can still serve a function – it can still be of *use*. Many people possess firearms as a means with which to defend themselves and their families against the unlikely but by no means impossible eventuality of home invasion or personal assault; or a firearm might be maintained as an instrument of survival against natural or man-made disaster when the ordinary sources of food and protections from animal predators are not at hand. AR-15 and similar rifles are among the firearms commonly kept for such purposes by many Americans.

Objects can also serve less tangible functions for their owners, and can be possessed for more abstract, but no less legitimate, reasons. Objects can serve as instruments of education; as symbols of allegiance, identity and affinity; as monuments, memorials, and records; they can serve as the source of inspiration, purpose, and stimulation; they can be a source of relaxation, pleasure and fulfillment outside of the normal demands of work, family, and other duties; they can serve as expressions of belief, values, and points of view; and innumerable other social, psychological and spiritual functions. For many people, collecting as a hobby or avocation serves such a purpose. The 20th Century philosopher Ayn Rand was a collector – in her case, of stamps. One of Rand's former acolytes once observed that there are "those who worship Ayn Rand and those who damn her;"[842] she was, after all, a woman of rather eccentric views and a very flawed person who could and did inflict a lot of pain on those who she loved and who loved her.[843] Yet

---

[842] Barbara Branden. *The Passion of Ayn Rand* (Anchor Books / Doubleday, 1987), xiii.
[843] Two interesting biographies on Rand are Jennifer Burns, *Goddess of the Market: Ayn Rand and the American Right* (Oxford University Press, 2009); and that of former acolyte Barbara Branden, who broke with Rand in the late 1960s.

notwithstanding that, Rand was undeniably a brilliant and perceptive thinker with many keen insights into human nature. Of her own hobby of stamp collecting, she wrote that

> [t]he pleasure lies in a certain special way of using one's mind. Stamp collecting is a hobby for busy, purposeful, ambitious people... because, in pattern, it has the essential elements of a career, but transposed to a clearly delimited, intensely private world. A career requires the ability to sustain a purpose over a long period of time, through many separate steps, choices, decisions, adding up to a steady progression toward a goal. Purposeful people cannot rest by doing nothing nor can they feel at home in the role of passive spectators. They seldom find pleasure in single occasions, such as a party or a show or even a vacation... What they need is another track, but for the same train... collecting fulfills that need. It establishes a wide context of its own, interesting enough to hold one's attention and to switch one's mind temporarily away from exhausting problems or burdens. ... A collector is not a passive spectator, but an active, purposeful agent in a cumulative drive ... In collecting, there is no such thing as too many stamps: the more one gets, the more one wants. The sense of action, of movement, of progression is wonderful... and habit-forming.[844]

All of this can be said with equal application about virtually any form collecting and about gun collecting perhaps most of all. Firearms are powerful cultural symbols; captivating artifacts of the past; emblems of great historical struggles; relics charting the technological development of society; heirlooms and sentimental attachments to ones' personal and family history; and much more.

---

[844] Ayn Rand. "Why I Like Stamp Collecting." *Minkus Stamp Journal*, Vol. VI, No. 2, 1971, 2 – 7.

For all these reasons, AR-15 and other military-style semiautomatic rifles (as are all other types of firearms)are the object of an avid collecting community, supporting a great deal of research, study, and scholarship. Many publications and websites track the evolution and development of the AR-15 and its selective fire counterpart, the M16. Examples include *Retro Black Rifle*, which provides a comprehensive summary of the development of the M16 and Colt AR-15, with photographs;[845] *Colt Commercial Variants*, which as the name suggests, provides information on the evolution of Colt AR-15s as opposed to the M16;[846] and the informal *SP1 Database*,[847] *USGI Colt Carbine parts variation guide Edition IV*,[848] and *Retro M16 Parts Timeline*[849] at *AR-15.com*. One interesting subset of the AR-15 collecting circuit focuses on so-called retro versions of that rifle and of the M16. Hobbyists in this field devote substantial time, study, work and resources to assembling semiautomatic replicas of historic versions of the US military's M16 rifle. The rifles are often built on specially made, new manufacture semiautomatic AR-15 receivers that replicate the external appearance of the earlier military models in great detail but are capable of only semiautomatic operation,[850] and they incorporate as many original components as possible (*sans* components necessary for selective fire such as the auto-sear and the full-auto receiver itself) to produce highly authentic and historically correct, semiautomatic only versions of historic weapons. These

---

[845] *Retro Black Rifle*. http://www.retroblackrifle.com/. Retrieved June 23rd, 2019.

[846] *Colt Commercial Variants*. /variants/#Definitions. Retrieved June 23rd, 2019.

[847] https://www.AR-15.com/forums/ar-15/-/123-304266/?. Retrieved June 23rd, 2019.

[848] https://www.AR-15.com/forums/ar-15/-/123-296919/?. Retrieved June 23rd, 2019.

[849] *Retro M16 Parts Timeline*. https://www.AR-15.com/forums/ar-15/-/123-602896/?page=1. Retrieved June 23rd, 2019.

[850] One well known supplier of retro receivers and other retro parts is NoDak Spud, LLC, https://www.nodakspud.com/AR%20Lowers.htm. Retrieved June 23rd, 2019.

"retro builds," as they are called, fill an important gap in the collecting market left by the near impossibility for most people of obtaining the genuine selective fire originals due to the strict licensing requirements, the ban on registration of new examples of the weapons for private ownership, scarcity, and resultant prohibitively high cost of the originals.[851] Such retro builds hold strong appeal for collectors interested in the firearms as much for their historical significance as for their practical utility. One remarkable collection of such retro builds can be viewed at *Weapons of the World Photo Albums / US Colt/ArmaLite AR-15/M16 (5.56)*.[852]

---

[851] A collectors M16 rifle on the ATF civilian registry can cost in the vicinity of $25,000.

[852] *Weapons of the World Photo Albums / US Colt/ArmaLite AR-15/M16 (5.56)*. http://imageevent.com/willyp/firearmsalbums/uscoltarmalitem16AR-15556. Retrieved June 23rd, 2019.

Chapter 8
Conclusion: The Spores of Rot

In September 1958, the US District Court for the Western District of Virginia ordered the integration of the public high school in Warren County, Virginia,[853] pursuant to the decision of the US Supreme Court in *Brown v. Board of Education*.[854] In response, Governor J. Lindsey Almond declared the high school "closed and removed from the public school system."[855] The Commonwealth of Virginia then embarked upon a policy of "Massive Resistance,"[856] in which desegregated schools were closed and grants made available to educate the children previously enrolled in those schools in nonsectarian private schools.[857] Defending this arrangement before the Virginia Supreme Court of Appeals,[858] Virginia Assistant Attorney General Robert D. McIlwaine III dismissed *Brown* as "'a mass of gratuitous dicta' without specific reference to situations like that in Virginia."[859]

In the recent case of *American Legion v. American Humanist Assn* Justice Kavanaugh declared that the US Supreme Court "fiercely protects the individual rights secured by the US Constitution."[860] True enough – but only, it would seem, to a point. For since the *Heller* decision, states and municipalities across the United States have treated *Heller* as if it were nothing more than "a mass of gratuitous dicta," as Attorney General McIlwaine dismissed *Brown* before it. Unlike the courts that passed upon Virginia's egregious school

---

[853] Benjamin Muse. *Virginia's Massive Resistance* (Indiana University Press, 1961), 68.

[854] *Brown v. Board of Education*, 347 US 483, 74 S.Ct. 686, 98 L.ed. 873 (1954).

[855] Muse, 68.

[856] *James v. Almond*, 170 F. Supp. 331 (E.D. Va., 1959).

[857] *Harrison v. Day*, 200 Va. 439, 106 S.E.2d 636 (1959).

[858] Now simply the Supreme Court of Virginia.

[859] Muse, 165.

[860] *American Legion v. American Humanist Assn.*, 588 U. S. ____ (2019) (Kavanaugh, J., concurring).

segregation laws[861] however, many of the courts considering Second Amendment claims post *Heller* have indulged – have even aided and abetted – state and local authorities in their attempts to render *Heller* impotent. In his concurrence in *American Legion*, cited above, Justice Kavanaugh wrote that "the Constitution sets a floor for the protection of individual rights."[862] Yet numerous courts, such as the *Kolbe* majority, have sought to erect a low ceiling above the Second Amendment, contorting themselves as if in a game of *Twister* to pen up the right to keep and bear arms in as small a space as possible. Whereas these courts would lodge some of our rights in a capacious mansion fit for an emperor, they do all they can to cram the right to keep and bear arms into a dog's kennel. They seek, in short, to so constrain the right guaranteed by the Second Amendment as to render it an impotent and empty promise. As Akhil Reed Amar has noted,

> [b]y declining to address the Second Amendment, the Warren Court never had to answer … tough questions about its general approach to incorporation and thereby explain why its selective approach was principled across all clauses. Conservative critics may be forgiven for wondering whether the liberal members of the Warren Court were simply more personally sympathetic to antiestablishmentarianism than to gun rights.[863]

As Amar goes on to note, the *Heller* decision went a long way toward vindicating the Court's Incorporation Doctrine,[864] as did the Court's more recent holding in *Timbs v. Indiana*, which held that seizure of an automobile via civil asset forfeiture was a fine and that the Excessive Fines Clause of the Eighth Amendment is

---

[861] See *Harrison* and *James*.
[862] *American Legion* (Kavanaugh, J. concurring).
[863] Akhil Reed Amar. *America's Unwritten Constitution: The Precedents and Principles We Live By* (Basic Books, 2012), 166.
[864] *Id.*

incorporated against the states.[865] But the Court's profound reluctance to accept Second Amendment cases and to correct plainly defective reasoning such as that in the *Kolbe* opinion nonetheless invites speculation that on the Roberts Court, some enumerated rights are "more equal than others."[866]

One of the most galling aspects of the current state of Second Amendment jurisprudence is that restrictions on semiautomatic rifles like the AR-15, magazine capacity, and so forth rest upon foundations of sand. Most or all of the "facts" about such firearms and accessories put forth in support of such restrictions are demonstrably erroneous and provably false – nowhere more so than in the absurd reasoning of the *Kolbe* majority. Whence comes the flood of misinformation that courts use to constrain the right to keep and bear arms? Indubitably, some of it is purely well-intentioned naiveté. By way of illustration, consider the following anecdote relating to a wreck at sea:

> We arrived on scene and all five of them were in the water; some clinging to debris, some not. As we hovered above the scene, two of the victims appeared to be looking up at us, treading water. I hurriedly changed into my wetsuit when I heard the pilot say, 'They don't look like they are in any immediate danger. They can wait for the boat.' I said 'No Sir, they look like they are drowning!'[867]

This quote is drawn from a Coast Guard publication explaining that most people cannot recognize a drowning person.

---

[865] *Timbs v. Indiana*, 586 U. S. _____ (2019).

[866] George Orwell. *Animal Farm* (Harcourt, Brace, and Company, 1946). 112.

[867] Aviation Survival Technician First Class Mario Vittone and Francesco A. Pia, Ph.D. "It Doesn't Look Like They're Drowning: How to Recognize the Instinctive Drowning Response." *On Scene: The Journal of the US Coast Guard Search and Rescue*, COMDTPUB P16100.4, Fall 2006, 14.

While "a person in the water that is shouting and waving" may be in aquatic distress and in need of assistance,[868] they are not yet drowning. One who actually is drowning cannot yell and cannot wave their arms, even if they want to; it is all they can do to tread water and keep their mouths in the air for a few more minutes, which is what inborn instinct forces them to do.[869] Most people have not experienced a drowning directly, but have only seen them depicted or described in the media, or extrapolate how they think a drowning person would act from their own experiences in other contexts. Thus conditioned, they may not recognize a person on the verge of death from drowning. Their life experience has blinded them to the truth. Misperceptions about firearms generally, and AR-15s in particular, can and likely do arise by just such a process: the emotional reaction to the tragedies of violent crime and mass shootings can easily cement such ill-informed perceptions into articles of faith.

Mere misperception is not necessarily a sufficient motivator to drive people into the courts and to inspire those courts to disregard contrary evidence in imposing misguided policy based on these erroneous views. Hubris often plays a role. Dalrymple describes this process in a different context, but his description is apt here as well. Describing an influential medical journal, he writes that

> [w]hen it pronounces on social philosophy, as it often does, it reads like *Pravda*, not in the sense that it is Marxist-Leninist, of course, but in the sense that it takes its own attitudes so much for granted, as being so indisputably virtuous and true, that other viewpoints are rarely if ever expressed in its pages.[870]

A classic example of such thinking is a 1994 *Washington Post* editorial which declared that "[assault weapons] ought to be banned –

---

[868] *Id.*

[869] *Id.*

[870] Theodore Dalrymple. *False Positive: A Year of Error, Omission, and Political Correctness in the New England Journal of Medicine* (Encounter Books, 2019), x.

it's ridiculous that the banning should even be an issue."[871] Writing upon an event discussed in the medical journal previously referenced, Dalrymple observes that "[t]elling the truth would threaten not just a few individuals and institutions, but an entire worldview that was more difficult and painful to give up than a bad habit."[872] Such describes a great swath of what passes for debate on firearms policy.

It is regrettable that the Supreme Court has so far allowed false information and erroneous beliefs to erode the protection afforded by the Second Amendment in the lower courts. Justice Gorsuch recently addressed problematic evidence in the context of an appeal for disability benefits, in which the Supreme Court found that an Administrative Law Judge had relied upon "substantial evidence" in making his ruling, and that the petitioner's claim was thereby barred. Dissenting, Justice Gorsuch wrote:

> [C]onsider what we know about this standard. Witness testimony that's clearly wrong as a matter of fact cannot be substantial evidence. Falsified evidence isn't substantial evidence. Speculation isn't substantial evidence. And, maybe most pointedly for our purposes, courts have held that a party or expert who supplies only conclusory assertions fails this standard too.[873]

Justice Gorsuch went on to assert that "[i]f clearly mistaken evidence, fake evidence, speculative evidence, and conclusory evidence aren't substantial evidence, the evidence here shouldn't be either."[874] If an Administrative Law Judge ought not to rely on defective evidence in adjudicating a claim for benefits, an Article III

---

[871] "Hyping the Crime Bill," *The Washington Post*, September 15th, 1994.
[872] Dalrymple. *False Positive,* 3.
[873] *Biestek v. Berryhill,* 587 U. S. _____ (2019)(Gorscuch, J., dissenting)(internal quotations and citations omitted).
[874] *Id.*

court certainly ought not to rely upon such evidence in reviewing restraints upon an enumerated Constitutional right.

Also concerning is the Court's toleration of plainly pretextual claims put forward in support of banning AR-15-style rifles and accessories. The Violence Policy Center virtually admitted that its arguments were pretextual in its 1988 report *Assault Weapons and Accessories in America*. So have others, such as the *Washington Post*, which in supporting the 1994 Assault Weapons Ban admitted that

> [t]he [crime] bill also includes a ban on assault weapons … but no one should have any illusions about what was accomplished. Assault weapons play a part in only a small percentage of crime. *The provision is mainly symbolic; its virtue will be if it turns out to be, as hoped, a stepping stone to broader gun control*[875] (emphasis added).

More recently, the Virginia State Senate Majority Leader, Republican Tommy Norment, said in response to the May 31st, 2019 mass shooting at a Virginia Beach government office that

> [a]n extended magazine is optical, but does it change the outcome, I'm not sure, but it's something the citizens like this would say at least it's an incremental effort to do something. At least that is an issue that it's very easy to resolve'… 'Nothing would have helped us in Virginia Beach,' Norment told the crowd to jeers. He told the crowd he thought the General Assembly would act nonetheless.[876]

---

[875] *Washington Post*, "Hyping the Crime Bill."

[876] Steve Roberts, Jr. "Norment expects GA to consider legislation to limit large-capacity magazines after Virginia Beach shootings," *Virginia Pilot*, June 3rd, 2019. https://www.vagazette.com/news/va-vg-ebbins-norment-extended-magazines-0604-story.html. Retrieved June 30th, 2019.

These advocates all propose bans on so-called "assault weapons" or "high capacity" magazines, not for any benefits that such bans might actually confer, but as a stalking horse for other objectives. In Senator Norment's case, that other purpose would seem to be nothing more than the placating of angry constituents. For others, the real purpose of bans on AR-15 rifles and other accessories seems to be, not to obviate any special harm or threat, but rather to prepare the ground for much more Draconian firearms proscriptions later. Dr. Winslow, quoted above, illustrates the point. In the Senate testimony that torpedoed his nomination for a position in the Trump administration, he expressed dismay that private citizens can purchase weapons such as the AR-15.[877] Early in his *Washington Post* opinion piece, he wrote that he did "not support unrestricted ownership of semiautomatic assault weapons by civilians."[878] By the end of the article, he was not merely advocating banning AR-15s, but was openly declaring that "[h]aving semiautomatic weapons makes no sense,"[879] with no qualification as to type whatsoever.

The US Supreme Court opined in 1887 that

> [t]he courts are not bound by mere forms, nor are they to be misled by mere pretenses. They are at liberty, indeed, are under a solemn duty, to look at the substance of things, whenever they enter upon the inquiry whether the legislature has transcended the limits of its authority. If, therefore, a statute purporting to have been enacted to protect the public health, the public morals, or the public safety, has no real or substantial relation to those objects, or is a palpable invasion of rights secured by the fundamental law, it is the duty of the courts to so adjudge, and thereby give effect to the Constitution.[880]

---

[877] Winslow.
[878] *Id.*
[879] *Id.*

The Supreme Court ought not, therefore, yield to the mere incantation of "public safety" when confronted with firearms restrictions.

In *Department of Commerce v. New York*, Chief Justice Roberts, writing for the Court, temporarily blocked the Trump administration's decision to add a citizenship question to be asked of all respondents to the 2020 United States census. Though overruling the lower courts on the substantive questions of whether the Secretary of Commerce had the power to add the question and whether he had relied upon substantial evidence in so doing (the Supreme Court found in favor of the administration on both points), the Court nonetheless returned the proposed question to the Department for further consideration on the ground that it had not fairly stated the basis of the proposed change. As Chief Justice Roberts wrote,

> [w]e do not hold that the agency decision here was substantively invalid. But agencies must pursue their goals reasonably. Reasoned decision making under the Administrative Procedure Act calls for an explanation for agency action. What was provided here was more of a distraction.[881]

If the Court subjected the administration to such scrutiny over implementation of an administrative action that the Court itself found that the administration had the power to take, then the Court's review of constraints imposed upon the exercise of an enumerated right – including that protected by the Second Amendment – ought to be all the more searching, and restrictions imposed for pretextual reasons ought to be called out and overruled.

From whence the deference of so many courts to the unfounded claims put forward about AR-15 rifles, so-called "high

---

[880] *Mugler v. Kansas*, 8 S.Ct. 273, 123 US 623, 31 L.Ed. 205 (1887).
[881] *Department of Commerce v. New York*, 588 U. S. _____ (2019).

capacity" magazines, and related items? In addition to the foregoing, one factor that undoubtedly contributes to the judicial reticence on the Second Amendment is deference to the states' exercise of the police power – their traditional power to promote the public safety, morals, and welfare: some judges – particularly those with little experience with or exposure to firearms – might be reluctant to overrule the judgment of states and localities seeking to constrain firearms ownership. But the police power is not unlimited and, in light of the considerations set forth above, the excessively deferential position taken by the judiciary with respect to firearms is unwarranted.

That the state's police power is not unlimited was reinforced recently by the US Supreme Court in the case of *Tennessee Wine and Spirits Retailers Association v. Thomas*.[882] In that case, the Court noted that

> [t]hroughout the 19th century, social problems attributed to alcohol use prompted waves of state regulation .... One wave of state regulation occurred during the first half of the century. The country's early years were a time of notoriously hard drinking, and the problems that this engendered prompted states to enact a variety of regulations, including licensing requirements, age restrictions, and Sunday-closing laws.[883]

Observing that "[i]t does not at all follow that every statute enacted ostensibly for the promotion of the public health, the public morals, or the public safety is to be accepted as a legitimate exertion of the police powers of the state," the Court overruled Tennessee's residency requirements for entry into the business of selling alcoholic beverages.[884] If the Court is willing to strike down state regulatory

---

[882] *Tennessee Wine and Spirits Retailers Association v. Thomas*, 588 U. S. _____ (2019).
[883] *Id.*, internal quotations and citations omitted.

actions as offending a Constitutional right that is merely implicit in the text of the Constitution, how much more willing ought the Court to be to intervene to vindicate a right expressly enumerated in the Bill of Rights itself?

"The phrase 'gun violence' may not be invoked as a talismanic incantation to justify any exercise of state power,"[885] and with good reason. For, as securing the safety of the public is the principal function of government, it is therefore (along with its sibling, national security), the rationale most likely to be invoked in defense of government corruption, abuse, and overreach.

In justifying infringements upon our rights, the incantation is often recited that the right to free speech does not empower one "to shout fire in a crowded theater." An examination of the history of that memorable phrase is illuminating. The expression is drawn from the 1919 case of *Schenck v. United States*, in which Justice Holmes declared that "[t]he most stringent protection of free speech would not protect a man in falsely shouting fire in a theater and causing a panic."[886] Undoubtedly truer words were never spoken, but those words do not remotely describe the conduct of which the appellants in *Schenck* had been convicted. Charles Schenck and Elizabeth Baer were members of the Socialist Party opposed to American participation in the First World War. Acting on that opposition, they had circulated letters through the mail condemning conscription as unlawful and encouraging recipients to exercise "your right to assert your opposition to the draft."[887] For these acts they were convicted of violating the Espionage Act of June 15, 1917.[888]

---

[884] *Id.*, internal quotations and citations omitted.
[885] *Duncan v. Becerra*, 265 F. Supp. 3d 1106 (S.D. Cal. 2017).
[886] *Schenck v. United States, Baer v. Same*, 249 US 47, 39 S.Ct. 247, 63 L.Ed. 470 (1919).
[887] *Id.*
[888] *Id.*

However justified the conviction of Schenck and Baer may have seemed when Justice Holmes passed upon it, with the perspective of time we can only view it as a wholly unwarranted exercise of government power, in no way analogous to the very real danger caused by shouting fire in a real crowded theater. Schenck and Baer would be far from the last victims of government abuse carried out under the pretense of providing for public health and safety. Some such abuses are comparatively mundane and primarily implicate economic interests. As the Institute for Justice has reported,

> "[o]ccupational practitioners, often through professional associations, use the power of concentrated interests to lobby state legislators for protection from competition though licensing laws. Such anti-competitive motives are typically masked by appeals to protecting public health and safety, no matter how facially absurd."[889]

Another area rife with abuse, justified on public safety grounds, is civil asset forfeiture, as recently addressed by the Supreme Court in *Timbs*. While the defendant in *Timbs* had committed an offense, many completely innocent people are caught up in the civil forfeiture net, as in the case of Tonya Smith and her husband, Demitrios Patlias, from whom West Virginia state troopers seized more than $10,000 in winnings from Baltimore's Horseshoe Casino. Although the couple was never charged with any crime, West Virginia authorities refused to return their cash until the couple went public to the media.[890]

---

[889] Dick M. Carpenter II, Lisa Knepper, Angela C. Erickson, and John K. Ross. *License to Work: A National Study of Burdens from Occupational Licensing* (Institute for Justice, May 2012), 29.

[890] Deanna Paul. "Police seized $10,000 of a couple's cash. They couldn't get it back — until they went public." *The Washington Post*, August 13th, 2018. https://www.washingtonpost.com/nation/2018/09/01/police-seized-couples-cash-they-couldnt-get-it-back-until-they-went-public/?utm_term=.a95e9d2e9d02. Retrieved June 30th, 2019.

Other abuses are far more sinister, such as the Supreme Court's "grotesque error[]"[891] in *Korematsu v. United States*.[892] A whole train of abuses of freedom of speech and the press attended the desperate efforts to prop up the institution of slavery in the antebellum period, justified on the basis of a purported fear that criticism of slavery would encourage domestic disturbances and servile insurrection. One example is

> [t]he fact that a virtual censorship of the mails crossing the Mason and Dixon line was established after 1835 [to counter] [a] powerful, concerted effort of propaganda [that] had been launched ... by the abolition societies of the North,

a censorship that "could not be maintained without the acquiescence of the Federal Government."[893] In 1836, Virginia enacted a law that "provided severe punishment for any member or agent of an abolition society who should come into the state and maintain that the owners of slaves have not property in the same, or advocate or advise the abolition of slavery."[894] The first person prosecuted under the act was Lysander Barrett, against whom the Commonwealth's Attorney moved for a rule to show cause why a criminal information ought not be entered against him for "violations of 'the act to suppress the circulation of incendiary publications;'" his offense was having "signed a memorial to Congress, which prayed the abolition of slavery in the District of Columbia," such "being a sin against God, a foul stain on our national character, and contrary to the spirit of our republican institutions."[895] The Court ruled in Barrett's favor, not on the ground that his free speech rights had

---

[891] *Gamble v. United States*, 587 U. S. _____ (2019) (Gorsuch, J., dissenting).

[892] *Korematsu v. United States*, 323 U. S. 214 (1944).

[893] Clement Eaton. *The Freedom-Of-Thought Struggle in the Old South* (Harper Torchbooks, 1964), 197.

[894] *Id.*, 127.

[895] *Commonwealth v. Barrett*, General Court of Virginia, December 1839, *Reports of Cases in the Supreme Court of Appeals of Virginia*, Volume IX, 1872, 665.

been violated, but rather, because the law required that one charged under it be a member of an abolition society, which he was not, and that the offense, being a felony, could not be brought by information.[896] In 1854, Mrs. Margaret Douglass was tried for having taught black children how to read and write. She argued her case *pro se*, and "being of bold spirit," mounted an effective defense, such that "the jury recommended a nominal punishment."[897] Unmoved, the judge sentenced Mrs. Douglass to a month in jail, *"justif[ying] the Virginia law prohibiting negro education as a necessary measure of self-defense against Northern incendiaries"*[898] (emphasis added). The ultimate manifestation of this line of reasoning was set forth in that greatest of all American judicial heresies, the odious *Dred Scott v. Sanford*, in which the Chief Justice Taney held that "Congress had no power to naturalize" African slaves and their descendants, and further that no state could vest such a person with state citizenship, either.[899] It would have been bad enough had Taney left the matter thus, but no. In an astounding exercise in judicial activism, Taney emitted what must be the biggest barnacle of gratuitous dicta ever to encumber the American ship of state, holding that "the act of Congress which prohibited a citizen from holding and owning [slaves] in the territory of the United States north of the line therein mentioned, is not warranted by the Constitution, and is therefore void"[900] – thus overturning the Missouri Compromise and speeding our land toward civil war.

The relevance of this infamous case to the topic at hand lays not it its subject matter, but rather in its rationale; for Chief Justice Taney justified his holding, in part, by an appeal to public safety:

> [I]t cannot be believed that the large slaveholding states regarded [African slaves and their descendants] as included in the word citizens, or would have

---

[896] *Id.*
[897] Clement, 137.
[898] *Id.*
[899] *Dred Scott v. Sanford*, 60 US 393 (1857).
[900] *Id.*

consented to a Constitution which might compel them to receive them in that character from another state. For if they were so received, and entitled to the privileges and immunities of citizens, *it would exempt them from the operation of the special laws and from the police regulations which they considered to be necessary for their own safety.* It would give to persons of the negro race, who were recognized as citizens in any one State of the Union, the right to enter every other state whenever they pleased, singly or in companies, without pass or passport, and without obstruction, to sojourn there as long as they pleased, to go where they pleased at every hour of the day or night without molestation, unless they committed some violation of law for which a white man would be punished; and it would give them the full liberty of speech in public and in private upon all subjects upon which its own citizens might speak; to hold public meetings upon political affairs, *and to keep and carry arms wherever they went.* And all of this would be done in the face of the subject race of the same color, both free and slaves, and inevitably producing discontent and insubordination among them, and *endangering the peace and safety of the state*[901] (emphasis added).

Taney then justified the execrable "special laws" and "police regulations" applicable to African Americans on the ground that "such laws were deemed by [the slave states as] *absolutely essential to [their] own safety"*[902] (emphasis added).

Providing for the safety of the public is the core, fundamental, and most legitimate function for which governments are constituted. Being the principal function of the state, it is also the strongest rationale to which the state may appeal in justification of its

---

[901] *Id.*
[902] *Id.*

measures. As we have seen above, however, the very strength of the appeal to the public safety and welfare is itself an invitation to abuse – abuse in which our courts have, from time to time, been tempted to acquiesce. In his dissent in *Carroll v. United States*, Justice McReynolds wrote that

> [t]he damnable character of the 'bootlegger's' business should not close our eyes to the mischief which will surely follow any attempt to destroy it by unwarranted methods. To press forward to a great principle by breaking through every other great principle that stands in the way of its establishment; in short, to procure an eminent good by means that are unlawful, is as little consonant to private morality as to public justice.[903]

Although the automobile exception to the Fourth Amendment's warrant requirement has not proven as troublesome as Justice McReynolds feared, other cases have shown that his warning was both prescient and warranted. When our courts have succumbed to the temptation, whether for the sake of expediency or other motive, to downplay or disregard our Constitutional guaranties, embarrassing errors such as *Korematsu* and *Plessy v. Ferguson*[904] have sometimes been the result. Such errors have often been justified as promoting public safety or national security. The cramped reading many courts force upon the Second Amendment is also justified as necessary in the interest of public safety. Such a justification is as ironic as it is unwarranted, for

> [i]mplicit in the concept of public safety is the right of law abiding people to use firearms and the magazines that make them work to protect themselves, their families, their homes, and their state against all armed

---

[903] *Carroll v. United States*, 267 US 132, 45 S.Ct. 280, 69 L.Ed. 543, 39 A.L.R. 790 (1925)(McReynolds, J., dissenting).
[904] *Plessy v. Ferguson*, 163 US 537 (1896).

enemies, foreign and domestic. To borrow a phrase, it would indeed be ironic if, in the name of public safety and reducing gun violence, statutes were permitted to subvert the public's Second Amendment rights— which may repel criminal gun violence and which ultimately ensure the safety of the Republic.[905]

I do not intend to question the validity of the state's public security function. My first military deployment was to Somalia during Operation *Restore Hope*, where I learned, if I had ever doubted it, that freedom cannot exist without security, and that liberty is extinguished in a state of anarchy as surely as bacteria are destroyed in boiling water. But many forget that *the reverse is equally true*: the people cannot be truly secure if they are not free, for the absence of freedom implies coercion or worse.

One of the most interesting courses that I took during my undergraduate years was a colloquium course on militarism in Latin America. The most enduring imprint of that course on my mind was the impression that many Latin American military leaders conflated their own interests – institutional and personal – with those of their nations, thus providing a rationale for frequent forcible interventions into politics. Some say that to a man with a hammer, everything is a nail. And so it can be for any entity charged with maintaining public safety in the absence meaningful restraints; in such a case, that entity can attack the very security and freedom it purports to protect, like a political auto-immune disorder, wherein the state's antibodies attack the healthy tissue of the state itself – the people and their liberties. Hideous results can ensue, as in the case of Argentina's Dirty War, wherein "[t]he end of terrorism came ... through another campaign of terrorism conducted by the state."[906] In that nasty episode, the

---

[905] *Duncan v. Becerra.*

[906] Maria Rasmussen. *Argentina: The End of Terrorism Through State Terrorism (Fundación Manuel Jimenez Abad, des Estudios Parlamentarios y Autónomos del Estado,* 2010), 2. http://www.fundacionmgimenezabad.es/sites/default/files/20101115_et_r

ruling military junta "disappeared" tens of thousands of people between 1976 and 1983 in its campaign to destroy two terrorist organizations, the Montoneros and the People's Revolutionary Army (ERP).[907] It was not only the supporters of these groups that felt the sting of repression in this war. Friends of mine were university students in Argentina during this period. They have reported that even being found with academic textbooks in one's car was enough to arouse the suspicion of inspecting soldiers. So concerned were they over the state of affairs that they ultimately fled the country, never to live there again. And these were *opponents* of ERP and the Montoneros – ardent anti-communists who had come to Argentina as children as refugees from communist regimes in Eastern Europe.

In his 1981 volume on the Royal Navy during the Napoleonic Wars, Dudley Pope wrote that

> [f]or all the romance in the building of the Royal Navy's ships, the waving flags and the sound of bands playing at the launching, a ship was often rotten as she slid down the ways ... the shortage of compass timber often meant that some timber from an old ship was used in the building of the new, and although the wood looked sound it almost certainly contained the spores of rot – 'that little soft patch' which was considered unimportant but which carried what might be termed 'wood cancer' to new timber.[908]

The spores of rot can infect structures other than ships; metaphysical spores of rot can erode the moral and intellectual foundations of an institution or a system of law. Like a necrotic organ in an otherwise healthy body, an atrophied, choked off or defunct Constitutional provision can leach out its infection and rot, compromising even the healthy portions of the body politic. The

---

asmussen_m_en_o_0.pdf. Retrieved July 14th, 2019.
[907] *Id.*, 3.
[908] Dudley Pope. *Life in Nelson's Navy* (Naval Institute Press, 1981), 53.

manner in which so many courts have snubbed, stifled and chained the Second Amendment threatens to spawn such an infection in our own Constitutional system. Indulging the temptation to choke off and kill a provision of the Constitution that one deems awkward, embarrassing, cumbersome or obsolete compromises the majesty of the document as a whole. Having once taken such a step, taking it yet again will be all the easier.

While it is not to be expected that outrages as extreme as those described above will befall the United States, the slippery slide away from liberty is not an idle fear. We live in an age when even our most cherished liberties, such as freedom of speech and the free exercise of religion, are themselves under serious challenge. As Justice Alito recently opined,

> [v]iewpoint discrimination is poison to a free society. But in many countries with constitutions or legal traditions that claim to protect freedom of speech, serious viewpoint discrimination is now tolerated, and such discrimination has become increasingly prevalent in this country. At a time when free speech is under attack, it is especially important for this Court to remain firm on the principle that the First Amendment does not tolerate viewpoint discrimination.[909]

Such discrimination – and worse – is advocated in the name of security, as political extremists promote the suppression of speech on absurdly tenuous claims that opinions they deem offensive could lead to violence, or worse, that such opinions constitute violence in and of themselves.

---

[909] *Iancu v. Brunetti*, 588 U. S. _____ (2019)(Alito, J., concurring).

The Supreme Court has admirably stood against such abuse of free speech in recent years. It is not enough, however, for the Court to remain steadfast in its enforcement of a mere subset of our Constitutional rights. *Weakness is a provocation*: Equivocation in the enforcement of one provision – in this case the Second Amendment – invites calls for equivocation in the enforcement of others. Water seeping into a crack in masonry freezes and expands, widening the crack; this repeated action of freezing, melting, and freezing again can weaken and destroy the strongest edifice. Infirmity in sustaining the rights guaranteed under the Second Amendment cannot be quarantined to just that provision. Having once prevailed upon the Court to avert its eyes to the evisceration of the right to keep and bear arms – one of the rights enumerated in the Bill of Rights itself – the enemies of liberty will be emboldened to press for concessions in other ways anathema to freedom. It has happened before; it is being attempted with respect to our First Amendment rights as this is being written. In sustaining and enforcing the right of the people to keep and bear arms, as guaranteed by the Second Amendment, the Court would set an example of firmness that would redound to the benefit of all our rights. Capitulating in the face of challenges to any one of those rights creates a precedent in the minds of the people; it erodes the majesty of the Bill of Rights, making the next incursion easier, and so on by degrees.

Now is the time for resolution in vindicating of the rights guaranteed by the Constitution. If our Republic can sustain the right to keep and bear arms in the face of the social challenges with which we struggle today and against the smug disapproval of other Western democracies, then we can sustain all of our liberties against all comers for all time. If, however, we become weary of well-doing, and sacrifice this portion of our inheritance for the illusory promise of security, then the temptation to sacrifice other liberties in the face of transitory troubles or ephemeral passion will be all the greater. "Enforcing the Constitution always bears its costs. But when the people adopted the Constitution and its Bill of Rights, they thought the liberties promised there worth the costs."[910]

Remember the defenders of
Xuân Lộc, April 1975.

---

[910] *Gamble v. United States*, 587 U. S. ____ (2019)(Gorsuch, J., dissenting).

Made in the USA
Monee, IL
03 November 2021